DOMINIQUE
The Case of an Adolescent

DOMINIQUE
The Case of an Adolescent

Françoise Dolto

Translated from the French by Ivan Kats, revised by Lionel and Sharmini Bailly

DIVIDED

DIVIDED

Published in the United Kingdom by Divided in 2025.

Divided Publishing
Rue de Manchesterstraat 5
1080 Brussels
Belgium

Divided Publishing
Deborah House
Retreat Place
London E9 6RJ
United Kingdom

https://divided.online

First published in France in 1971 by Éditions du Seuil as *Le Cas Dominique*. Published in the United States in 1973 by Outerbridge & Lazard as *Dominique: Analysis of an Adolescent*, translated by Ivan Kats. The publishers acknowledge the assistance of Catherine Dolto in the realisation of this edition.

Designed by Alex Walker
Printed by Printon, Tallinn

Cover image: Mike Kelley, *Untitled*, c. 1975. Unique two-colour lithograph on newsprint, 61 × 43 centimetres.

ISBN 978-1-7395161-9-2

Contents

Foreword

Michael Ryzner-Basiewicz

At this time, the child is all receptivity, but is destined to autonomy.
—Françoise Dolto

Like all of us, psychoanalysis has mixed feelings about childhood. If, in one way, we may see childhood as a moment of spontaneity, playing, profound intimacy and, of course, pleasure, we may just as easily see it as a time of terror, fragmentation, trauma, and hopelessly frustrated desires. Psychoanalysis (and this of course means psychoanalysts themselves) has been torn between these kinds of 'good' and 'bad' mythologies, by what the French analyst J.-B. Pontalis admonishingly calls 'rough and normative typologies'. In the canon of psychoanalytic theory, these myths help us make sense of ourselves and the situations we often (begrudgingly, repeatedly) find ourselves in; they are stories about ourselves and others *for* ourselves and others. But what gets overlooked amidst its admittedly bizarre cosmology of vaguely and not-so-vaguely sexual terms is that psychoanalysis – at its best – offers us a way of thinking about childhood (and therefore adulthood) that goes beyond any one myth, any one story we or others may recite. As both a method and set of ideas, psychoanalysis is at its most compelling when tasked with complicating these mythologies: asking every question, retracing every step, and exploring even the most insignificant moments of our early lives – in effect, when it is preoccupied with *everything*. This kind of task is, as Freud famously decided, impossible. But it is because of this investigative power and its grip on our imagination that psychoanalysis remains, at the very least, interesting, if not useful; it is at once a technique and a worldview, premised on taking extremely seriously the smallest details of so-called everyday life. It replaces one static mythology with the possibility of rediscovering a diversity of mythologies – the meaning and function of which can appear and disappear as needed. It may be impossible to be completely cured, to change everything, but it's not impossible to discover a better life. This is, I think, among the many things that make Françoise Dolto's *Dominique: The Case of an Adolescent* so remarkable; an impossible labyrinth of stories about suffering, as well as an attempt to find a way out of them.

Somewhere between a unified theory of everything, a detective novel, and a homily on the unconscious, Dolto's *Case of an Adolescent* can at first come across almost as a caricature of 'psychoanalysis' – a kind of fantastical pastiche of concepts and interpretations. But the more we read this book, the more it becomes clear that *Dominique* is really unlike any other piece of psychoanalytic literature. Far from being constrained by the idiom and dogma of psychoanalysis, Dolto seems to have been liberated by it; finding in terms like 'castration', 'ego ideal' and 'cannibalism' (among many others) a vocabulary to express something about the most inarticulable parts of our early lives. Dolto shows us that this strange psychoanalytic language provides a way of describing experiences – of the nascent body and mind, as well as its place in the world – that are impossible to articulate otherwise. Take for instance the following passage: 'Is this a representation of the image of his own body as having "swallowed an umbrella" . . . Does the "umbrella" signify the prohibition against wetting one's bed . . . Is it the oral desire for the mother's "udder" . . . Or does it represent the paternal penis disappearing into the mother?' Reading this, we realise that what starts as an odd, technical-sounding question turns into an index of life-and-death dilemmas plaguing Dominique: *What does it mean to have a body? What happens when I take things into my mind? What am I allowed to do? What does my mother want from me? Where is my father and what has happened to him?* The magic of reading Dolto's language, her observations and inter-pretations, is that we implicitly start to wonder about our own versions of these questions, about what kinds of umbrellas we ourselves might have swallowed, and why.

But if we take Dolto very seriously – if we believe she has something to say about the suffering of today's children and adolescents (whenever today might be) – we should also address the aspects of her thinking that may at first appear to be at odds with our own. Dolto's references to homosexuality, gender identity and 'stereotypes' may alarm us if we take them to be prescriptive, if we read her as advocating for a return to a kind of idealised vision of childhood and family life. It is true that Dolto frequently points to the necessity of 'the law', to the castrating 'prohibition' of Oedipus; likewise, throughout the case, we find countless allusions to the roles of Dominique's mother and father – to his 'masculine' and 'feminine' ego ideals. There is, of course, the temptation to read Dolto here as saying that these are natural, immutable social categories and bonds that are there to be reified, but I think this would be to miss the point. The power of what Dolto has to say does not come from a valuation of these categories, but from her description of their failure – of the consequences of their impossibility and the solutions the psychoanalyst helps the child find. Today, it is clearer than ever that the mythologies surrounding the family have become suspect. Dolto is reminding us that – among many other reasons – the failure of these structures becomes especially destructive for children when they go unspoken, are dehistoricised, and when adults (consciously and uncon-sciously) dramatise their own wants through their children – when they deprive them of a chance to realise something of their own desire. In this way, we are reminded that the things we con-sider 'developmentally inappropriate' for children to talk about are, invariably, the things we as adults are too anxious to hear.

If psychoanalysis with adults is about reminding them that they have a choice, that they have say over their lives, psycho-analysis with children, according to Dolto, is about showing them that they have a choice to begin with, that what they say matters. While for Dominique the solution to his suffering involved a re-finding of his 'masculine structuration', assuming an identification and position that had been prematurely foreclosed for him, we shouldn't think that this is the only solution available. Desire is not destiny, biological or otherwise. In an enigmatic footnote, Dolto writes: 'Natural castration, normally called primary castration, results from the fact that the human body is monosexual and mortal. Cultural castration has a structuring force only if the subject has first valued the parent of his own sex from the social angle: if he has valorised eroticism and human fecundity.' Reading this, it is impossible not to think about the implications of what Dolto is saying for trans and gender-nonconforming children and adolescents – the current subjects of seemingly inexhaustible adult fantasies and mythologies. While we may have our doubts about Dolto's insistence on 'fecundity', just as we may question what she means by 'monosexual', what should strike us are the stakes of being able – or not being able – to 'valorise' an ideal, to unconsciously cohere as an image of oneself in the image of an other. If we take natural castration simply to mean that, because we have bodies that change and die, we can never *really* have it all, that, as we grow up, we need to give up the fantasies we covet the most – occupying the centre of our parents' universe, being perfectly understood, having our every need satisfied – then we can understand our valorisations (of whoever they may be) as the way out of this crisis. But we know that it is exactly this ability to valorise trans people that is so often forbidden for children and adolescents. Maybe here we can understand the failure of 'cultural castration' and its 'structuring force' as the anguish so frequently described in the testimonies of individuals prior to transition: the incorporeal, derealised sense of suffering that is so often dealt with by suicide; the feeling that one's body is not one's own, or even real. It is also impossible to avoid noting the racialised dimension of this kind of alienation: that is, whether one's body is considered a body to begin with, and according to whom. French colonial racism and its living legacy haunt Dominique's story, intersecting with the Bel family's history of subjugation at the hands of their Nazi occupiers. History and state-sanctioned racism *literally* disintegrate bodies, deteriorating our ability to shape unconscious images of ourselves. Whereas a psychoanalyst like Jacques Lacan – Dolto's contemporary and uneasy ally – underscores the illusory nature of our identifications and the misrecognition they engender, Dolto counts them as precious. In this way, reading Dolto reminds us that we need images, identifications and valorisations to live.

Returning to Dominique, if his survival – finding a way out of what Dolto describes as a 'vegetative' existence – coincided with a heterosexual object choice and masculine identity, then it follows that other choices and identifications are just as viable should they follow from our desire. (In this way, the double meaning of 'identify' should stand out to us.) Many clinicians are, after all, very familiar with the stabilising effects of transitioning for suffering young people, just as they're all too aware of the myriad psychiatric debates associating gender-nonconforming and transitioning with mental illness. Of course, in *Dominique*, Dolto is herself no stranger to speaking about illness and pathology. In fact, Dolto most frequently (and consequentially) refers to Dominique as psychotic – a term that has been largely dissociated from mainstream descriptions and diagnoses of children. This word, moreover, may also make non-psychoanalytic readers uneasy insofar as its everyday use is usually derisive; more curse than diagnosis, a designation for the 'worst', or most 'incurable', kinds of mental illness. But for Dolto, this is obviously not the case. 'To the psychoanalyst,' she writes, 'every other person, whatever his behaviour, is a full-fledged member of the human race; the "psychotic" is the subject of an unconscious story which he actualises, rather than symbolising it in the form of a structured tale, as do those we classify as "normal" or "neurotic".'

What starts with Dolto's insistence on the treatability of psychosis – a notion contested then as now – turns into something of an ethical treatise: a call for what she names a 'human encounter'; a recognition of psychosis as an orientation to living on equal footing with 'normal' (that is to say, neurotic) life, only one that is often fraught with greater challenges. The scare quotes around the words 'normal', 'neurotic', and 'psychotic' should make us wonder about what we are trying to say when we invoke such terms. The arguments Dolto makes in Part III, 'The Psychoanalysis of Psychotics', are, I think, perhaps the most beautiful part of this amazing book. Dolto's writing reads as so purely associative that it feels like many papers superimposed over one another; ideas connected through an unconscious logic, not writing convention. While we see Dolto digress, become side-tracked, we always get the sense that something of her own desire is being articulated; we get the impression that she is working through something for herself and on our behalf. There are so many little inexplicable moments throughout *The Case of an Adolescent* that it's easy to forget that the brilliance of Dolto's interventions and ideas comes from the fact that she was so wholly attentive to what was being said, consciously and unconsciously, to her. Reading Dolto today is a reminder that, if we really listen, we may also be able to hear something.

DOMINIQUE
The Case of an Adolescent

I

Clinical History

Twelve Sessions of a Psychoanalytic Treatment of an Adolescent, Apragmatic since Infancy: Frame and Theoretical Considerations

Contemporary literature offers a multitude of short or tiny vignettes drawn from a series of several hundred sessions. At the same time, the written or graphic records which Freud has left of certain cases (such as the case of Little Hans or of the Wolf Man, for the analysis of children) are of considerable help, independent of the theoretical implications he derived from these cases. Freud invited our own personal thought and our constructive criticism through these detailed records.

Contemporary literature offers a multitude of short or minute extracts drawn from a series of several hundred sessions. These represent selections from the dreams, the words or the behaviour of patients, and mostly serve to justify technical research or some discussion of transference or counter-transference. The clinician is left to wonder about the basis of their selection.

At the same time, I have always thought that the help of other psychoanalysts in therapeutic work could be of considerable interest with regard to specific case work, in clarifying one's own theoretical direction, which draws its meaning from the closest listening and the greatest respect for everything that the analysand expresses of their unconscious. Participation by others makes it possible for him to evaluate critically the unconscious receptivity that exists in himself as listener, at the same time as it makes possible a fair reconstruction of the analytic encounter, which is always hidden from him by his own counter-transference.

My hospital work has shown me that the presence of witnesses only hinders the subject when it disturbs my own spontaneity and receptivity.

At each of the sessions attended by assistant psychoanalysts, it was our practice for one of those present to record everything that was said, whether by the patient or by the analyst. We made a point of keeping the child's drawings; I myself made sketches – in front of the child, and during the session – of successive states of his clay models. The role of script-girl may seem unrewarding; it turns out to be of considerable critical interest: the patient's and doctor's mimicry, their unconscious matching gestures and acts, are readily observed. Having recorded and documented the sessions in this way, the analyst can later return to them for a clearer understanding.

In this modified application of the analytic 'encounter', transference reactions must take into account the presence of third parties, who may visibly affect the transference, or, more precisely, its emotional components. Third parties are present and listening. The psychoanalyst takes this openly into account in her interventions.

Anyone who has witnessed hospital treatment is aware of how much is to be learned from such observation. He will have witnessed the demystification of analyst and analysis alike. He will also have witnessed his own counter-transference reactions, and the forms of residual narcissism ever present in the analyst during the analytic encounter.

It is regrettable that this technique cannot be generalised, both because of resistance (in the psychoanalytic sense) and for reasons of confidentiality. We often have to make do with narratives that have been worked over and summarised both by our own deliberate selection, and according to a narcissism which either allows us or checks us in the recording of our counter-transference. The problem remains of truthfully communicating our professional experience.

I have thought it worthwhile to contribute to psychoanalytic research by writing up a case study from beginning to end. This document, recorded in detail by me in a more or less telegraphic style, has simply been transcribed here. As stated, I made sketches of the subject's clay figures during the sessions, noting the successive stages of the modelling which accompanied the patient's talk. This way of working has become a habit to me; it is almost automatic and frees my 'floating' attention.

The case presented here is not the outcome of a public consultation in hospital. The details of transference onto several observers introduces greater problems and I have preferred to publish a case viewed as a 'meeting of two minds' in a consultation at a medical teaching centre. I selected the present case because the number of sessions was limited. This made the reading easier and allowed me to present the case in its totality, thus placing an authentic and complete document before the reader.

The difference between this case and those treated privately is that the fee is paid at the dispensary cashier's desk, and not to the psychoanalyst himself. (We shall see later how this manner of payment will appear in the transference, one day, in the fantasy of the ticket at the station. A sum is given to a cashier who hands back a receipt.) The appointments and the rhythm of the sessions are agreed upon by the patient, his family and myself. Missed sessions are not paid for. I must add that Dominique missed sessions, not through any fault of his own, but because of the person accompanying him, or because of school holidays which coincided with the appointed day, when he was away. Only one appointment was changed to another date for my personal reasons.

As to my having chosen this case, the reader may think it is because it includes some particular real-life events, but this would be a mistake. Any man's life, whether he is neurotic or not, involves unusual circumstances. From the viewpoint of psychoanalysis – that is to say within the unconscious dynamic which structures the subject's development – it is not these events that are significant; it is the way the subject reacts to them, according to the organisation of his drives and personality structure at the time. Events within family life acquire a traumatic significance only when, because of them, the subject

has escaped humanising castration at various levels of the evolution of his libido.*

In the case study which follows, the development of the
psychic agencies did not find in the parental environment the
minimum support – verbal or in gestures – characteristic of
human symbolisation to overcome the mutilating impotence
that was the source of his anguish. On the contrary, it was
his anguish with regard to his family and society that became
the principal reality, the suffering image of anxiety. But this
remained unanswered by echoes in the words or gestures of
others.

If this book leads its readers to critical and constructive
thinking – polemic, to my mind, being outside the field of critical psychoanalysis – my work will not have been in vain.†

---

*   These words will become clearer in context, I hope. What I mean is
       that during his development, each human being meets with trying, if
       necessary, limits to his desires. The reality of these limitations leads
       to real or imaginary suffering, to sensations of bodily mutilation and
       to anguish. There follows a pathogenic regression or progression
       (cultural and social sublimation) determined by the subject's uncon-
       scious body image, his level of language, and the reactions he meets
       with in his environment: language, bearing; words, and concomitant
       anxiety.

          These processes are very different before the mirror stage, since
       the child is not then aware of the existence of his face. The pathology
       of psychotics seems to refer to preverbal and prescopic experiences
       of their own body. Such is Dominique's case. —F.D.

†   To ensure professional confidentiality, I have made some changes in
       the names of people and places. These have not changed the associa-
       tive value which they held for the subject. —F.D.

First Session:
15 June

1. *Interview with the mother*

After having welcomed Dominique and his mother, I send Dominique to the waiting room to prepare his modelling and drawing. Madame Bel stays with me.

Dominique Bel is a boy of fourteen who has been referred to me for diagnosis and advice about his educational placement. He reached puberty a year ago: his schooling has been quite erratic. For two years now he has been under observation in a special school, but has made no progress there. His stereotyped behaviour seems rather to have been getting worse.

The physician of a medical teaching institute where he was under observation for several years viewed him simply as learning-disabled. Since the onset of puberty this doctor has feared an evolution to schizophrenia. Experienced observers in the most recent school shared this impression, which was also my first impression.

Dominique had to repeat year four of primary school three times. He then went on to the special school mentioned above. He has made no progress there, but neither has he made trouble in class. He keeps busy making drawings: a sample of his *stereotyped drawing* follow (see fig. 1, pp. 12–13). They have been the same for years: always a mechanical contraption – planes, cars (never boats). The drawings have a block-like quality. They are almost always drawn two to a page; in opposite directions, the top of the page for the first drawing serving as bottom for

Fig. 1
Drawings brought in by Madame Bel, made
by Dominique before treatment

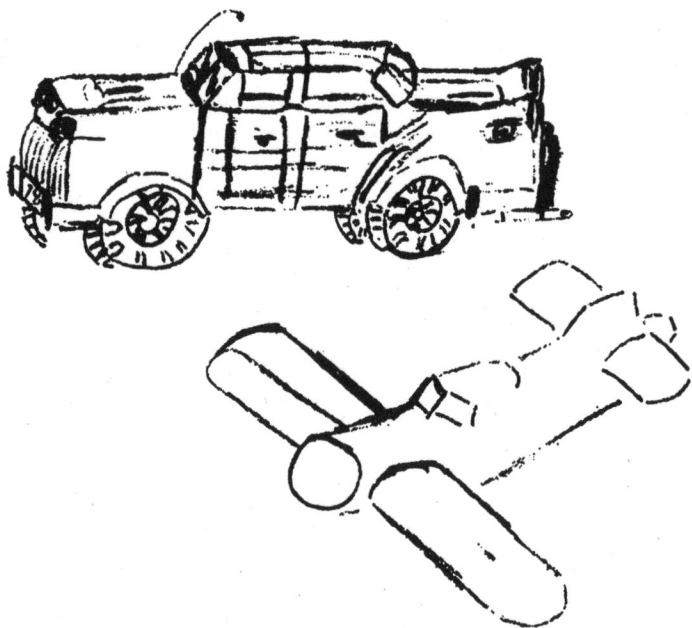

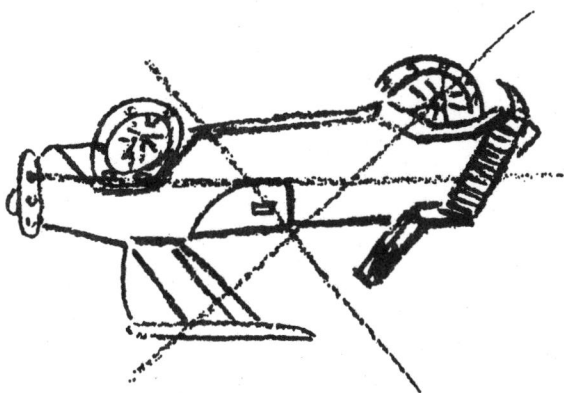

Ghost train at the fair

Fig. 2
Clay figure typical of Dominique's modelling
before treatment

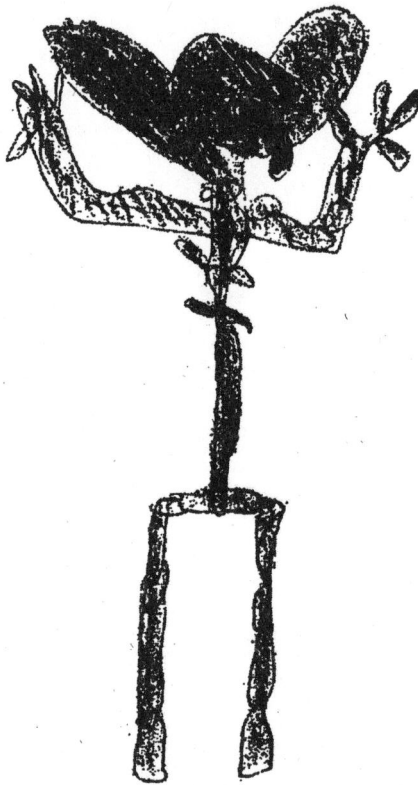

Figure made of modelling clay, 40 centimetres high.
Dominant colour: green. (These figures invariably
cover a considerable surface.)

the second. Examples of Dominique's modelling are also stereo-typed, as the illustration shows (see fig. 2, p. 14). To him, these are people. They take up a huge surface, the smallest being over 40 centimetres long. He moves them as if he were handling cooked macaroni, with affected care.

Dominique looks his age. He is lean without being thin. Brown hair, thick and crew-cut, fairly low forehead. Some fuzz is beginning to appear around his mouth. He does not stand straight, but rather like an ape. He has a stereotyped smile. His voice, high, bi-tonal and 'sugary', sounds as if it had not changed. He walks behind his mother, his arms bent, hands dropping much in the manner of circus dogs who have been trained to walk on their hind legs. He is totally disoriented in time and space. 'He is incapable of living by himself, or even of running small errands for his mother. He is so absent-minded that, if he weren't told, he would go outside in his pyjamas or keep on his topcoat and mittens while eating lunch at home.' His eyes are half-shut and an enigmatic smile wanders over his frozen face.

He has been attending the same school for two years. He is brought there and back by his brother. One day when the brother was absent-minded (and this happened only once!) Dominique strayed onto the wrong train. He then found him-self in some provincial town, but somehow he did manage to have himself sent home to his family, who had spent an anxious day. Dominique is likely to follow anyone when school lets out, unless the schoolmistress is there to check on him. He doesn't seem to know why he does this. Although he talks, as we shall see, he fails to answer questions put to him. He has learned to read – we will see how – and that is about all. As for mathemat-ics, he fails to respond even to the most pedagogically advanced methods; he understands exactly nothing. He is obsessed by this, so he is forever going over his multiplication table, very conscientiously, but to no purpose. His mother says that he occasionally displays a real resolve to learn, but at other times he gives up in despair, since he can remember nothing.

Though he lacks friends, he also has no enemies. At home, he plays a little with toy cars, but does nothing practical. Still, according to his mother, he is not all that clumsy with his hands. What he likes best is to draw. When modelling clay, he likes to produce long strings and then put them together. According to his mother, he is 'troubled by puberty', though he seems to lack any sexual modesty and is not curious about his sexuality. But, she adds, hers are only 'a mother's feelings. He likes to read and for some time now he has been making up stories, probably to show that he has a lot of imagination. We listen to him in order to please him, or really we pretend to listen so as to give him the pleasure of talking, but we can't make anything of what he says.' In fact, he is more a delirious rambler than a storyteller.

Dominique is the second of three children. The eldest is a boy, Paul-Marie, two and a half years older. The third is a girl, Sylvie, two years and nine months younger than Dominique. Reports in my possession from the school which Dominique has been attending for two years describe him as gentle, easy-going, co-operative, devoid of any ability; he is said to be nice (*sympathique*).

Dominique's mother says he is in good physical health. He has had the same children's diseases as his brother and sister, but only very mild cases. He tolerates food of all sorts and doesn't mind any kind of weather.

School reports describe Dominique's psychic health and character as good until the birth of his younger sister. He then seems to have experienced strong reactions of jealousy, reactions to which his present behavioural problems are traced. Very early, even before the birth of his young sister, Dominique was placed in a kindergarten that followed the active Montessori method. He was welcomed there and enjoyed school. However, after he spent two months away, with his father's parents, at the time of the birth of his little sister, the kindergarten would not take him back. The mother tried many other kindergartens, but none would let him stay.

Here are the detailed facts concerning this period, obtained from the mother: When Dominique returned from his grandparents' house, he discovered that his place in the baby's cot in his parent's room, the place he had always slept in until the time he left home, had been taken by his little sister. He was put in a grown-up's bed in his elder brother's room. He displayed no reaction to this, but later showed a very strong reaction of anxiety when he saw his little sister nursing: he tried to wrest his mother's breast away from the baby because he didn't want to see her 'eating mother'. He began to soil himself again at night, and during the day he wet and soiled his pants. This was the reason he was expelled from the kindergarten in which he had been very much at home before his departure: when he came back from his grandparents' house Dominique dirtied everything, was unbearable, unstable, aggressive. He had to stay at home.

The following summer he went away on holiday with his mother, his brother and his sister to visit grandparents – this time his mother's parents. He had a terrible summer: continual fits of stubbornness, anger and rage. These crises worried the mother by their sheer excessiveness. Both Dominique and his sister had to be continually protected during these crises. He maintained a period of mutism during this period and suffered from insomnia. The situation improved when they returned home. Dominique continued to live with his family and was easier to live with. When he was six years old the time came when his parents were obliged by law to send him to primary school. He proved extremely unstable there, having no contact with the other boys. He was not aggressive, but dirtied up his notebooks, and started soiling himself again, a habit his mother had succeeded in checking. In face of this failure to adapt, the schoolmistress sent Dominique to his first sessions at the neuropsychiatric children's ward of a Parisian hospital.

Dominique was given a number of psychotechnical and other tests, including an electroencephalogram. These brought out nothing of a pathological nature. The doctor then prescribed medicines that made Dominique excitable and hard to handle; up to that point he had been easy to get along with, if unstable. A period of therapy with a psychoanalyst was then decided on. Dominique underwent this treatment for six months, twice a week. The old jealousy, which had not been clinically perceptible for quite a long time, surfaced again. This was why the mother could now speak so readily about this period of jealousy: at the time of Dominique's psychotherapy she was led to remember all the details of Dominique's behaviour between the ages of two and a half and three. She recalled everything that she had earlier attributed to a sort of passing fatigue caused by the trip and by Dominique's development: she had not at first drawn a parallel between her son's character disorder and the birth of his little sister. This was easy to miss since Dominique's jealousy had not surfaced.

Thanks to the psychoanalyst, she had retraced and under-stood the different steps of the trial her son had gone through, and even now she spoke of her son's crisis with compassion. At the same time, she was wondering if it was really 'this' (mean-ing psychotherapy) that was needed: it seemed to her there had been no improvement. The boy was very nice before his treatment and very nice after. They said his mental ability was good. He was a boy who expressed himself well. He just wasn't sociable, he didn't like school. He still wet his bed and didn't do much of anything. He was passive and a dreamer; he refused human contact, but he didn't bother other people.

After six months of psychotherapy which brought no real improvement, the psychoanalyst apparently ordered the treat-ment stopped. She said things would improve little by little; Dominique should be reassured that he was loved as much as his sister; they should be treated the same and Dominique should be sent back to school. This was done.

So Dominique went through the first two years of primary school, from age six to seven and seven to eight; he did not learn to read and had little to do with the other pupils. He was well behaved and seemed rather afraid; he kept apart. At home he was very 'nice' with his little sister, wholeheartedly admir-ing, in imitation of the rest of the family, of every advance she made. The psychoanalyst had apparently also advised sending Dominique to the country after a while, if this seemed neces-sary and if conditions proved favourable; the boy, after all, was very fond of animals. The parents recalled this advice when

Dominique failed in school, so they sent him to spend a year with his father's parents, who lived in the vicinity of Perpignan in the South of France. There Dominique was in contact with the children of his father's sister. He was very pleased with this and was apparently very happy there. When he came back at the age of eight, he was able to read. But coming home, he found a little sister who had also been going to school and who had made progress in his absence. He lost what skill in reading he had acquired. It is to this episode that the mother traces her understanding of the fact that Dominique became jealous as soon as he was no longer alone with her. She took care of him as much as she could. Remembering the advice she had been given, she spoiled him as much as possible – to show him that his sister was not being favoured. But he did no better at school, even though his mother had found an understanding woman teacher at the primary school. With the help of this teacher Dominique slowly learned to read again, and for four years, from the age of eight to over twelve, he remained at a level of reading which allowed him to immerse himself in books of history and short stories, his only reading matter.

Dominique's character has not changed since he was eight. He is still an easy-going child, except that everything has to be done for him; he is absent-minded and fails to take care of himself. This goes so far as forgetting to eat, to dress or to wash. He has no memory and has remained enuretic, which is a nuisance. It seems – but one can't be sure – that this enuresis was not a problem when he was eight years old and 'living in the country' with his father's mother. He plays by himself, telling himself stories that no one else can hear, but which seem to amuse him greatly. He likes to frighten others and winds himself up in bed sheets to 'play ghost'. He is very disappointed that people no longer pay attention to him, and so do not take fright at him, though people occasionally pretend to be frightened in order to please him. He has no nightmares and sleeps well. Food has never been a problem with him, even at the time of his initial crisis, when he presented with mutism, insomnia and total incontinence. He wolfs down any food his mother puts on his plate, cleanly and absent-mindedly. His mother also says that he has 'what doctors call phobias', fits of panic. For example, he is afraid of bicycles. Nothing in the world will make him go near one or try to get on one. He also has a phobic fear of merry-go-rounds. When he panics, he clings to his mother and will not move forwards or backwards. Still, he was fascinated by the ghost train at a country fair: he was ecstatic, and not at all panicky. His mother says that he also has tics, that he repeats the same actions (which actions?), meaninglessly – or, rather, that he has obsessional habits, does odd things. Certain objects must not be moved; dirty underwear must be put back in the drawer, as it is, without being washed. He hates to have his socks and underwear put in the laundry. He doesn't mind changing them, but he would like his dirty underwear to be put away in the drawer directly so it can be put on again, as it is, the following week. As for himself, he panics at taking a bath, but doesn't mind having his hands and face washed, for which he still needs his mother's assistance.

Not only does Dominique have no notion of arithmetic but he has no idea of proportions. He thinks that a big or bulky object can be put in a small box as readily as in a large one. He is not able to infer from the shape and dimensions of a package what its contents might or might not be. Nor does he have any understanding of the value of money. He lacks any sort of logical structuration. The only thing he does well is draw. His sketches are good, the objects are easy to recognise (always the same few objects), and the parents hope that they will be able to find him a job 'that has something to do with drawing'.

Dominique has been given many electroencephalograms, and all the specialists who have seen him tell the mother the same thing: that the case is incomprehensible. This includes the specialists of the social services (*sécurité sociale*; see footnote to p. 238), where he was recently examined for two days. Dominique was expected 'to be all right' when eleven or twelve, but only the enuresis stopped during the summer between his twelfth and thirteenth year, as puberty came on. His mother noticed this by traces of discharge on his sheets, but the boy never mentioned it. He never masturbated. All the doctors asked the mother the same question. She didn't know this existed, and never saw him do anything like it. He has no sense of sexual shame, and his mother, as we shall see later, is very pleased about this.

Dominique is 'fixated' on his father, she says. It is the first time we hear any reference to the father, but we are told no more about him. It appears that Dominique resembles his mother's father, who is dark, like the mother. She says her son is very hurt by this resemblance. His father and brother and all the father's family — the Bels — are tall and blond.

Ever since early childhood, Dominique has shied away from physical contact with his mother, as with everyone else. When she thinks about it, this shyness seems to date back even before the birth of his little sister. This is his usual bearing, except when he panics — at a merry-go-round or a bicycle, when he clings to her or, when she is not there, to anyone who happens to be present.

The schools he has attended since he was six have no complaints to make about him, but at home he makes life impossible — it is hard to say just how. What is meant by impossible is that he upsets everything. It is not that he cries or complains: his sheer presence makes life difficult. It isn't easy to say why; he doesn't seem to be doing anything particularly objectionable. His mother doesn't seem to be quite able to explain how he makes life impossible. Her mother — Dominique's maternal grandmother — says that all this stems from the fact that Dominique was spoiled when his little sister was born: he should have been taught a lesson. If he didn't want to speak, his parents just should not have spoken to him. If he soiled himself, they should not have washed him. If he didn't want to sleep, they should not have bothered about him, and so on. In fact, Dominique's mother has been made to feel very guilty by her own mother for having been a bad mother to Dominique. This guilt feeling has been strengthened by the experience of the earlier psychotherapy: she feels guilty for not having suspected that her son was suffering from jealousy. She is now unsure about the further treatment which I suggest. She is also afraid her husband won't accept it because he doesn't much believe in 'medicine'. He is pretty much resigned to the fact that his child will remain backward. A few weeks ago the social welfare services made their medical report without recommending treatment. Madame Bel has come here to the child guidance clinic, not to have her son cared for, but to solve the problem of schooling in the coming year. 'What are we to do?' The elder brother is leaving school and will no longer be able to take Dominique to the special school, where he could have remained. He is unable to go by himself because he has to take a train morning and evening. The mother cannot take him: she says she 'has her daughter, whom she cannot leave by herself'. For these reasons she is hoping to find a boarding or part-boarding arrangement with a suitable school. This is why she has come to the child guidance clinic. The first person to see the mother and son together sent them to me for my opinion. Madame Bel expects me to tell her where her son can be sent to school.

I ask the mother for more detailed information about herself and her husband. This follows:

Madame Bel is an only child. Her parents lived in Africa, where her father was working. They are now living in the East of France, where their families originally came from. She spent her childhood in French Equatorial Africa, where her father was a builder, and then she went to boarding school in the Congo. She has led a very unhappy life. The only happy period of her life, she says, was at school in the Congo, where she was living with nuns and spent the first part of her baccalaureate studies. When the family returned to France because of the war, she decided to follow in the footsteps of the nuns who had brought her up and go into teaching. She passed the second part of her baccalaureate and went on to do her bachelor's degree in German, in the unoccupied zone of France. At eighteen she was so bored that she wanted to die; she started to become obese. She weighed more than 15 stone (and was only 5' 4" tall). She was very unhappy, didn't know how to dress or how to fix her hair, and was very shy. She was already making her own living

teaching German, while completing work on her degree. She
met her husband at this time; he himself was an escapee from a
German prison camp, studying at a school of engineering, alone
and far from his family. She feels that meeting her husband was
an extraordinary bit of luck. Her husband and she were 'twins
in the misery of youth'. She had intended to finish her degree,
but immediately found herself pregnant. Paul-Marie was born
without difficulty. Then came Dominique, who was very much
wanted (though they had really hoped for a girl), also without
problems.

There is little to be said about Dominique's early years.
He was a beautiful baby, big and lively, though Madame Bel
must 'admit' she found him very ugly: he was hairy and brown
like her father. She breast-fed him for a year. Dominique started
walking at the age of one, cut his teeth very early, and learned
to speak at the normal age, perhaps even a little earlier. In fact,
she recalls, he spoke quite well even before being weaned. On
the other hand it was difficult to toilet-train him, a habit which
the eldest boy had learned immediately; he had almost never
soiled his nappies. This comparison should be taken with some
reservations: the mother also says Dominique 'again started'
soiling himself at the time of his sister's birth, when he was two
and a half, and this would imply he was clean before.

The mother refers to a transitory period of 'dirtiness'
(which she calls 'encopresia') around the age of twenty months.
Thinking back on it, she recalls, it was just when she was
beginning to carry the girl. Dominique, she recalls, was again
toilet-trained while at the Montessori School, and later when
staying with his paternal grandmother, where she had sent him
towards the end of her pregnancy and at the time of Sylvie's
birth. But as soon as Dominique came home and discovered his
little sister, he not only began to display all the regressions that
we have described: he also asked to be given diapers like his
little sister, and insisted on being nursed like her. The mother
gave in to all these demands, to no avail. At the same time,
Dominique almost lost his ability to speak. Speech, however,
returned to him by degrees, his mutism lasting only briefly,

at most one month. The mother remembered all this because she had had reason to recall it at the time of Dominique's first analysis, when her attention had been drawn to the period of Sylvie's birth.

The mother adds that there seems to have been a sudden change, sometime after the sister's birth at the end of the summer holidays, when they moved to a larger apartment. Dominique started talking again when they moved to this new place. He also began to behave well again and regained control of his bowels, except at night.

Dominique is even-tempered. He never laughs except when by himself, and never cries. He is occasionally agitated by or even furious at people for doing what he doesn't want them to do, but he says nothing. She can see it nonetheless: she knows his ways.

As for her husband, Madame Bel tells us that he has been 'in the industrial export business' since Dominique's birth. She has been very lonely since her husband took on this job. 'She is both father and mother to her children.' Her husband is around, she says, 'very unpredictably': she never knows whether he will come back at night, and he sometimes remains away for two weeks or a month without warning. He doesn't want to be called at his office because it disturbs him. 'This seemed hard at first, but luckily I have the children. Since we get along perfectly well, the children don't see the difference, and in fact, they lack nothing, even when their father isn't there.'

There are no financial problems: her husband makes good money. To give an example of the way they live she tells me: 'Last night for example, my husband came home at midnight. We talked until two in the morning, he left for work at six in the morning with his suitcase. The children didn't get to see him, and he hadn't been home for two weeks.' Another example: 'We had decided that he would be spending Whitsunday holidays (Pentecost) together with us. The children were looking forward to it. Well, at seven o'clock in the morning there was a phone call. He had to leave. His suitcase is always ready.' He is an engineer and often has to go to Germany for work, mostly on short

notice. He is always on call. He is one of a team of two associated engineers. The other is an enterprising man born poor, but
graduated from one of the *grandes écoles*,* which gives him a title
superior to that held by her husband. She believes this other
man is unhappily married. He married a rich wife, their children
have been at boarding school since they were little, and the man
is interested only in his work. He and her husband are friends,
not just business associates. They can count on one another.
'Still, my husband, although he is so busy, always manages to
be home when he is needed: he has always been there when the
children were born. I can count on him when necessary. He stays
with the children and takes care of the house and while there
he is very motherly with them. Last year we were able to spend
two weeks of the holidays together, as we had done the year
before. It was the first time we all took our holiday together, the
children and he. When he is home, my husband potters about:
he likes gardening, fixing things and boating. My husband likes
children when they are babies, but he doesn't like to have them
help him because he likes to do productive work and to do it
well, and children always tend to be in the way. Since he is home
for very short periods of time, he can't take care of them, or
speak to them very much. But through me he knows everything
that happens, and he has all the faith in the world in me.'

I asked her how she felt about her husband's frequent
absences from home. 'Luckily,' she says, 'I am very busy; I have
three children; I do everything for myself. I like that, and my
daughter takes up much of my time. I help her with her studies, she needs me a great deal. And then there is the house-
work to do. Of course, hardly anybody ever visits. As a result,
Dominique doesn't see any men other than his father, and he has
always had women teachers in school. Once or twice a year, on
Sundays, we pay a visit to the engineer my husband works with.
We take the eldest boy and Sylvie, but we don't take Dominique
because my husband would feel embarrassed about him in front

---

*   These elite schools, of limited enrolment, are the major ladder to
      professional eminence. —Translators.

of his boss's wife. The three children admire their father a great deal; they like to sail on the boat with him during holidays, except for Dominique who, though he knows how to swim, is afraid of the water. So he stays and plays on the beach in a supervised kids' club while we go off sailing with my husband.'

What about the mother's parents? Their character?

She says nothing about her mother. She tells me that her father was extremely strict with her when she was young. Since she has been married, however, he does everything he can to please her. But, she says: 'I'm sure that if there was a quarrel between me and my husband, he'd take my husband's side. My father and mother both took my husband into the family; they saw him as they would the son they had always hoped for. My parents didn't want a girl.'

Her husband's parents?

She tells me her in-laws live in the Pyrenees. Her father-in-law is a retired officer with a mind of his own: he is always right. Still, he seems to be a man of good heart. But her husband doesn't get along with him. They both have their own ideas and they prefer not to speak to one another. Her husband, Georges, is the eldest child: he is forty-two years old. He had a difficult childhood: the son of a high-level officer, he moved seventeen times in his youth: he was not a very good student, but this mattered less at that time. Poor marks did not keep a child from going on to the next class; they mattered even less since the Bel children changed schools every year. There were several dramas in the family: 'The brother who came after my husband died of an accident when he was a year and a half; my husband was then five. The baby had swallowed a part of a toy train my husband was playing with.' Her husband has told her that he remembers this incident clearly, and that the empty cot impressed him enormously. We should bear this in mind. It is the same cot which later Georges Bel did not want to leave unoccupied from one child to the next. Paul-Marie left the cot only to give it over to Dominique. An empty cot in the parent's bedroom would have upset the father. Dominique took Paul-Marie's place in the cot without any delay, and Sylvie took Dominique's when he left home to stay with his paternal grandmother. The Bels did not buy Dominique a new bed in preparation for this third birth. Similarly the children were not allowed to play with electric trains when small because of the earlier accident and the possible danger; 'But it seems that my husband's fear has passed: for a few years now we have had an electric train at home, and my husband doesn't seem to fear accidents anymore.'

After the accidental death of the father's baby brother, there was a sister, seven years younger than Georges Bel, called Monette, which is practically the same first name as Madame Bel's. Monette is married and lives with her parents. She has five children and would have had six, but here too a drama occurred. A boy, born blue, died at the age of six months during a visit from Dominique. As Madame Bel, unlike her own mother, believes in telling her children the facts of life, she took Dominique to see his little dead cousin. She explained to him how he would be buried and how his body would be transformed into earth. Dominique was eight years old at the time.

So now there are only the husband and his sister left in the Bel family, two children out of four. Monsieur Bel did have a brother twelve years his junior, but he disappeared in the mountains at the age of seventeen. It was the same year as Dominique's birth, and it was a terrible drama, which Madame Bel relates in these terms: 'He set off with his sister and a young man into the Pyrenees. When they were on a path along the side of the mountain the friend dropped a good knife which slipped down among the bushes on the slope. My brother-in-law said: "I'm going to look for it and find it, you go right on. I'll take a short-cut and catch up with you." He was never seen again. It was thought for a while that he had been taken for a Spanish runaway or struck with amnesia. His parents looked for him in Franco's prisons; for three years they kept up hope. He couldn't legally be given up for dead because I think this requires a period of three years. It was a terrible time for us. I was then expecting Dominique. It was only three years later, when I was expecting my daughter, that we placed a marble plaque at the graveyard to commemorate Bernard. We could never hold

a religious ceremony because there was always a vague hope
that someday he would be found again. My parents-in-law are
strict Catholics, while my own parents don't go to church. I do
because of the nuns who brought me up.'

Madame Bel's other children?

She tells me the eldest boy would like to become a painter.
He hasn't been doing well at school in the last two years, but his
father wanted him to pursue his studies, contrary to the advice
of his teachers, who thought he would never get through his
secondary studies. He is now in the second year of the *lycée*
(year eleven) and will have to give it up. This is in fact what has
been decided for the next year, in spite of his father's wishes.
And this is why a place must be found for Dominique. The
father, who became an engineer after his escape from jail in
wartime Germany, would himself rather have become a dentist
or decorator, but the required course of study was too long.
The mother says that the eldest son, Paul-Marie, has good taste
in clothing, like his father, while she herself has little taste.
(Note that Dominique says that he has no 'taste' for foods.) Of
her eldest son she says: 'He is fairly mature for his age, and he
doesn't like girls. He cannot understand that young men flirt
with girls. He cannot imagine that a man and a woman could
sleep together.'

He is too 'prudish' and, she repeats, he is very mature for
his age: 'I think it comes from the fact that we are together a lot.'

She often uses the word 'we'. She and her eldest son form
a couple. 'Is she worried about his becoming a misogynist?' 'No
I'm not very worried about his attitude towards girls: my husband feels the same way. He thinks it's a very good thing for a
man to know only one woman in all his life, and that this should
be his wife. Anyway this is the case for us, and my husband is
not interested in women. I'm quite at ease in this respect. He has
only me and his work.' Paul-Marie goes around with his friends,
plays the guitar, likes to dance, but he likes girls only from an
aesthetic viewpoint. He is going to take up drawing at art school.

*She goes on to give me some more details about Dominique. She
says:* 'He has a good sense of rhythm. When his brother has

friends over and they put on a dance record, Dominique dances by himself in the room next door. But he stops right away if anyone sees him. Dominique is quite shy. In the street, when we go out together, he always walks ten metres ahead of us, slinking along the wall for fear of the cars, or ten metres in front of his brother when his brother is with him. And his brother doesn't like that because it's always easy to take the wrong bus or the wrong train. Dominique has been very anxious all day today. He was told that he would be going to see a lady doctor. He was afraid it was a doctor for crazy people and he was afraid of being detained and locked up.' He told his mother: 'I'm intelligent, but I'm uneducated and they put me into a school for backward children.' Madame Bel comments: 'This proves that he doesn't understand the meaning of the sentences he says, he just repeats them.'

Madame Bel's daughter?

'She is much like my husband. She likes to be of use. She would like to be a doctor. She is not very good with her hands, but she is good at cooking and at taking care of babies. She likes to study and has many friends.' Does the mother have friends? 'Oh no, I don't have time and I lived abroad in the colonies too long; the girl friends I've had live in all four corners of the world. I would have liked to stay in the colonies at a boarding school, if I hadn't had to make my own living so soon after. For me, boarding school was paradise. We wrote to our parents only once a month and that was good enough. I liked being a cub scout leader with the black children. I never was afraid of going around with Blacks. Anyway, I had a dreadful upbringing. I didn't learn anything. I don't know whether my mother is right. She feels that Dominique may have been spoiled. I don't know.' Madame Bel adds that she would have been very happy as a nun, leading the life of a teacher in Black Africa; but she is also very happy in her life as a wife and the mother of a family.

This is the end of the interview preliminary to my first contact with Dominique. Madame Bel warns me, before my seeing him, and whatever my opinion and my advice may be, that she will make no decisions before speaking with her husband.

2.   *Interview with Dominique alone*

Dominique comes in with the clay figure he has been modelling for 'the lady at the clinic'. He has chosen green clay (see
fig. 2, p. 14). The figure is typical of the stereotyped manner in
which he has been modelling for a long time. Dominique has
the bearing I described earlier: he speaks through his nose in
a mannered, extremely shrill voice. He doesn't look straight at
me – is he deliberately avoiding my gaze? – instead, out of the
corner of his eyes, from under the eyelids, he glances towards
his clay model, which he delicately pats and touches with his
fingertips. I introduce myself and ask him if he has anything he
wants to say to explain his own feelings. With a frozen, anxious
smile he says: *Well, me, I'm not like everybody else. Sometimes when
I wake up, I think I've lived through a true story.* (These are his first
words to me, literally transcribed.)

I SAY TO HIM: *Which made you untrue.*

DOMINIQUE: *That's it! But how do you know?*

ME: *I don't really know. That's what I think when I see you.*

DOMINIQUE: *I thought I was in the room as a little boy again,
afraid of burglars. They can take money* (argent), *they can take silver-
ware* (argenterie). *You can't imagine what they could take.*

He stops talking. I think to myself: Would the dining room
(*salle*) not be the dirty (*sale*)? And I say: *Or even your little sister?*

DOMINIQUE: *Oh you, how do you know everything?*

ME: *I don't know anything at first, but it's because you're saying
things to me in your own words and I'm listening as well as I can. It's
you who knows what has happened to you, not me. Together we might
be able to understand.*

Silence. I wait a long while, then:

ME: *What are you thinking about?*

DOMINIQUE: *I'm trying to figure out what's wrong in life. I'd
like to be like everyone else. For instance, when I read a lesson several
times over, I still don't know it the following day. Sometimes I feel I'm
dumber than everyone else, or I say to myself that I can't go on like
this. Things are going wrong. I'm talking nonsense.* (He cuts the last
word into two strongly accented syllables, in a very shrill tone.)

ME: *But it's true, you are talking nonsense. I see you know it:
maybe you're pretending to be a loony so as not to be scolded.*

DOMINIQUE: *That must be it. But how do you know?*

ME: *I don't know. But I see that you've disguised yourself as
a loony or an idiot. But you aren't, since you notice it and you want
to change.*

He comes back several times to his obsessions with the
multiplication table. I tell him once and for all that *this doesn't
matter to me, that his school maths isn't what interests me; that he
hasn't come to see a schoolteacher but a doctor, to find out how he might
stop being crazy and become like anyone else, if he wants to, everywhere
and not just in school with numbers.*

I ALSO TELL HIM: *What's important in life isn't what you do
with your lessons, your notebooks and schoolbooks, it's your way of
being, your way of being not true. Everything that happens in your
heart and that you don't want to talk about. I saw your mother before
and I spoke to her. I'll also speak to your father.* Then I explain to
him — but is he listening? — about confidentiality, and that we
won't begin anything without the father — at least without his
wishes, or his permission. His father will have to accept that
Dominique is coming to see me, and that we are trying to understand what keeps him from being like everybody else.

I see Dominique again in his mother's presence and I tell him
that I will see him with his father. Or, if in two weeks' time the
father cannot come to the appointment with his son and wife,
then I shall want to see him alone, on a day and at a time that he
is free, before the summer holidays. Even late in the evening, or
at my office, away from the clinic. *My seeing him is indispensable.
I repeat to Dominique in front of his mother that his father's absences
don't mean that he doesn't matter: that in any case his mother has
always acted after consulting her husband.* I repeat for Dominique's
sake that the director of the clinic (whom he has met) and I,
and perhaps also his mother, may decide on his working with
Madame Dolto — myself — but only if his father agrees.

At this point, Dominique no longer seems interested and
wants to leave. He goes out to wait for his mother in the waiting

room. Now alone with me, Madame Bel asks what I think of
the case.

The reader will agree, on the basis of this conversation,
that some contact has been established with Dominique. The
general impression which he creates is nevertheless psychotic,
though intelligent; witness his distant appearance, his mannered voice, his frozen smile, his way of holding himself at a
distance, his inability to look me in the face or to shake hands,
his not saying good-bye but instead escaping like a cat or a baby
who is bored when I speak to his mother.

I explained my views to Madame Bel. 'This isn't simple
retardation, but a psychotic, intelligent child. To my mind the
problem isn't Dominique's schooling, but his mental equilibrium, and his total lack of social prospects. I think we absolutely must try psychotherapy before trying to enrol him in an
institution that would accept him. I'm not thinking of a school
but, considering his age, something like a specialised training
centre for social problem cases. But I think we should resort to
this only if psychotherapy fails. We can still attempt it, since he
has just entered puberty, a favourable period for psychotherapy.
It is his lack of contact in any setting, his isolated life, which
are Dominique's real problems. Whether educated or illiterate,
it will always be this which makes him a misfit, although he is
intelligent.'

She says: 'My husband will tell you anything you want to
know, but you know, he is sceptical. He believes only in surgery,
not at all in medicine. It's a shame we can't operate in a case like
this.' She adds: 'When my husband and I don't agree, we never
tell the children. We always appear to be of the same mind. My
husband won't keep me from sending Dominique back to you,
but he still has a poor impression of psychotherapy from when
Dominique was younger. At that time we were told to treat him
just like his little sister, to show him our love. Then everything
would be all right. My husband feels that since we did everything we were told, to no avail, it means there is nothing to
be done. He has resigned himself to this. And then we were
told things would get better with time, patience and love, but

Dominique is getting stranger and stranger. Now it's getting so people notice it, where before it used to be overlooked.' I tell her, 'That's exactly why I think we should stop this evolution towards "madness".'

A week after this consultation we receive a letter from Madame Bel, which says among other things:

> I admit that I was very deeply shaken when you calmly told me that Dominique was mad and that he would have to be treated as such, when for the last twelve years we were told that he was merely retarded and that he would be all right with patience and much love. Now that the first shock is over, I think I tend to agree with your diagnosis because it corresponds to many things that worried us. I don't know why the Commission of Mental Hygiene which examined him for two days didn't tell us that. If only they had told us: we must do everything we can to cure him, he can still get better. But they told us we had to find him a school, to keep him at home as long as he didn't cause any trouble. With time, they said, everything would be all right. But I can tell you that since he saw you Dominique's behaviour has completely changed. Until then he had been living like a stranger at home. Now he is always trying to be of help, without our even asking him anything. He does the house-work, puts the cupboards in order, rushes to the kitchen to fetch anything that may be missing on the table, just to save me the trouble. He is extraordinarily thoughtful and nice to each of us. He is always seeking to please and be helpful. I must say it is touching. When I don't hear him moving about in his room, I go up to look and I find him desperately repeating the multiplication table in his book. He would so much like to be a success in school. In view of all his useless attempts he asked me the other day: 'Do you think I'll ever be able to do my work?' I told him: 'Don't worry, leave that maths book alone. The summer holidays are coming and Madame Dolto said it wasn't worthwhile

troubling your head with all these things. It's not that
you're stupid; just that something has gone wrong in your
head, and maybe it could get better.'

Since no one had yet proposed a date for meeting with her
husband, who is quite determined to come and see me, there
follows *another troubled letter.*

I suggest a time for the appointment.

*On 30 June, Monsieur Bel, Dominique's father, comes to see me
with his wife and son.*

Second Session: 30 June

Two weeks after the previous session

1.   Interview with the father

I see the father alone and let him talk. He tells me that he is never home and describes his job in approximately the same terms as his wife. He gets along very well with his boss, who is a friend. There are no set hours. He must always be on call. It's that kind of job but it pays very well and is very interesting. As for Dominique, he tells me that even when he was very small, before the birth of his sister, he was a difficult and demanding child. He used to hammer his head against the cot to make his mother come and, his father notes, he used to bruise himself so badly that they had to give in to him out of pity. And as for his wife, says Monsieur Bel, she takes care of everything, she is extremely active, and she has a great sense of duty. When he comes home, 'there is real rejoicing'. She isn't only a wife, but '150 per cent a mother'. She does everything the children ask her to. 'Has she no defects?' I say, smiling, 'not the smallest fault?' He laughs and says: 'She's sometimes a little angry, but that's all. She gets excited and shouts and then everything is forgotten.'

I ask Monsieur Bel to speak to me about his youth. His *first younger brother*, two years younger than he,* died in an absurd accident: 'He swallowed a part of the train I was playing with.'

---

*   Monsieur Bel says two years younger, Madame Bel had said four. Four is correct. Monsieur Bel's slip shows that he is identifying himself with Paul-Marie, and his younger brother with Dominique. —F.D.

I asked him what effect this tragedy had on him: 'My parents didn't blame me for it too much, because this baby put everything he could get hold of into his mouth. We spent two days asking ourselves whether he had swallowed the missing piece or not and we kept on looking for it. Finally we had an X-ray taken. The missing piece was in his stomach, and an operation was thought necessary. The baby died on the operating table.' Monsieur Bel's *other brother* disappeared when he was seventeen years old. He relates the story in the same terms as his wife. He tells me that his mother used to dream that the boy had been eaten by bears: the experience was a terrible trial, especially for her. What was particularly dramatic was that no trace of the boy could ever be found. 'My brother was twelve years younger than me, he was really a nice fellow. He was just the opposite of me.'

I ask him: 'What do you mean, the opposite?'

'Well, he was a *tightwad*, where I'm very generous. He was closed up inside himself, where I'm outgoing. There used to be great battles between my brother and my younger sister, who was seven years younger than me and five years older than him.' Of *his sister* he says she resembles his daughter, but has more self-confidence. But then his daughter is more enterprising than his sister was. On the other hand, *his eldest son Paul-Marie*, he says, 'is like me, timid but open once you get to know him; he doesn't dare knock on a door.' And *Dominique?* 'That's not easy to say. He's from another planet. He isn't one of us.' He doesn't manage to say anything else.

'Is he affectionate with you?'

'He's especially fond of his Uncle Bobbi, my sister's husband.'

Monsieur Bel tells me that his sister was the first girl to be born in the Bel family for 150 years. As a result she was extraordinarily spoiled. Because of this lack of girls, his daughter was similarly welcomed with great joy by all the Bel family. *His wife?* He tells me that 'she's extremely unsociable when it comes to visiting others, but our house is the house of God, anyone is welcome; my wife is too easily influenced. She's forever giving in to the children and sometimes they drive her up the wall.'

He adds: 'Dominique has changed very much in the last two or three weeks. My wife thinks it's related to his talk with you, I don't know whether this is so or whether it's a coincidence. He's always asking if he can't be useful in some way or other. The other day he got hold of a cookbook and made a clafoutis, all by himself, it was really quite good and it gave me a lot of faith in him. You see, when it comes down to it, being a cook is quite a good trade. Maybe this will really interest Dominique. I've also thought that he could become a shoemaker. It's a trade that isn't unpleasant or too difficult, and it doesn't take too much training.'

The father has no illusions about Dominique's possibilities but he has more confidence now. 'Dominique may learn to mix with people.' The father says that he was present at the birth of all his children and that he even took care of Dominique's delivery by himself, along with his mother-in-law, who is present at all her daughter's deliveries. '*My mother-in-law* is very good-hearted, she'd give up the shirt off her back. She was brought up as a peasant and is superstitious. For instance, she believes in cutting off a marmot's paw and tying it as an amulet around babies' necks, and she's done all kinds of things like that for my children. I let her do whatever she wants. She has a rough, peasant character. She brought up her brothers and sisters herself because her mother died young. Life hasn't spoiled her. I remember my wife used to quarrel with her endlessly, but since we got married, my presence has made things much easier. My father-in-law is a very good man, a little rough, he was in the colonies and it shows . . .'

He speaks of Dominique's birth: he remembers it 'as if it were yesterday'. They had all gone to the Rex cinema ('when my mother-in-law is here, we take her out a bit'); Madame Bel began to feel labour pains and they came home right away. The baby was born before the doctor had a chance to get there. Dominique was born covered with fuzz. He even seemed to have hair all the way down to his eyes and down to his cheekbones. He looked like a monkey, Monsieur Bel said, laughing. His wife found him so ugly that he had to cheer her up.

'*My eldest son, Paul-Marie?* He loves children, especially other people's. Anyway, he's good-natured at home. He's lazy, passive. My wife tells me he's different when I'm not there.'

'*My daughter?* Now she is very hard-working. She likes to work, and she's a good student. She has many friends. *Paul-Marie* is quite a loner. My wife says that he has friends, but I don't know them. He doesn't open up to me.'

'*Dominique* doesn't readily make friends, but when we're at the beach, he plays with children seven to eight years old.'

'He plays?'

'Well, let's say they're the only ones he doesn't run away from. But he really prefers to be alone and can entertain himself with nothing but talking to himself. He keeps away from others and they don't seek him out.'

After the interview is over, Monsieur Bel says he quite agrees to having Dominique make a try at psychotherapy with me at the beginning of the school year. He is ready to do anything for his son. However, he doesn't have much hope, and will not be disappointed if we merely succeed in keeping him the way he has been for the last two weeks. He has been behaving like a boy who is waking up.

From this meeting, Monsieur Bel comes across as a man who is very busy, easy to get along with, and who doesn't have much of a sense of intimacy with his family. He is nonetheless good-hearted and hard-working. He may be emotionally attached to the man who is his associate, boss and friend. He has a lot of respect for his wife, and a grudge against no one, but I can say no more about him. I asked him whether he thought that Paul-Marie knew the facts of life, knew about sex and women. He told me that he had had a brief talk with him recently and that he was happy to see that his son had decided not to go around with girls before getting married. This is what he himself had done and he was proud of it. But they don't talk much. Monsieur Bel is at home too rarely, and when he is home he is very busy.

Monsieur Bel left after having told Dominique, at my request, that he agreed to our starting work together at the beginning of school next year. Since he was leaving for Germany, he said good-bye to his wife and son. There followed a session with Dominique, which I had been planning to make rather short, but which I prolonged because of its interest from the viewpoint of diagnosis.

2.   Interview with Dominique

Dominique comes in saying in an affected, nasal and rather trumpeting voice: *I've got to get out of this to keep them from following me all the time.*

Me: *And you want to get out of it?*

Dominique: *Oh yes, certainly. And then I had dreams when I was ten years old.* (I told him at the first session that he could tell me about his dreams.)

Me: *Long ago?*

Dominique: *Oh yes; long ago.*

Me: *But how old are you?*

Dominique: *They say I'm fourteen, but I think that it was very long ago that I was ten. But you know, I just don't understand maths. And so the dreams, well, I got lost in a railway station and I met a witch and all she said was crack, crack, crack* (with his hands he makes a gesture of cracking something). *I was looking for some information and it was getting on my nerves, I didn't want any trouble, especially since I was in a station. Once in a while I managed to help out, but I didn't succeed and nobody needed me. And then, you see, whenever I have 500 francs, all I have to do is wait until I have 500 francs and then I'll be rich. But you know, it will take a long time. What's needed is patience,* he adds in an altered voice, as if it weren't he who were speaking. (His natural voice, as noted before, is already quite nasal and artificial-sounding.)

When he stops talking, I speak to him about his father's visit. I stress the trouble his father had gone to, and the interest his father has in him. I ask Dominique to tell me what he made for me while he was waiting. (In my technique I ask children to make a drawing and a figure out of modelling clay before the session.)

His clay figure (see fig. 3, p. 41). *It's a 'person'. What about this person? He must have some ideas of his own.*

There follows a long, nasal presentation, seemingly delirious and difficult to follow or even to make out, and which I couldn't take down. I only know that it was near a station, that his father was involved, and that cars climbed into trees. All this is delivered in a very loud voice; the tone of his voice occasionally dropping, as if he were communicating a secret. I understand this secretive tone no better than what he is saying aloud. I simply say yes to everything he says until he stops speaking, and then:

ME: *I've got to learn to understand better all the things you say. Let's see your drawing.* (His drawing isn't quite finished.) *What is it?* (See fig. 4, p. 42.)

DOMINIQUE: *It's a boat of the Trojan War, a Trojan boat. They were in it, they might have been dead, the dead too. Houses too, on the boats, they take everything, they couldn't believe it, it isn't water.* I think of Egypt, of the ship of the dead, of the Trojan horse. There follows a series of words in which I seem to hear the number (*trois*), and not the city (*Troie:* 'Troy').

I ASK HIM: *The number three, is that what you're talking about?*

DOMINIQUE: *Three times three is nine and nine divided by three?* And in another tone of voice: *He doesn't know, but they say it's the same thing, that all you have to do is put a division upside down in order to make a multiplication and he doesn't understand anything about threes.*

I then draw a series of lines on the paper, to have him count along with me. There are twenty lines. I group them in fours or fives to show him the process of multiplication and division. Dominique displays a total inability to take in any concept consisting of three elements: $20 \div 4 = 5$ to him means $4 = 5$; but $20 \div 4$ is meaningless. Or else the meaning is that $20 = 4$. There are no relations between figures other than adding and subtracting; as for the signs $\div$, $=$ and $\times$, he refers to them as 'is'.

I repeat my question about his choice of words. *The Trojan War? It's the story of a boat that came in loaded with dead people in order to win the war.*

Where?

No answer. Nothing is to be got out of him.

Fig. 3
Clay figure made by Dominique
before the second session

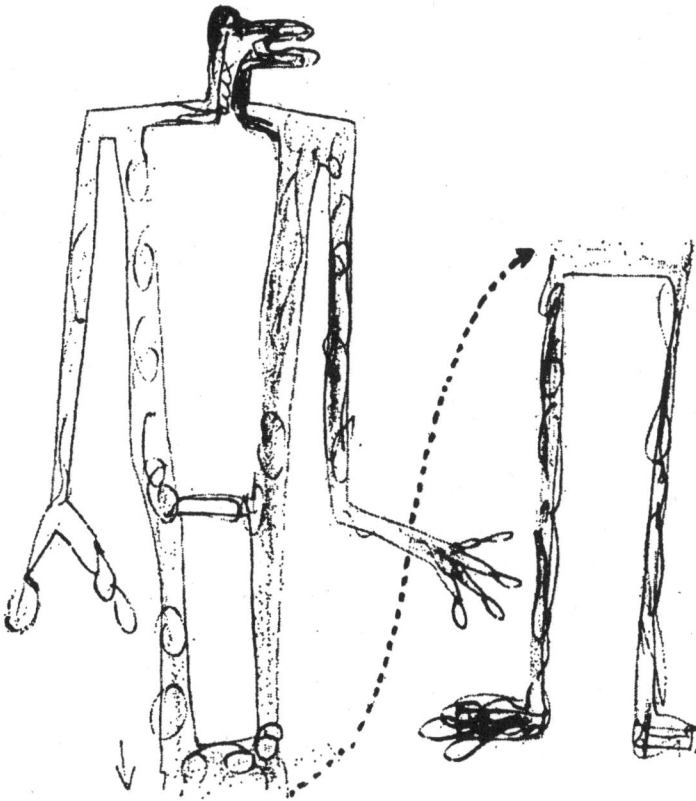

A man made of small pellets of modelling clay, stuck together
end to end, about 40 centimetres long.

Fig. 4
Unfinished drawing made by Dominique
before the second session

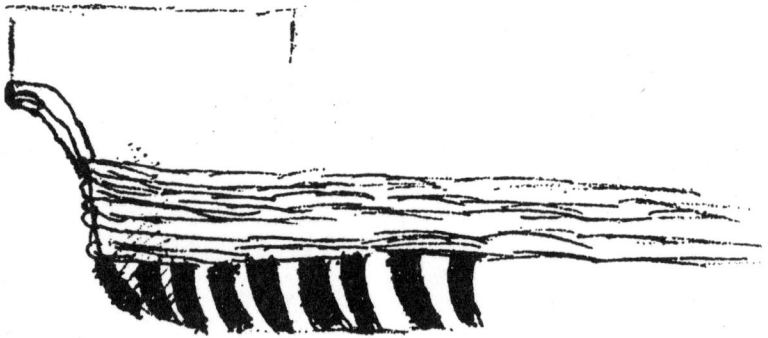

Trojan boat, about 10 centimetres long: 'They were in it, they
might have been dead, the dead too (half-raving). *Houses*
too, on the boats, they take everything, they couldn't believe it,
it isn't water.'

There is, properly speaking, no exchange between us. He talks to himself, stops talking, starts talking again. I have the impression that he is in a world where I cannot find him, when he is addressing me, I cannot find any meaning in the literal meaning of his words. They obviously stand for something else. For example. One comes to the clinic (a kind of station, waiting room, front desk: you pay and use your receipt as a ticket) for some information, some re-information,* and there one finds a witch (Madame Dolto) who speaks about three 'cracks' or who 'cracks' herself. (Later it will be said of the sister that she is a 'crack'). A 'crack', accompanied by a gesture of cracking, is, for me today, the only movement that represents the impression of a body: being put between grinding jaws. No doubt that is what he transfers onto my bizarre and valorised self, as in any attempt to establish contact. This is what I understand of this form of dangerous contact which he feels in relation to orality. What there is between us is mutual consumption (*inter-consummation*), according to what he understands of libidinal relations.

I give no advice for the holidays. But his mother and I decide that Dominique and I will meet again in October, and I inform Dominique of this.

As to his schooling? The mother asks what is to be done with him next year. Dominique doesn't want to stay for this discussion and goes slinking off, like last time, without saying goodbye. I recommend he take a special educational needs class at the primary school in his neighbourhood. Or else he should continue at the special school where he has been the last two years, if proper arrangements can be made to have him accompanied to and from school. I add that the *present treatment*, rather than the finding of a perfect school, may perhaps allow Dominique to adjust into the educational system. His failure in the last two years while attending an excellent school with a flexible, specialised teaching philosophy is proof of this. Since financial means are limited – at least so I am told – I feel it is

---

*   Read *renseignement* ('information') as *re-enseignement* ('re-teaching').
—Translators.

better to choose the free primary school and make something of an effort to afford the treatment, at least for a trial period.

The clinic received *several letters from the mother* during the month of September. The first, which never reached me, said that a special educational needs class would be given in a neighbouring school for children of Dominique's age, but that the headmaster was formally opposed to his admission. These letters of Madame Bel's implore Madame Dolto to send in word to back Dominique's application for admission. It is the only chance. It would be beyond their means to continue schooling in the special school, which would mean getting someone to see Dominique to and from school, while the school where the special educational needs class is being given is only a few minutes away from home. The headmaster feels that he cannot admit Dominique in view of the information he has received from the child guidance clinic where Dominique had been examined. The class is not equipped to deal with character troubles or madness. 'Yes, yes,' the mother was told, 'we are always being told that the children are very nice and then they make life impossible. This school is open only to children who have fallen behind their class for reasons of absence, or for some other simple causes, not to problem children.' I give in to Madame Bel's request and write a letter. A return letter says that Dominique will be admitted for a few weeks, on trial, as I had requested. *Another letter from Madame Bel dated late September* confirms that she will be coming to the appointment set for the beginning of October. She tells me that Dominique started school a few days earlier; the teacher has never seen a child try harder. He literally drinks in her every word. She is very pleased with him as a student, and if he keeps up this way, she is certain he will catch up, since he pays attention and is very willing to learn, which is a rare quality. And not only does the child behave differently in class, reports Madame Bel, but the dog, which Dominique used to terrorise, is now delighted to see him come home and welcomes him more effusively than he does any other member of the family. Dominique says: 'See how this nice dog likes me and how happy he is at my coming home,' and it is quite true. The dog behaves towards Dominique the same way Dominique now behaves towards other boys. 'I had noticed how terrified he was of anyone approximately his own height and age, and how he would play only with small children and distantly. And now he plays with his own peers, and when his sister complained that the boys from the boys' school across from her own bothered the girls when school let out he told her: "You know, from now on I can hurry over on my bike and meet you when school's over. I'm big and strong like the others now and you can count on me." He used to have a phobia of bicycles but this summer he has been doing a lot of bike-riding. He learned as soon as he tried.' Madame Bel adds: 'When I told Dominique that we had an appointment to come and see you, he wasn't at all happy. I'll tell you what he said: "Oh damn it. I'm going to miss school. I really wonder why we have to go to see Madame Dolto. I'm doing fine, I don't need a doctor at all." I answered that his papa and I wanted him to be taken care of. I'm writing all this to show you the change in his behaviour. He is still just as helpful and affectionate at home, not only with me, but with his sister. For instance: before, when he took a bath, he took all the time in the world, and he left the bathroom dirty; well, now he actually brings in the hot water himself. We don't have running water, and have to have the water heated and carried into the bathroom. He brought in the hot water for his sister, he laid out a dry towel on the radiator, and he even went so far as to spread toothpaste on her brush. My daughter can't get over it. Dominique, who never even thought to say good-morning or good-evening, kisses us good-night now every evening.'

When I received the letter with all this news, I said to myself: the boy has sensed that his deeper mental structures were about to be touched; he is now defending himself in another way.*

---

*   Some psychotherapists in a similar situation are satisfied with a child's apparent progress, by his better adaptation to school or family, and they tend to stop treatment at this point. This presents a danger. An enclave of unconscious resistance may well endure behind the screen of obsessive rituals erected by the superego for the purpose of pleasing others. —F.D.

Third Session: 18 October

There is no preliminary contact with Dominique's mother. I have to take him by the hand to get him to follow me. He probably expected that I would speak to a grown-up first, as I did before the holidays. Or else this is his way of expressing refusal.

Dominique comes in and sits down. He does not tell me that he didn't want to come, as his mother wrote me, or that he was annoyed to have to come: this is already clear from the situation. He will tell me his fear that if he exposes his discontent I may become very angry (and perhaps bite him?). I remind him of the decision to have a series of meetings two weeks apart during which he is to tell me everything he thinks as well as the dreams he remembers — by means of words, drawings and modelling. I assure him of the confidentiality about what happens at the sessions, a confidentiality which he himself will not be bound by. Then I wait.

Dominique speaks in the same affected tone, with the same nasal voice. He still avoids my gaze, as before, but this time I am able to understand and note down everything he says. *There is a little girl who is extraordinarily strong, Fifi Steelstrand* (Brin d'Acier).* *She has very strong arms. She's funny. She sleeps with her head upside down. She's very nice. She's very funny. She has two little friends in the zoo. Two tigers who've run away. The guard and the policeman too want to catch 'him' again* (the tigers are no longer two) *but Fifi says to the tiger, 'If you bite; I'll bite you too.'* He was

---

*   'Fifi Brindacier' is the name given in French to the children's book
    character Pippi Longstocking. —Translators.

bold, but not very brave . . . and he was very scared of her. Then she sang to him, 'It was a little "cha-cha-cha"' * *in order flatter him and he wasn't very pleased, but he let her stroke him . . .*

Dominique adds some other things about Fifi Steelstrand, who is courageous, daring, true and not true. At first he identifies me with Fifi, but later he identifies himself with her by saying: *His mother was a little troubled to see 'him' befriending tigers, but 'she' said to her: 'Don't worry, mother, when I'm a grown man, I'll take care of myself.* (Note the alternation of the masculine and the feminine for the same person.) And then in a lower pitch, as if telling me a secret: *You know the teacher made four groups, there are those who are ahead, and those who are behind, and I'm in a group too, but you don't know what group you're in. She makes up groups like that. Then she gives an assignment and then you know you're in a certain group.* Then he continues more loudly: *Fifi, 'he' has red hair and his mother died when 'she' was a baby. She performed a lot of tricks which would never have occurred to anyone else. Some of them aren't too bad. One day she made a red and blue dress with a brown hem. It happened to be her birthday.* In a low tone: *She put on her father's shoes and she put on green ribbons.* Then, loudly: *What strikes me was when I turned to look at my little chest of drawers, I'd put the soldiers of the Middle Ages there. The kind of people you wouldn't like to meet in the street. I put them in the chest of drawers. And then I was afraid at night. And I wouldn't go to bed before the end because I want to see her again. It's me that she's going to do things to*—† Dominique stops talking. I think to myself: he is putting things in order; whatever frightens him he is now enclosing in his fantasies: it is he who represents the middle age in the family, between the eldest and the youngest child. Is this a dental, phallic aggressivity which he is repressing?

I say: *Who is going to do things to you?* No answer. Nonetheless, it is obvious that in his delirious-type transference, he is talking about me. I wait a fairly long time and then he says:

---

*   Also: *cha = chat*, 'cat'. —Translators.

†   Note that the phobias that from the observation of daily behaviour had supposedly disappeared (bicycles, dogs and peers) have in fact become focused upon the present transference. —F.D.

Let's say she's back from her holiday and that she's a little tanned. (This describes my complexion, as compared to last June.) *Or that she has made a little cruise in her cellar (?). She has a black side and a red side. Myself, when I've got a friend I ask 'her' what she wants to play at.* (This is an allusion within this transference to the fact that I propose nothing to him, that I remain quiet. See the clay figure represented as a two-colour lollipop, with sticks for legs: fig. 5, p. 50.)

ME: *What about this friend. Is it a boy or a girl?*

DOMINIQUE: *Why no, it's a boy. And you, do you have television, because there are some districts where they don't have any . . . And what colour were his eyes? Yes, what colour?* He asks the question while looking at the black and red clay figure in the shape of a tongue or a slab . . . He keeps looking at it. *Well, they had no colour. They were bright . . .* He brings out the word forcefully, with emotional intensity. Then there is a silence. He goes on: *Once at my grandparents' house, I was in a room with my cousin and there was a noise in the attic. My grandfather had said it was a cat, that the cat was fighting or that there were rats. It's an old memory you know, in 1960, but it was in our time, it's not prehistoric.*

ME: *Who is your cousin?*

DOMINIQUE: *I think it's the daughter of my father's sister.*[*] *Babette is her name, she is seven* (his cousin was in fact seven years old when he was eight, as I will learn later). *She wasn't afraid, but she was asking, and me too, we were asking, what did I have on my head?* And then, sotto voce: *I often see mice, myself. I don't know where I see them, but I see them . . . But once I carried everything into my battlefield in my head, then I camouflaged my military truck and then the soldiers and then if a mouse comes through, it disturbs all the soldiers.* (This is a memory connected with something he knows in reality, the only experience he seems to know: that of relations between the members of his family. He is now describing *hallucinations or hallucinosis*). Silence. He has started modelling

---

[*] *La fille à la soeur à mon père*, instead of *la fille de la soeur de mon père*. Dominique uses very childish language language [*fille à*] for genital relations. —F.D.

Fig. 5
First version of Fifi Steelstrand made by
Dominique during the third session

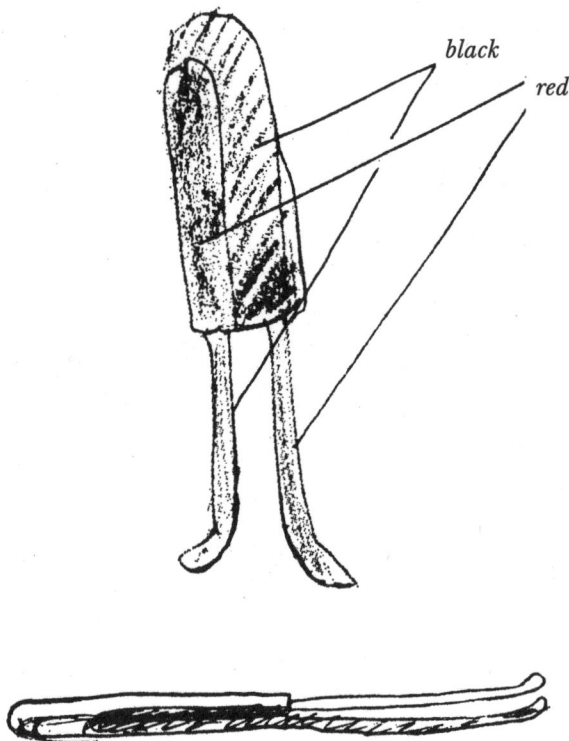

Black and red modelling clay, very thin legs, no heels.
The figure at first resembles a lollipop or a tongue,
lying flat on the table. Dominique then breaks it up,
and using different colour clays, makes it into
the little girl of fig. 6.

Fig. 6
Second version of Fifi Steelstrand

*Intermediate stage between first
and second versions*

*Purple clay used instead of black, and pink used instead
of red. The buttons and eyes are small balls of clay.*

*The blob that represents the right arm is formed out of a
bottleshaped mass of clay. Dominique spends a long time
handling this without telling me what it is: 'It's nothing.'*

*Dominique purposely puts in pointed holes 'for the pockets'
and adds high heels, but makes no hands. He tries to make
the figure stand by holding it up.*

another clay figure (see fig. 6, p. 51). Then, loudly, he trumpets: *My teacher says that when a rat walks across the room, they always thought there were many. They say if you walk on a viper's foot. But anyway, vipers are hidden in the trees.* (I remember the cars too were hidden in the trees, but I don't tell Dominique.) He goes on: *But you see she has pigtails. But I didn't make any knots in them, because I rolled them up . . . and then, you know, Babette, well, it's better to get along with her than not. Two boys made fun of her red hair and then she tied them to a branch of a tree by the skin of their necks and then, you see, she put on the big shoes of her mother's high heels.* (Here is Babette again, his cousin, who has the daring character which the father attributed to his daughter – the very picture of his own sister but more enterprising.)

DOMINIQUE: *Right now I've got a collection of soldiers of the Middle Ages, and a collection of match boxes and a collection of Gringoire stamps.* And then at home I had a whole farm . . . With my cousin, we say we're a cattle dealers.*

ME: *Your cousin?*

DOMINIQUE: *Yes, Bruno. He's the son of my father's sister.† Trouble is, my cousin, wow, she was spoiled by my grandmother. Now it's different. It's my mother of my father because the other one is called Mémé* (Granny). *You know she carries a pony under her arm because her father gave it to her, it's a well-known fact* (?). *A little horse, stronger than a foal. But strong, is she strong! Oh là là!* He looks at his clay figure, a little character some 12 centimetres high, lying on the table: its legs wouldn't hold it up.

One can see that this figure differs from the stereotyped ones of the last two years. At this session I merely listened, trying to understand as well as I could what was taking place, that is, the transference of dependence to myself. Dominique is expressing

---

*   Gringoire, a firm that manufactures gingerbread, encloses stamps
         representing coats of arms in each of their packages. —Translators.
         As expected, Dominique is attempting to set up obsessional defences.
         —F.D.

†   The same infantile genitive (*fils à la soeur*) as noted on p. 49.
         —Translators.

his fear of the female members of the family, the fascinated interest which he has long had in his cousin Babette — an interest which he now also feels towards me — as well as his phobia of animals, of any kind of fighting aggression. He is saying something about sexuality — though completely foreclosed inside — that relates to Babette, *alias* his sister: the story of the snake associated with Babette's rolled-up pigtails; with the rats that drive off the dangerous soldiers hidden in the chest of drawers or cabinet;* with the motor impulses hidden in the trees;† with sexual impulses which are punished by the tempters (myself in this case).

This, it will be noted, is the characteristic language of the psychotic. But one might also say, one who knows children, that it is the language of a child of under three. They often speak this way, particularly when by themselves, when there is no one in the room to listen. They then speak about themselves in the third person, at least until the time of the discovery of the first person, when this 'he' begins to alternate with 'I' (or their first name) and designates them as subjects. Is this the talk of an ordinary learning-disabled person, as was diagnosed following IQ tests that assigned Dominique a mental age of four or five? No. No child of this age, and as disoriented as Dominique obviously is in time and in his own space, could be as certain of the place of things and of family relationships. In these matters he shows no confusion whatsoever, as we will see in all the following sessions.

---

*   It will be remembered that a chest of drawers or cabinet can represent the abdomen and that Dominique wants his underwear to be put away in the chest of drawers without having been washed. —F.D.

†   In the imagination of children trees are an anthropomorphic presentation of their experience of the world. The inner organs are quiet in a body in a state of well-being; they are troubled during periods of anxiety. —F.D.

Fourth Session: 16 November

Four weeks after the previous session

Sessions had been scheduled for every second week; the previous one was cancelled because of All Saints Day (a holiday in France).

From Dominique's mother, whom I meet in the waiting room with Dominique, I hear that everything is going all right and that the teacher is pleased with him. But Dominique says nothing at all himself. He comes in and as soon as he has sat down: *I'm going to make a sheepdog. You know, Ironstrand: well I've finished the story.* (The reader will recall that earlier on he had called her 'Steelstrand'.)

ME: *Oh, yes?*

DOMINIQUE: *She left with my father and when she found out that her friends were crying, she wanted to stay with the friends. Though it didn't appeal to her, to live in a bamboo hut.* * *But she stayed with them so they wouldn't cry. I'm reading a fascinating book right now. It's the story of a sheepdog. The mother dog had little pups, including a lovely red-haired one.* (His tone is bizarre, with some affected mimicry.) *And the boy said: 'This one I'll keep.' The father wouldn't let him. He sent it off by truck in a box with the others. Then there was a bump.* (No doubt the truck hit a hole in the road and the box was thrown out, but Dominique provides no details.) *The dog came back: it was in the station and he asked his way.* (He, too, returned after having been lost for a day.) *And*

---

*   *Cabane à bambou* (instead of *de bambou*): an infantile form of expression. —Translators.

the boy, Paulo was his name, said to his father: 'You see, we want to get rid of him, then he comes back.' (His brother Paul-Marie is sometimes called Paulo. In the parents' mind, our clinic should have given them the address of a specialised institution to which Dominique would be sent.) I say nothing, and Dominique goes on after a silence: *Oh yes, the beginning of the dog's training was a failure, but if we take a lot of trouble and it works, there's a chance he'll get a prize. Next year he'll take another dog's place.* At this juncture Dominique becomes quiet and works on his clay model: *Paul-Marie won't let anyone talk, me or my sister because we're little. He's the only one who talks to Mama.* I, on the other hand, allow Dominique to talk and I listen to him. He is working on his sheepdog (see fig. 7, pp. 58–59), struggling with the 'tail' and the rear end, which remains disconnected from the rest for a while. He doesn't know whether to put the tail pointing up or down. Finally, he leaves the tail up; he continues work on the trunk, then on the head and the ears. The whole thing is set up very solidly, fixed, set on the table, on its four feet.

DOMINIQUE: *Paul-Marie always has to be right. Otherwise he's nice enough, but he's especially nice with children of other families . . . Still, he should know there's such a thing as being brothers . . .* A pause. *Look, he's got a little mouse!* (He quickly shapes a small, long object.) Pause. Then in a low voice: *He is going to eat the mouse.* (He makes the dog 'eat' the mouse. This changes the snout: from long with a slit to short with no slit. Dominique puts a kind of terminal knob on the tail and does away with the eyes.) *Here's the head, and all the rest. There you are. Now he is going back to sleep . . .* (His father had said that Dominique was waking up.) . . .

And he's digesting. Look, we're going to teach him how to walk! But where is the mouse? (He pretends to be looking for it . . .) *Why, it's true, he's eaten it; it's all gone.* He puts the dog back on its feet. Now he removes the dog's head and extends the tail to the ground. Pause . . . *Oh, yes, then we started with a dog: well, we are going to end up with a cow. The dog has a dream where he becomes a cow. And then . . .*

At this point I notice that the dog has, in place of eyes, two oval half-eggs, set on the head in relief like a fly's eyes, one vertically, the other horizontally. This animal head, now lying on the ground, has no sensory organs except eyes and ears, and the ears lack holes. Dominique takes off the ears and puts on 'horns', that is, a crescent, and puts the new head back on the body.

DOMINIQUE: *There's a fly which is having fun pestering the cow. It's invisible. And this ox is dreaming that he is a milch cow.* Silence.

ME: *How old were you when you found out that what cows have between their legs were not 'wee-wees'* (fait-pipi)? Silence. After a pause during which he blushes, Dominique replies: *Oh, well, it was very late. I thought they had four. Well, one day in school . . . but I wasn't sure.* The first reply is glossed over, but has the force of an interpretation accepted; it relates to the felt need to manifest oneself as phallic. My 'association' has the value of an interpretation which rids him of the phantasy of urethral teats (i.e., an udder for urinating).

HE GOES ON: *Oh, yes. About this cow. She's dreaming she's an ox. The cow is the ox's dream. But the ox she's dreaming of is dreaming he's a cow.*

I INTERRUPT: *Do you think the cow is dreaming of an ox or of a bull?*

DOMINIQUE: *Oh, that, well, that, I really don't know.*

ME: *Do you know if there is a difference between a bull and an ox?*

DOMINIQUE: *Well that, I mean, I think that bulls are much meaner. So I was told. But this cow is a sacred cow. And what does she think she is! Well!* Very softly: *She thinks she's a sacred ox. But it's a mirage!* And then raising the pitch of his voice, as if it were a woman's: *You know, mirages are sometimes historical.**

ME: *I think that the sacred ox or the sacred cow — that may be because you have a crush on Madame Dolto. You want to make her sacred.* He blushes all the way to his ears and says: *Yes,* and then keeps quiet. *That's it!* he repeats in a hollow voice, with an intense expression.

ME: *And maybe you've had a crush on someone else before?*

---

*   Note that sometimes when speaking, Dominique becomes a mere tape recording of other people's speech. —F.D.

Fig. 7
The modelling of the sheepdog made by
Dominique during the fourth session

*First stage: Hind quarters. Dominique kneads
the tail, and moves it successively up and down,
repeating this gesture a few times as he speaks,
before going on to shape the rest of the dog.*

*Second stage: The whole dog. The animal stands solidly
on its feet, pointing.*

*Variation A: Muzzle with a slit for the mouth, and a
knob at the end of the tail.*

*Variation B: Muzzle shortened, no more slit; tail lowered
and ending in two prongs.*

*Variation B¹: Tail all the way down; paws, toes and claws very
realistic; note that the ears have not been hollowed out. Eyes:
two oval shapes, set in relief, the right eye vertically, the left
horizontally.*

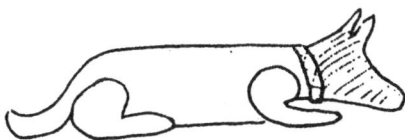

Third stage: The dog is sleeping: no more eyes. The head is then cut off at the collar. This headless dog body will now become the body of a cow.

Fourth stage: The sheepdog turning into a cow. Two rows of rounded teeth on the collar. Dominique stands the headless dog up on its dog legs; he lengthens the tail and the body, and transforms the legs.

Fifth stage: Sacred cow (sacred ox). About 8 centimetres high. Dominique demolishes and then rebuilds the ox-cow, and then leaves it standing on the table, as a witness to the rest of the session.

He speaks very low, with the same expression: *Yes, on my teacher.* Then changing his tone: *But me, you know,* (in an aggressive tone) *I don't want it, I don't want it, it isn't right. I want to love only my parents.* The tone of his voice now sounds much more involved. He seems anxious, agitated; the pitch rises and becomes shrill towards the end.

I TELL HIM: *You can love your parents as parents, but you can't have crushes on them. It isn't the same thing, loving one's parents and loving others, or women.* And I tell him the law that love has to find its object outside the family. *It's all right to have crushes, it doesn't remove love for parents, it isn't the same sort of thing. Later after many crushes like that, there comes something much stronger. Strong enough for a boy to get engaged, to be married and to have children. This is how your father met your mother when he was a young engineer and she a young teacher. They were married and had children.* He listens very carefully, and then says in a modulated, calm voice: *Oh well, so that's it! Well! Well! My cow just woke up . . . And she isn't sacred anymore. She's like any other cow . . . She dreams that she belongs to a nomad.* (I wonder: is it his father with his little suitcase always ready?) He hums a tune that I don't recognise: *'pam, pam, pam, pam'.* He destroys the cow.

ME: *What's that song?*

DOMINIQUE: *That's the nomad's song. While she was chasing the flies with her tail, the nomad was sleeping.* He then becomes quiet and reconstructs the cow, which he had completely taken apart the moment that I gave an interpretation of the transference onto me of his ideal ego – a self phallic, mammary and urethral all at once. *Well, now I am going to make the nomad. A little fellow with a beard who was sleeping in a tree. Whenever he laughed, he was laughing in his beard, and his beard was in the tree.* (See the first state of the nomad figure: fig. 8, p. 60.)

The beard may be a reference to the marmots whose feet Dominique's maternal grandmother used to tie around his neck when he was a baby; the nomad bears some resemblance to a marmot. Remember also the dynamism of the cars and serpents, in the branches of trees. I say nothing and wait. He goes on: *One day he had to get rid of his cow, because he was a poor beggar,*

Fig. 8
The nomad made by Dominique during the fourth session
(about 2 centimetres high)

First stage: The nomad as Maharaja.

Second stage: The nomad leading his cow (he is called 'Mademoiselle'). A blob for the head, a blob for the body, a hat; two eyes, two pigtails, and a beard that grows and trails along the ground.

His 'kiddie-goat' cow

Third stage: The evil man or the tired-out nomad? Only one eye, one opening, a slit in the hat, a flattened-out blob for the head, two other cube-like masses, something sticking out of the chest or abdomen.

The camels.

and anyway he was fed up with drinking milk. So he went off drag-
ging his cow along . . . (The nomad figure in its second stage:
see the so-called cow, a vertical thing topped with a toothless
jaw, and its tie-up with the nomad by an 'umbilical cord'.) *He*
found a lot more grass than food for himself. Finally he was forced to
eat leaves, like the cow. He was thin, poor thing. Once he used to be a
Maharaja, but that because of his unfailing determination, and also
once his cow instead of making a calf, used to lay gold. But then this
jealous fakir took her and gave her a shot and then some poison grass,
and she couldn't make gold anymore. And one day she made a calf,
like any normal cow . . . Then she became skinny three times, and the
calf fat three times. And of course, she done died (elle a mouru).* *So*
now the poor man found it all quite lonely, and people were mean and
turned the poor old man out the door. For several months he walked,
he walked three times for several months, his long beard to the ground.
And everybody on the road said to him: 'Good morning, Mademoiselle.'
And that, he was getting fed up with that, and people were saying it
to flatter him. One day he saw, far off, a caravan of camels. (He is
now modelling some very small camels which reach to about the
nomad's feet: see fig. 8, p. 60.) While modelling these camels,
he sings a rhythmic melody. The 'camels' are bound together
by a very thin cord.

Then he says: *Oh what's going on?* (All this in a very mannered voice.) *My poor little kiddie-goat* (biquette),† *I've got to sell*
you. (He places the so-called camels right next to the so-called
man.) *And then the cow fell right down, she was so tired. No I don't*
want to sell you right away, I'm going to ask for some water from that
man over there. See you later . . . He goes on with the story while
kneading the little bits of clay, whose meaning I don't quite
understand. *Then he tells the nomad everything, that my poor kid-*
die-goat (ex-cow), *she's thirsty: that I've got to have some water, that*
I'll sell him the kiddie-goat, who had the place of honour. Bye-bye, my
little kiddie-goat! Well you see, the nomad had lost his camel, who'd
kicked the bucket. So he bought the kiddie-goat. No, you've got to follow

---

*   The correct French would be *elle mourut.* —Translators.
†   Dominique's word for 'penis': see p. 104. —Translators.

this man. But the kiddie-goat wouldn't follow him. Then for several days she wasn't allowed to speak to the man. The man who'd bought her was much meaner than he was. While saying these last words he puts on a very severe look and a strange, deep voice. He also transforms the first cow, the four-legged one which had been left aside all this time, greatly lengthening its snout in order to pull it by the nose. He says: *The man was strong, he told the animal that he must obey the man. Animals are made to obey. And she had to carry him along on her back because the poor fellow had only one foot left.* (See the third stage of the nomad model.)

This half-raving session is interesting because of the shifting back and forth of identifications. At the beginning, there is the fantasy of the daughter (reference to the last session) who went away with the subject's father. One can't quite make out what happened. It seems that the little girl became two, that part of her stayed, out of pity, with some beggars in a hut, and those two wild animals, who had run away from the zoo, of which Dominique speaks in the singular (this may be his cannibalistic instinct towards his mother's breasts, unprotected by any taboo).* Dominique is not aware of the contradictions. Then comes the sheepdog. It should be noted that this favourite animal has red hair, as did the little girl of the last session. People want to get rid of the sheepdog, but they can't. This is what happened to Dominique. 'They' sent him to Perpignan, but he came back and 'they' couldn't get rid of him. And then at this time Paulo (*alias* Paul-Marie) thought 'they' would get rid of him by sending him out as a boarder, but Dominique is still at

---

* Uncastrated cannibalistic wishes or rather wishes that were arti-
ficially reactivated when Dominique's mother put him to the breast
again when the sister was born. Dominique's mutism seems to have
resulted from the destruction of verbalised speech, which symbolises
the oral relationship after weaning has ended the bodily contact of
breast-feeding. The identification made by the two-and-a-half-year-old
boy with the cannibalistic behaviour of the baby girl decapitated his
body image and dismantled its structure, so much so that it affected
not only the body image as linked with language but also the bodily
schema as linked with mouth-to-breast–udder–teat sensations. —F.D.

home. Then there is the matter of the dog's collar. It is green,[*]
just like the shoelaces which the little girl put in the shoes
which she had taken from her father and which were trans-
muted into her pigtails (second version, when the little girl was
phallically valorised), and then into the mother's high-heeled
shoes. Projected into the dog – as represented by Dominique
in his game with the modelling – is the fantasy of losing one's
head just as one is beginning to walk . . . Isn't this what happened in Dominique's life? To walk is to stand up, the phallic
posture of the body in relation to its support, the ground. Two
things are confused here: the fact of having supposed control
of one's phallic posterior, and that of having shoes on one's
feet – human feet whose sex is undifferentiated because of the
undecided phallic identity – as between man and animals, man
and woman. Then there is the change-over from dog to cow
through the 'tail', after the loss of the head and eyes. There
is the cow that dreams of being an ox, and the ox that, in the
cow's dreams, dreams he is a cow. What is present here is a
suspicion, a doubt, an inability to choose the sex dreamed of,
the desired sex, to know the sex of other people and his own
sex. When Dominique projects himself into an animal, or when
he projects me or his woman schoolteacher, of what sex are we?
We are sacred, that is to say 'adorable' (crushes), divine, outside the reference of sexual desire as far as marriage and procreation. We also see that there is an obliviousness to, a foreclosure of the question of the fecundity of horned animals, of
the castration of oxen, the question of the bull. This despite the
fact that Dominique has lived in the country with his uncle, the
cattle farmer, and likes animals. He says the bull, the male, is
mean. Dominique himself used to butt (with his horns) against
his cot and the walls of the house; and he triumphed over his
father by taking away the phallic, nourishing mother, a mother
who still breast-fed him, even though he had already learned
how to speak.

---

[*]   In French *en vert*, 'in green', perhaps a pun on *envers*, 'towards' or
'backwards'. —Translators.

Then there is the story of the sacred cow, no doubt derived from something he has read — the sacred ox Apis,* like the Egyptian boat and the Trojan War. The cow is obviously identified with the schoolteacher or with myself, with special people who are not like others, who are neither male nor female, but above others. This mythic transference, from the moment of interpretation, returned this 'idol' to its status of normal female who gives birth according to the laws of her kind, and not just anally to gold, to 'value'.† And there is the story of the bearded man in a tree, the story of the bearded man who has fallen, who was once a Maharaja and a Prince. This is really Dominique's own story when he was born, we were told: small, his mother's little king, shaggy, covered with hair, long-haired. He was as gentle as a lamb, a kid, a *biquette*.

·Once Dominique's trauma was definitively confirmed, he became nothing more than a thirsty little goat, a kid (pissing cow: *vache qui pisse*); and his mother limited the amount he drank because of his enuresis. First the lean, thirsty cow, ready to drop from tiredness, and then in its place a camel, the most sober and untiring of animals. (It is obvious that these comments did not come to me until I re-read the account of the session. During the session itself, I was all ears and eyes, conscious of the significance of a truth that was surfacing in all the ways it could.)

But Dominique goes on. I listen. When he is quiet, I just wait.

DOMINIQUE: *The man tells the nomad everything, then he comes back to his cow-kiddie-goat and says to her: 'My poor kiddie-goat, this man will give me water only if I sell him my kiddie-goat that used to have the seat of honour. Farewell, my kiddie-goat.'*

In this story where the kiddie-goat (or phallic part-object)‡ occupies the seat of honour, and where the man wants to give the kiddie-goat life by giving it something to drink (fresh running

---

* Worshipped by the ancient Egyptians. Also, *Apis = à pisse*, 'pissing'.
    —F.D.

† In French *vaut*, 'is worth', 'value', and *veau*, 'calf', are homonyms.
    —Translators.

‡ For its phallic nature see p. 104. —F.D.

water), he is forced into an absurd predicament: having to sell his prize possession in order to secure water, i.e., nourish what he will no longer need if he loses this precious object. It's a fool's bargain. To me this fantasy portrays allegorically what actually happened to this child: not a castration that initiates him into culture, but a mutilation. There was no symbolisation after his renunciation of the part-object, the urethral penis – only a losing bargain. The way in which the erotic pleasure of oral absorption which results in urethral emission was renounced did not allow for the preservation of an access to the phallus. Instead the satisfaction of his need resulted in his altogether losing the object, in his giving up love and even desire, in order just to survive. This matter of a part-object is not only the story of his penis in relation to his own body, it is the story of his whole self, insofar as he had been the part-object, his mother's fetishistic part-object, or imaginary penis, until the birth of his little sister.*

This precious part-object, which is now separated from the subject, its owner, can only survive by being sold, that is to say given over to a bad master who will no longer provide it with what it needs to live on (to drink), but will lead it by the nose (see the umbilical cord, the tip of the nose in the clay model). This kiddie is Dominique's sex organ at the time of nursing, since then foreclosed to its living desire, and whose dead weight he must now bear. In other words, at the same time that the maternal object leads him by the nose, he, Dominique, straddles it as a mount between his legs; but this can only be done if the object so straddled has lost all personal initiative. This means the alienation of the subject's desire in order to satisfy the perverse desire of the

---

*   It will be recalled that Sylvie's birth modified the mother's libidinal
      economy. Madame Bel as a child and young girl had been disavowed
      by her parents on account of her sex. Her mother had shown no
      interest in her daughter's studies. Madame Bel married a 'twin in
      suffering'. She witnessed the Bel family welcoming Sylvie just as
      Sylvie's paternal aunt had been welcomed. The father says this of
      his daughter: 'She is like my sister, but more courageous.' Sylvie
      is clearly a Bel. The mother says: 'I am busy with my daughter, very
      busy, I have to see to her studies: she needs me.' It is she who
      needs Sylvie. —F.D.

other, co-narcissistic and unable to stand alone. Another point
made by the story is the kiddie-goat's having itself to drag along
its new and cruel owner, who no longer even takes care of it: for
this second owner has only one foot left, a former breast now
used as a foot, a single 'odd' member on his trunk. Dominique
found himself with no one like him, no one he could identify
with; in his interhuman relations he was obliged to regress to
bodily dependence. He had become himself only insofar as he
accepted his own body as a penis, the part-object of another: a
typical metaphor for the foetal relationship (see the two 'camels' and their curious minuscule shapes, p. 62.). These are the
defences against the invading phobia of threatening death in a
falsely transferential situation. The result is regression to the
preverbal stage of primary process. Any real solution is excluded
since it would imply self-cannibalising whereas at the real time
of the primary process, cannibalism was but a fantasy during
which the absorption of real mother's milk maintained the flow*
between the presubject as a part-object, and its pre-object: the
total image of the adult with whom he can go on identifying in
the totality of his body and erogenous zone, because of mutual
attraction.

We shall now stop to summarise the clinical picture presented
by this boy before going on with the session notes. We have
noticed a miscognition of space, time and their mutual relation;
that is, a failure to recognise the means of measuring time and
(by experimental means) space. Thus, seeing feels dangerous
to Dominique. His miscognition keeps him from being able to
represent, in space, dimensional differences, that is, palpable
differences. As his mother pointed out, Dominique is under the
impression that a small package can be made to hold a very
large object, and that distant things are really small. (Illusions
of perspective have become reality to him.) As far as time, or
relationships in time, are concerned, Dominique likes history
very much, and I am told reads historical novels. But though

---

*   The bend of mutual dynamic participation (*la vie d'échange*). —F.D.

preoccupied with history and prehistory, he is unable to appreciate which events follow which. This will also appear in the coming sessions.

Taking into account these miscognitions sheds light on the system of defences with which Dominique has sought to protect himself from attack. Dominique has a phobia of being looked at, of seeing and of being seen: this is what gives him his shifty look – he will not look you in the face, but casts a sidelong glance under lowered lids. He also has a phobia of hearing and of being heard, which manifests itself in sudden drops in his voice, as if he were suddenly telling a secret, or speaking from far off and drawing nearer. All this points to a fear of being caught, or bitten: of being the object of aggression. These two phobias must bear a relation to the primal scene which he witnessed and lived through. (Till he was two and a half years old, that is, until Sylvie was born, Dominique's cot stood in his parent's bedroom.) He seems to be in a state of latent panic, fearing he will be seized, bitten, displaced, separated. This leads him to avoid things, to avoid encounters; it is mirrored in others, both people and animals, by a reaction of discomfort and non-contact towards him. Dominique never runs; he is afraid of children who are running, as of dogs. Any kind of sudden movement approaching him he perceives as predatory, as threatening to break him up. His normal expression – frozen, reserved, with a smile that seeks to please – expresses how unbearable this state of constant persecution is to him. He preserves himself from having to display initiative of any sort through his naive and disarming mien of incapacity. This approach, however, is totally ineffectual, because it is so uniform that others view it, not as expressive, but as the mark of mental retardation. Dominique displays the way of being and appearance, the features, of total powerlessness. The appearance is derived from a magical, propitiatory language, as are his posture and his speech.

The acts of the oral stage of mutual devouring and drinking (the child takes milk from mother, who takes faeces and urine from him) are usually renounced by a symbolisation into acts expressive of a tender relationship – cuddles, kisses, caresses that are not sexually explorative but explorative of the world and the body of the self and not the mother, which has been renounced.* For Dominique none of this has ever been possible. All the elements of the situation conspired to drive him to an all-devouring contact, to an eroticised and devouring relationship with an equally devouring and spoiling Other. The way in which Dominique has been fed so far has prevented any valorisation or devalorisation of food, whether with regard to taste, quality or quantity. He has never displayed any preferences for, or rejection of any specific foods. In this family, one is allowed to take food *in the name of need* at any time of day, at one's pleasure and without asking for permission. It is the mother who prepares all the food, but she places *no restrictions on the children's oral desires*. The same holds true for the gestures of anal symbolisation: to leave or to drop, to throw things on the ground or into the water, to mould (see the style of his modelling). Dominique is never destructive, never makes a violent gesture, a shout, or systematic bickering. He wants nothing and asks for nothing. Both in his family and in society he is 'absent'.

This child presents phobias, some of which are sufficiently characterised to be objects of general comment. But no one talks about his miscognitions, or the phobic structure that underpins them. It is said of Dominique that he tends to get lost, that he is so absent-minded that he hardly knows how he is dressed, etc. But the threat of persecution under which he lives – the fear of all that exists in time and space, of all that moves – this is never mentioned. We have noted his phobia concerning things that turn: merry-go-rounds, bicycles. He also has 'obsessive habits', rites about how to put things away, and hidden, hardly perceptible rages. Finding that familiar objects have been moved from their usual places will overwhelm him with anxiety. He has a phobia about washing and laundering. Anything that moves or changes or is modified becomes a threat. Any dynamic image

---

*   Remember that Dominique learned to speak before he was weaned; that he weaned himself, and that then later, he was again allowed to breast-feed as often and as much as he liked, as long as his young sister was still being breast-fed. —F.D.

gives him away, gives him away as living, signals his existence *as far as being still alive, and so apt to be cancelled out, killed* (if he is alive).*

These miscognitions exist and are normal in very small children; their usual defence mechanisms generally succeed and don't offend. In front of people they don't know, young children become silent and keep their mouths shut; 'they lose their tongue', as the French expression has it; they revert to a regressive preverbal behaviour. They see, hear, I would even say sniff out everything that is going on, but say nothing of it. Or else, when facing threatening things or animals, they exemplify the kind of regression represented by becoming part of the mother's body again: they hide in her skirts, they hide behind her . . . they stay on the lookout, shielded behind the mother's body, sometimes with their back to her. Or else they keep out disquieting perceptions by hiding their face in her skirts. But this kind of behaviour, which we have all witnessed on the part of young children, is usually met with a comforting gesture from the mother (a chaste gesture as opposed to a gesture of sexual provocation). Some children, in addition to the tendency to nest, also revert to thumb-sucking, to stroking their ear, while taking a foetal position, by themselves, or in their mother's arms, or on her knees, and turning away from what is going on. Now Dominique as a child never acted in this way. He very early developed a verbal relationship with his mother, since, as we have noted, he learned to speak distinctly even before he was weaned at the age of one. His father confirms this. Even before his sister's birth he did not enjoy bodily contact with his mother; Dominique dominated his mother (fitting in with his first name). He mastered her by his will, through his masochistic behaviour.† He made her his attentive slave and so took her away from his father. All the while in his cot, and until the birth of his sister, he had patiently to bear his parent's

---

*   If he is alive: *s'il vit* and Sylvie (the little sister). —F.D.
†   It will be recalled that at night he used to butt his head until he was
        black and blue while in his cot (butting like a horned beast). —F.D.

love-making whenever the father came home. The father's comings and goings were unforeseen, unannounced; for the child
they were quite magical.

I have shown elsewhere, in a theoretical and clinical paper
on so-called jealousy reactions to the next-born,* that the troubles of an elder sibling under four were invariably due to a
conflict in the structuration of the subject's identity – a hypoth-
esis which has since been confirmed in all cases brought to my
attention. This structuration is a function of those aspects of
the child's personality whose ethical, oral and anal organisation is shaken by the birth of a younger brother or sister. In
Dominique's case, this identity conflict is evident: when Sylvie
was born, he was no longer the same, his role had changed,
since he was no longer the favourite, the most protected: there
was someone else now. We see this sort of jealousy in daily
life, when a dog who is attached to his master becomes jealous
when he sees him diverting his attention to another object. He
is being dispossessed. But what happens in a human being is
far more complicated. The love that a human being bears his
mother and his environment during the structuration process
of his personality leads him first to identify with and to imitate
these other objects of love, and then to introject their value.
The human child behaves as he sees his elders of both sexes
behave, and whoever his familiars may be, they are ahead of him
on the road of life. When he introjects them, when he symbolically incorporates them, he is, literally, developing into a more
mature human being. When the infant gives up the breast, he
gives up cannibalistic incorporation, but in its place he finds
the introjection connected with the assimilation of sound and
image, a structuring symbolic process. By means of this introjection he wins the approval of those who surround him, and
achieves the exchange of speech, which bears witness to his
membership in the group.

---

*   Françoise Dolto, 'Hypothèse nouvelle concernant les réactions dites
       de jalousie à la naissance d'un puîné', *Psyché* 7, 9–10 (1947).

But suddenly a little sister appears, as if by magic, and becomes an incontestable phallic prize: the cynosure of all the family. The law of his own oral identification and introjection will force him to *introject her*: that is, the boy aged twenty or thirty months will have to valorise the ways of this infant who can neither speak nor find food elsewhere than at her mother's bosom: this incontinent infant who, strange to say, delights a mother who so far had been so upset at the sight of soiled pants.

In this case of jealousy of the next-born, we are, through Dominique, confronted with the derealising consequences of an unacceptable reality. If we now try to understand why things turned out as they did in this particular case, we find ourselves equipped with enough elements to follow the process up to the age of two and a half, when Dominique had his breakdown. Dominique reacted to the birth of his little sister with defence responses which were not recognised as such by the people he lived with, but which they tolerated in view of their own anxiety. To the child this meant they approved of them – which did not help matters. Even more perverting was the return to breast-feeding and baby-talk, which was further exasperated by the seductive, overheated libidinous elements which (unknown to her) stemmed from the mother, and which in the absence of castration destroyed other possibilities for structuration in later development, during the anal, urethral and genital stages. But this will become clear to us only through the analytic work of later sessions.

Let us return to what happened when the little sister was born: to the revolution which this introduced within the family, in the behaviour of Dominique's familiars, in the emotions they expressed, and in his own structure.

Dominique was his mummy's own little phallus. He was the king of the parent's bedroom. By indulging in a whim, by banging his head against the cot, he could get his anxious mother to leave her husband's bed, do all her little boy's will and satisfy, not his needs, but his desire to separate her from her husband. This infantile despotism she excused as a royal prerogative. But it must also be said that the mother had tried to enforce an early toilet-training, that she had been successful as far as defecation was concerned, that the threat of soiling himself or wetting his bed in a tantrum represented a real threat to his mother, who, it will be recalled, had a phobic fear of dirt and was obsessed with cleanliness.

Do not forget that this little phallus of Mummy's was very precocious. He began to speak before his teeth grew in, and spoke correctly before he was weaned. He learned to walk at the time he was being weaned. Between his mother and his elder brother, the little fellow had a happy life. True he was not the lord of his sphincter muscles, which he had sold to mother for some satisfactions of her own. True, he could not yet speak to her quite perfectly, but his babbling enabled him to interject himself, like a listened-to parrot, between mother and brother, and play the role of Third Party all day long.

Do not forget further that Dominique started school very young — at the age of two years and three months — to be like his big brother, and that he successfully adapted to the Montessori school. All this before the birth of the little sister. He was sent to live with his paternal grandmother towards the end of his mother's pregnancy, both to lighten his mother's burden and to distract his grandmother who was mourning the loss of a son. Coming back home, Dominique found that he had lost his place in his parent's room, that there was another baby in his cot. This baby completely broke the equilibrium that had existed in the family. Father and mother found their greatest joy in the newcomer; even the elder brother apparently surrendered his prerogatives to concern himself exclusively with this little sister. Dominique's shock before the unwonted experience is understandable. What was he to make of it? Why was the little sister so important? Well, because her birth entirely satisfied the family on both sides. The new trio — father, mother, daughter — was thoroughly happy. Even the elder boy had to make sense of himself by 'doubling' his mother. The little sister, the second in the Bel family, came just after their acceptance of the death of a son. In the same way, some years earlier, the father's sister had been born after the death by accident of the little brother.

The father had lost precedence at the age of seven when his own little sister was born: his family's joy at that birth can be imagined; there had not been a girl in the family in 150 years. Monsieur Bel now experienced the same pleasure, but this time it was he who was the father, giving joy to his wife as well as to his parents. As he liked to point out, the little girl looked very much like him, but had the daring he lacked: 'she is ever so enterprising!' Of course, this isn't what he said when she was born, but at that time he liked to point out: 'She is 100 per cent a Bel, she looks 100 per cent like my sister.'

As for the mother, she admitted to me that she felt guilty towards the sisters who had brought her up for having got married; she had wanted to identify with them, to follow 'the ministry of teaching'.* She also felt guilty towards her own mother who, when she was thought to be unmarriageable because of her obesity, said 'So much the better, now you won't leave me.' According to Monsieur Bel, relations between the two women at the time were intensely aggressive. The fact that she had borne a girl who looked like her husband's people gave great satisfaction to Madame Bel, as well as to her own mother, who loved her son-in-law. From morning till night Dominique heard that this girl was much more beautiful (*belle*) and more 'Bel' (father) than he; and hence more highly regarded by both father and mother. The fact that the family name and the adjective characterising the power of seductivity sound alike made this little girl the phallically meaningful child. Dominique had always been told he was ugly, hairy as an ape, that he did not resemble his father, but the maternal grandfather: a vulgar man, a colonialist, and a brutal breaker of black people. Remember also that the little girl was named *Sylvie*, and that Dominique had been continually hearing these two syllables

---

*   'The sisters' refer to the nuns who brought her up; their minis-
        try includes the vows of chastity taken by the brides of Christ.
        —Translators.

(*Sylvie* or *S'il vit*, 'if he is alive') since the disappearance of his uncle and the subsequent arrival of his sister, referring either to her or to the hopes of finding him: '*S'il vit* – if Bernard is still alive we'll still find him, he'll be here or there . . .' Given the role played by language in a child who knew no other phallic manifestation of power and culture, these two syllables must have played a considerable role in building up the many confusions in Dominique's mind, and his schizophrenic attitude. Couldn't the little baby just be the uncle come back in the form of a little girl (see p. 79)?

What happened in Dominique's attitude towards his elder brother Paul-Marie when Sylvie was born? Could Dominique find support from this elder brother or identify with him? No: because no real relation existed between these two brothers, these two fetishes of their mummy's. The only sensible relationship between them would have been one of reciprocal aggression, but neither the father not the mother would have tolerated it. Still, I am certain that it is this companion of his own sex, apparently without influence, who contributed most to Dominique's autistic reclusion. Elder siblings by their very position play a role in the structuration of the younger who imitate them or try to hold on to them. But when will parents and educators understand that for the sake of both their children, they must not valorise the protective attitude an elder child may bear towards the younger? The elder child should be encouraged *not* to imitate either the mothering or the law-giving parent. This dominant parental role, coupled with the manifest inferiority of younger siblings, can only sap the defence mechanisms on which their structuring depends. We have barely mentioned the elder brother. Still it is because of the change in schooling of this elder brother that we came to know Dominique who, abandoned by his handler, was to be placed in a specialist boarding school. I shall study in a separate chapter the reciprocal relationship between the two brothers, whose personal oedipal structurations were interconnected at the time the little sister was born. We will see in some detail the role of libidinal dynamics within the family unit, articulated oedipally and orchestrated by the parents insofar as they are the supports of the adult imago for each of the children. Their own oedipal 'counter-transference' to their children interferes with this structuration, mostly by standing in its way. This result makes impossible the symbolisation processes of the pregenital libido.

We can now return to the description of the sessions, having outlined the elements that from the start seemed to us the most important for the understanding of this case.

Fifth Session: 4 January

Six weeks after the previous session: Dominique missed two sessions

1.

Dominque is accompanied to this session by his mother and his elder brother, but it is only later that I will hear that the elder brother is waiting in the waiting room. It seems that the elder brother has already asked the mother twice to 'see me', but Dominique didn't want him to come. The mother told me last time that her eldest son would perhaps come if I wanted to see him. I told her that I would see him if Dominique wanted it. Dominique told his elder brother that he would like him to meet me: I didn't refuse.

Madame Bel comes in first, with Dominique's knowledge. There is something she wants to tell me before I see him:[*] how happy she is that Dominique has had a Christmas holiday that was even better than last year's summer holiday. Her own mother came and stayed with them. This was the woman who could not stand Dominique, ever since the famous summer when he was three years old and, unbeknownst to anyone, became mad with jealousy towards his little sister. This grandmother blamed

---

[*] When a patient seriously wants one of his familiars to see his psychoanalyst, I think that this meeting is necessary to him, and accept it. When a minor is involved and he wants me to meet his parents or grandparents during his treatment, I accept only with his approval. I speak to them in his presence or alone, as he wishes, or as the parents accept. If I see them alone, I later inform the patient of the part of the conversation that concerned him. —F.D.

Madame Bel and her husband – Madame Bel in particular – for their lack of authority. This grandmother also had a marked preference for Paul-Marie, while she found Dominique ugly. 'It's true,' the mother had said, 'that at his birth he was covered with hair. It's true he was ugly compared to his brother and especially to his sister who is so pretty. I must admit he looks like my father, who is no beauty.' But the grandmother found him changed; he was very nice to her and they are now the best of friends.

We see that Madame Bel has been renarcissised by her son's treatment and improvement, that she is rehabilitating herself in her mother's eyes. There may be some other feelings beneath this satisfaction.* After this brief exchange, the mother goes back to the waiting room and Dominique comes in.

2.   Meeting with Dominique

DOMINIQUE: *Well, there is something that's bothering me. You know I've been sick in my head. And so I've never learned anything. And there's something I want to learn and that is to tell the time.*

I ask him about the day and the time of the appointment. I make a drawing on a piece of paper, a circle spread with the twelve figures, a 'clock'. With two 'hands' of clay Dominique himself marks the hour at which he came in, and then follows the progress of the hours and minutes. In less than five minutes he knows how to record time without having to make a single gesture. I abstain from congratulating him or making him conscious of the fact, and go right on.

ME: *Well, what have you got to tell me today?*

DOMINIQUE: *Well, my big brother is Mr Know-it-all.* (He repeats this and identifies himself as the very opposite, as Mr Know-nothing.) *Then there's the big story with the dog, Yap, he wasn't proud of himself when he made wee-wee everywhere. But he's making progress. At home we've always had dogs.* (This is true, but it is something I had

---

*   Madame Bel caused Dominique to miss two sessions. —F.D.

never been told by anyone, and that was not known in school.)
You know I talked to you about a sheepdog, well that's because I like dogs.
We've always had dogs. Before, we used to like Gouki a great deal, he
was as affectionate as Yap. Then one day we had to get rid of him. The
landlord had some cocker spaniels and it was like cat and dog.

ME: *But there weren't any cats?*

DOMINIQUE: *No, but they quarrelled. It was no surprise. I don't*
know what he said, but we had to get rid of him. We gave him to a ken-
nels. That was six years ago. And you see, for a while, I couldn't think
of anything else. Whenever I saw a dog, I thought it was Gouki even if
he didn't look like him. I thought it was him dressed up as another dog
or even as a cat. (So Sylvie could be *s'il vit*, 'if he is alive', Bernard
disguised as a baby.)

ME: *Oh really?*

DOMINIQUE: *Yes. I was really sad when I was six years old.*
Maybe it was when I was eight. (We know that the father's brother
who disappeared was declared lost when Dominique was three
years old, and that when he was eight years old a little cousin, a
blue baby, a brother of Babette, died almost before his eyes, at
the age of six months. The age of six, which Dominique refers
to is the time when he was expelled from school and admitted
for his first treatment.) *My grandfather and grandmother from the*
Meuse are Mummy's father and mother. Well at the postwoman's, there
were two little boys (slip?) *and I was very pleased because I stroked and*
tickled them as if I had a cat, because you see if I had had a cat . . .
and then we didn't have one anymore.

ME: *A cat?*

DOMINIQUE: *No, a dog. You see, I liked him a lot. But the others*
liked stroking a dog better and I wanted a German shepherd myself.

ME: *Oh yes, why?*

DOMINIQUE: *Because I'd known a family that's* (note that
Dominique knows how to say 'whose') *children held a German*
shepherd, and I was aching to hold the German shepherd, like all the
family. There's a real celebration for me now when I come home. He
likes me, our dog. When people see how Yap likes me they can't believe
it. Our dog, who's a dachshund, is a terror when he isn't affectionate,
he growls, because he bites, he's dangerous. With him you have to be

happy, because if you're not happy, he isn't happy and he can become dangerous. When mother explained things to me, it used to annoy me not to know. And I was especially annoyed because she was explaining it to me. Before I didn't like my name, 'Bel', I would have liked to have a name beginning with an O. I would have liked to be called 'Olax'. That's a nice one, Olax. When the teacher took the register and my turn came, she said 'Bel' and the others said, 'How pretty,'* so you see that annoyed me.* And very softly. *Why didn't they ever say 'pretty girl'?*

ME: *Would you have liked, that?*

DOMINIQUE: *Yes. But they made fun.*

These two experiences constituted humiliations very destructive of Dominique's narcissism. All the psychotics I have met have related under analysis real episodes or real situations which they experienced as humiliations, and which originated with one of the individuals who supported their ideal ego – a parent or a teacher, or an elder brother or sister who had taken the place of the parents as embodiments of the ideal ego.†

Dominique uses the verb 'to embarrass' (*vexer*) in the imperfect tense . . . He was embarrassed by his mother's teaching, embarrassed to owe his father a name which he feels makes him ridiculous. *The humiliation hidden behind this screen* of being embarrassed is more serious. What is involved for Dominique is the violation of the human personality (he has been robbed of the right to give his impotence a human meaning in terms of nature and culture); but principally, it is *a denial of what is initiatic in oedipal castration*: that which comes from the father, the valued model of genital and social power, and which is *experienced as an inductive trial into the social world of boys.* Beneath this experience of humiliation also lies the tempting and provocative

---

*   *Bel*: 'beautiful'. —Translators.

†   It is true that 'normal' people as well as neurotics also tell of their humiliating experiences. But such experiences are particularly telling for pathological cases. These events are particularly marking because they occur at key moments of structuration – moments where narcissism vacillates between the different needs imposed by the reality of a reorganisation of libidinal energy that is taking place: the imaginary value and ethos of the old libidinal investment had up until then provided security, but now turns out to be obsolete. —F.D.

emotions connected with parental persons — the very individuals who ought to be the supporters of the law against incest. We will see this in further detail later.

We note that in this session, Dominique, having reconciled himself with his family name, can also reconcile himself with dogs. The episode of the dog that had to be sent away — and was probably put to sleep — in order to please the landlord, seems to relate to the birth of his young cousin, the blue baby, and to his death soon after — as if to please the terrible cousin Babette, who practically owned the place. Babette is three years older than Bruno, her little brother. We also note that Dominique has been reconciled to the curious maternal grandmother, the rough peasant woman, with her magical rites.

In this session loaded with allusions, note also the reference to affectionate and erotic relationships with little boys (is there a slip here?), as if they were cats or dogs, to be petted. The situation which Dominique is relating and fantasising here is that of Dominique's experience with the grandmother from Perpignan, who used to take him in her arms to look at photographs of her beloved dead (or so Dominique tells it). Also, remember that the mother, reputedly on the advice of the psychoanalyst, again started to caress this big boy when he was six years old, caressing him as much as his little sister, and that she still does it. She has denied him the symbolic advantages of weaning and jealousy, and by so doing she frustrated him of the development of structural defence mechanisms that would have resulted from a real trial. What traumatised Dominique as the result of the birth of his little sister was not the frustration of tenderness, it was the fact that he was put back to the breast and deprived of the requirements for fatherly upbringing that would have preserved and supported his human identity. Furthermore, what follows later will show us the perverting role played for Dominique by a particular experience: the mother's habit of passive physical encounters with her children in bed, the outcome of her phobia of solitude. But we shouldn't jump ahead.

Having told me of these memories, Dominique goes on to make a model of a person (see the sketch of its first stage:

fig. 9, p. 83). Contrast its style to that of the previous model, the nomad, and to the 'people' made before the holidays (see fig. 8, p. 61).

ME: *Now who could this be?*

DOMINIQUE: *Maybe one of Mother's Blacks when she was a little girl. They were all naked and you could see 'it'.* (In fact one can see only a silhouette.)

ME: *And what is 'it'?*

DOMINIQUE: *Well, I made him all dressed up so you can't see it.*

ME: *Why, since you told me you could see it?*

DOMINIQUE: *Yes, they show it, they do. They don't think it's bad.* He puts a penis on it and says: *That's his udder.* (It looks indeed like a cow's teat in erection.) He goes on: *No it's not one of my mother's Blacks, it's a baby looking for popo.** And very softly: *I used to wet the bed, you know, for a long time. And look, that's called a man's sex too.* And he puts two balls representing breasts on the man. (See sketch, second stage: fig. 9, p. 83.)

ME: *No that's not what's called the sex. That's what you put on before. These two balls that you put on are something else: do you know what?*

He's quiet for a while and then says: *Mummy, for a while it was the Panthéon that interested me. You know, the Panthéon, where they buried Napoleon, where there was the hospital, a hospital of the tomb.* (His mother – all God, form, breast and dead, Napoleon, nurse of invalids, keeper of the crippled, glorifying the value of the Thing.)†

ME: *What is the hospital of Napoleon's grave? Does it have a name?*

DOMINIQUE: *Yes it's a name which says how they are. I don't remember.* He tries to remember.

---

*   Dominique uses the word 'popo' to refer to anything sexual.
     —Translators.

†   *Tout dieu*, 'all gods', is a reference to the Greek Pantheon, which
     houses all the gods. Also, the buildings of the Panthéon and Les
     Invalides, which are well-known Parisian monuments, are topped with
     breast-shaped domes. F.D. is linking together imagery suggestive of
     an all-powerful maternal imago. This links with the concept of *das
     Ding*, 'the Thing', from Freud's view of the primordial maternal imago.
     —Translators.

Fig. 9

Clay figures made by Dominique during the fifth session
(each about 10 centimetres high)

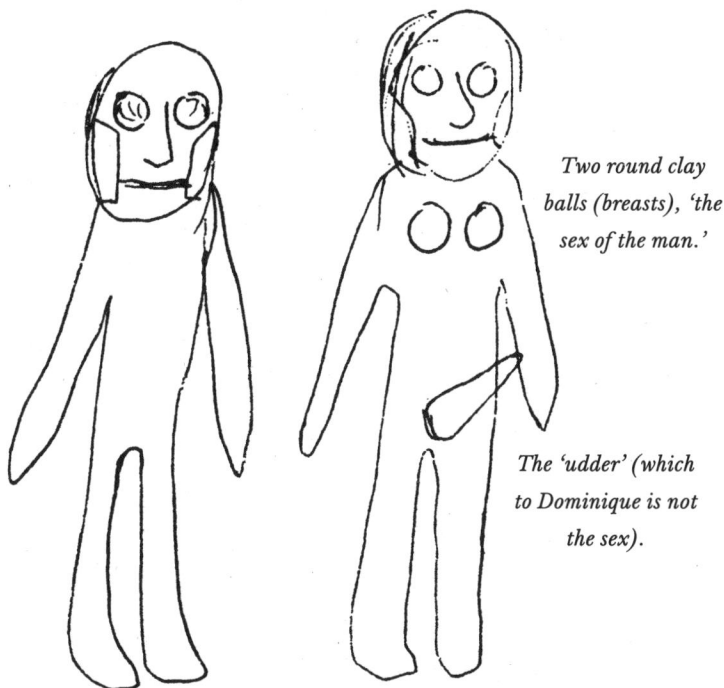

*Two round clay
balls (breasts), 'the
sex of the man.'*

*The 'udder' (which
to Dominique is not
the sex).*

*First stage: 'One of Mother's
Blacks. You can see "it" because
they are naked; but I made him
all dressed.'*

*Second stage: 'What do you mean
by "it"?' – 'The udder and the
sex' (referring to the breasts).*

*The eyes are formed in relief. Dominique says nothing
about the patches on the cheeks.*

ME: *Isn't it the Hospital des Invalides?*

DOMINIQUE: *Oh yes, you're right. Well then, that's an invalid. Me, I've got a lot less poultry than that (?). I made a trade and I also have a tractor that mother gave me. I like to play at being a farmer. When I stay with my cousins I feel more at home because it's a farm, and there you don't have to have any imagination, 'cause it's real. My cousin isn't even going to school.* Dominique is silent.

ME: *How come he isn't going to school?*

DOMINIQUE: *Well, he's six, or maybe eight, and all he does is multiplication. That's not studying.* (A little earlier it was he, Dominique, who was eight or six years old at the time of the death of this dog, *alias* his little dead cousin, that is, this cousin's elder brother.)

ME: *Well, do you think that isn't studying, doing multiplication?*

DOMINIQUE: *Well, you see, me, before* (before what?) *I saw* (sic) *the word study for grown-ups, schools for engineers.*

ME: *No, anything that has to do with learning is called studying. But, it is true that what your mother says about your elder brother is that he's now 'a student' because he's in a school where he's learning a profession. But you're a schoolboy, and so is your cousin, but a schoolboy studies at primary school or secondary school. 'A student' is more free. He doesn't do the same kind of studies, and not in the same place. In fact your father and mother were students at the university when they met and were married.* (Was Dominique listening? Perhaps my remarks were wasted.)

DOMINIQUE: *Well, you know this morning,*[*] *it surprised me, everything went better at school. I made no mistakes at all in dictation, or in multiplication either. But you see, it was the multiplication exercises of a group I wasn't in. And what about my group? Because, you know, the teacher made three groups. In my group, I don't know if I would have made any mistakes. Anyway I didn't make any mistakes in the multiplication that wasn't asked of my group.*

***

[*] In fact he didn't go to school that morning, since he came to this session with me. —F.D.

It is after this part of the session that Dominique tells me that his brother has come along with him and his mother, that his brother wanted to *see* me and that he, Dominique, was very pleased about this. He'd rather have me see the brother alone.

3.   *Interview with Paul-Marie*

I see Paul-Marie on my own.

He is a very polite boy, almost stiff, neat as a pin. Though seventeen years old, physically he looks like a fourteen- or fifteen-year-old, with even less of a beard than his brother. He sits up very straight. I ask him whether he has had to help his brother in life. He says that he has always had to 'transport' him everywhere. He has had to escort him because Dominique was forever getting lost. It is terrible to have a brother everyone notices. People are not mean of course, but he feels people make fun of him because of his brother. He feels his brother has changed a good deal since he's been coming here. He denies that he's been wanting to make my acquaintance when I inquire, though he blushes when saying it. It was his mother and Dominique who told him to come.

I ask Paul-Marie how he feels about his father's absences. He tells me it isn't fun. He thinks it's strange, a husband who is always away from his wife: but no doubt it's because of his work. Mother tells him it's his job. But still, he feels that 'Daddy could come home more often if he knew how it bothered Mother.' Because it bothers his mother a great deal when his father isn't there. How can he tell it bothers her? 'Because she's cold in bed, and then one of us always has to go and get in with her. You see, I don't want to, so it has to be Dominique or my little sister who gets into bed with her.' I ask him whether he's pleased with his work and with his friends. He tells me more or less the same things as his mother, using about the same terms. He doesn't understand why girls flirt. He says it isn't decent. He doesn't understand why men and women sleep together, but it has to be like that because without it there wouldn't be any children.

He likes a boy who is in his philosophy class because everything that this boy tells him interests him very much.

Paul-Marie seems glad to have talked to me. The interview wasn't very long, but a great deal was said.

Having spoken to his brother, I now see Dominique again.

4.   *Second interview with Dominique*

I tell Dominique that his brother told me that their mother liked to keep warm by taking them into bed with her, and that he, the big brother, refuses to go. Dominique is a little put off; he thinks, then:

DOMINIQUE: *You know, I was very surprised the other day to see my brother and sister at the skating rink. I was with my schoolmate, he's more than a schoolmate, he's a friend.* (The father's boss is more than a boss, he's a friend.) *And then, you see, my sister has some funny friends and my brother, well, my brother was with some very funny people.*

Note the defensive attitude at my allusion to the sleeping with his mother. He responds by making nasty comments about his brother's and sister's so-called friends. I have the feeling that the friend he was with is a friend with whom he does 'funny things', and I tell him so, I interpret what he says in this way. He lowers his voice and says:

DOMINIQUE: *Yes, we have fun with the bottom and with the slit. We do like the cows with their udder.*

ME: *What happens with your body, with what you call your udder, it isn't a cow's udder, you know very well it's your sex. That's just what we were talking about earlier, when you were making your little man whom you said was one of your mother's Blacks. Well, there are times when it is like the dog's tail at the last session, it can be up or down. It depends on what you feel in your body while you are having fun with it.*

DOMINIQUE: *Yes, it feels strange. Well my sister goes into my mother's bed, and I do too you know. Can she hear? Can Mother hear us?* He lowers his voice.

ME: *I don't think your mother can hear us, but you can speak softly if you want to. But since you sleep in your mother's bed, she knows it well enough. Why speak so softly? So that she won't hear you telling me about it?*

DOMINIQUE: *Well, it's because I don't want to sleep with her anymore. When I was seven, she wanted me to and me, I didn't know, but it made me feel funny, the way you said just now* (he's referring to an erection). *And then Mother would say to me 'Come on, it'll keep me warm.' And then it feels nice, but you know,* and he lowers his voice, *she doesn't want it when Daddy is there. She says it's for when Daddy isn't there. Because she's bored you see. It would be better if he were a grocer, because then he could always warm her up in bed. Mother says that girls have to sleep with women, and so my sister she always sleeps with Mother. You see, well, I still want to go into Mother's bed, but I don't know. And then she says that boys always have to sleep with boys because when they are grown-up, men sleep with men. In Germany, when he is working, father sleeps with gentlemen and he sees no ladies.*

ME: *And when you talk about this with your brother, what does he have to say?*

DOMINIQUE: *Oh my brother, he doesn't give a damn. Girls don't interest him.* (Implying, but they interest me.) *And then Mother doesn't ask him, so he doesn't give a damn. What I like, myself, is when my grandmother, my mother's mother, comes to see us. Because when she comes, she writes everything down: the restaurant, the knives and forks, the waiter, the menu, she writes down everything, everything we do. And I like it when my grandmother,* he *comes* (*mon grandmère il vient*; an allusion to me, who writes down everything he says; and again to me who, just like 'he' – the grandmother – separates the son from the perversely overprotective mother). *I'd like to be a mechanic and have a garage. I'd like to sell people petrol. I'd like to put petrol into their tanks.* * *And then I said to Mother, if Daddy was here, what would he say? It's true, she's right Mother, I don't know what. It makes me feel funny. So, I don't know.*

Obviously he is asking me a question here.

---

*   Note the association of 'fill her up' – the tank – with coitus, the sexual game and the transference onto myself, who takes everything down. —F.D.

ME: *But it is you who are quite right, and your father would agree
with you. Your mother never had a brother, she's always been brought up in
a convent with nuns. She doesn't know that when a little boy sleeps in his
mother's bed and when he is up against her nightgown and that he doesn't
have very much on, it does something to him. In his heart, he feels it's very
bad for him to take himself for his mother's husband, because then he takes
his daddy's place and it does something to him in his body. He doesn't know
whether he is an animal or a little baby boy or a little baby girl and it makes
him stupid, not to know what he is anymore. So you see, Mother tells you
that if Daddy were there you wouldn't go into her bed. Well, in the law of
all men, everywhere in the world, even with the black people who live all
naked, it is forbidden for a boy to sleep with his mother. The boy can never
be the mother's real husband. He can never love her to make real children.
Real children are made with the sexual organs of their two parents. The law
of men is that the boy's sexual organ must never meet his mother's. What I
tell you is the truth. Your mother wants you to know the truth. It is because
your mother has never had a brother and that she was brought up by the
nuns* (I repeat this) *that she has never thought of it. But ask your father,
he'll tell you the same thing that I'm telling you. It is the law of all men.*

During this second interview of the fifth session Dominique
models two shapes out of clay while he talks. (See the drawing
of the phallic form and of the Möbius strip: fig. 10, p. 89.) I copy
them without saying anything.

Following this double session with Dominique and the session with Paul-Marie, the mother asks me in front of Dominique
if I have anything else to say to her. Yes, maybe, I say. And I ask
Dominique: 'Maybe I should speak to your mother?' Dominique
strongly agrees. I have explained professional confidentiality to
him twice already: I think he trusts me entirely.

5.   *The mother alone*

I tell her that I have spoken to the two boys and that their
father's absence does indeed trouble them a great deal. And I tell
her that Paul-Marie has definitely been very troubled by always

Fig. 10
Work in clay made by Dominique
during the fifth session

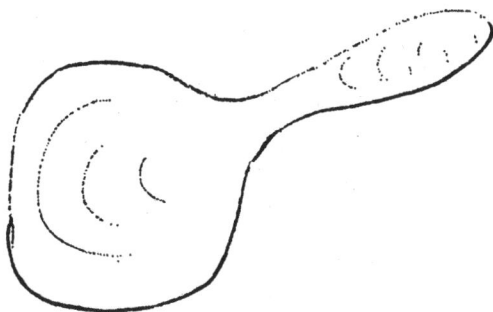

A voluminous ball with a protrusion or outgrowth,
swollen at the end.

A flat ribbon, closed into itself, so that the inner surface
continues the outer surface (a Möbius strip).

Dominique made these figures while he was talking
during the session — the session during which I told
him that incest was forbidden.

having to be in tandem with his brother. 'Yes,' she'd noticed this, 'but he was so nice, and it was brotherhood.' (That's a family word, brotherhood.) I tell her that I don't think Paul-Marie is too prudish with her; that his masculine sensitivity seems quite normal in defending itself against certain forms of intimacy with her, and that perhaps, having had no brothers of her own, she doesn't quite appreciate the level of intimacy at which a mother must stop with her sons. She answers with the sharp crafty air of a little girl who's been caught in the act. She says to me: 'Well don't you see, I like to have them in my bed, and I don't feel any shame showing myself naked to them, because I feel children need truth, and that everything is beautiful.'

I reply: 'But do you know that this may trouble your children, especially boys, and perhaps even your daughter?'

As regards Sylvie, she shows herself to be totally uncomprehending. Since the boys manage not to come into bed with her to keep her warm, well, too bad, she has to put up with it. So much the better if it doesn't mean that they're abnormally prudish, but as far as the girl goes, no. 'Sylvie keeps me warm you understand, cuddling up against me. But she's not pleased when my husband is there, because, of course, when he's there we have no need of them. As for Dominique, you know it wouldn't make any difference to me. Of course, Paul-Marie now says it would trouble him. He hides from me, even though I'm his mother! Imagine that. What can he have to hide from his mother?'

We have here a mother who is sexually infantile: once again it is the temptation to incest which is the main cause of regression, confusion of species and gender, and foreclosure of the oedipal self: of all that we are trying to track down, the mutilating experiences that mark Dominique's life.

Sixth Session:
18 January

Two weeks after the previous session

This time I don't ask Dominique to make a drawing or a model. Everything is going to be in words.

Dominique comes in happy and cheerful. *I'm happy now because I know how to tell the time.* Silence. *There's something which is a real miracle. It was enough for me to be nice with my godmother, no, I mean with my grandmother* (corrected slip) *and she's completely changed. She's for me now.*

ME: *You said your godmother? You never mentioned her to me, Who is she?* Dominique doesn't answer, closes up. (I'm being indiscreet.)

ME: *It's because you confused your grandmother and your god-mother while you were talking that I'm asking you this. It always means something when you say one word for another. That's why I'm asking you about your godmother. Godmother and grandmother: how can they be confused in your head? Is your grandmother also a godmother?*

DOMINIQUE: *Yes, she's Paul-Marie's godmother, but he calls her grandmother anyway. But that isn't it.*

ME: *What is it then?*

DOMINIQUE: *It's that she's just written to me, my godmother has. It's not her fault her forgetting me at Christmas time . . .* A moment's silence.

ME: *Who is she?*

DOMINIQUE: *She's a relative we don't see very often.*

ME: *Is this the first time she's forgotten you?*

DOMINIQUE: *Yes, that's it exactly, it's the first time, but she says she'll send me two gifts at once, one for Christmas and one for my birth-day. I was born on the 19th of January, you see.*

ME: *And your grandmother?*

DOMINIQUE: *She also wrote to me for my birthday, that she loved me. It's the first time she loves me. She sent me some money for my birthday. It's a miracle, it's a real miracle.* Silence . . . *I like to play at being a woman.*

ME: *Tell me about it.*

DOMINIQUE: *My cousin is the son of a cattle dealer.* (Is he talking about Uncle Bobbi today?) *His mother is also my aunt, she has two babies, she feeds the boy with a bottle and also sometimes the maid* (?) *. . . So, as soon as she gives the bottle, my cousin and me milk the cows and we go and give the milk to the one who's giving the bottle to the baby. It's funny. We like it. It's great fun. We pretend to be the woman who's giving the milk to the woman who's giving the bottle.*

ME: *The bottle, or is it the breast?* No reply. Silence.

DOMINIQUE: *I have a little well. Not quite like that one.* (He's referring to a clay model of a well, which is sitting on the table, left by another child.) He goes on: *Do you want me to play with that?*

ME: *With what?*

DOMINIQUE: *With the woman . . . like with my cousin . . . you're nice!*

ME: *Why? You thought that Madame Dolto would tell you that everything that's especially fun was prohibited? But now, do you think those games would be possible in front of your father?*

DOMINIQUE: *Oh sure, everybody laughs, the cattle farmer, my cousin's father* (père à mon cousin), *he laughs too when he sees us play at being women.*

ME: *Well you see then, if the father says it's allowed, well then it is.**

DOMINIQUE: *Yes, but it's fun anyway.*

ME: *Yes, but there are a lot of things that are fun and also allowed.*

DOMINIQUE: *That's right.* Silence. *Well, now I've solved the mystery! . . .*

ME: *Tell me about it.*

---

*   Being in doubt as to the perverse character of this game, I merely refer to the law of the father. —F.D.

DOMINIQUE: *Yes, my mother has an electric blanket and my sister likes it, she also likes Mother to keep her warm.* This grammatical mistake hides a slip:* like Mother herself, Sister likes the electric blanket which keeps her warm, in place of a mate. We will see this meaning confirmed later. So this is it: Dominique is still concerned with the taboo of incest, which he still does not accept. I remember the nomad with his blanket and little marmot arms around his neck.

ME: *What are you talking about?*

DOMINIQUE: *Well, about my sister who goes into Mother and Daddy's* (sic) *bed when Daddy isn't there; because when Daddy is there, Mother doesn't need an electric blanket . . . That's the mystery! The girl has a crush on the electric blanket.*

ME: *On the electric blanket or on Mother?*

DOMINIQUE: *Well, on both.* (We see that for the mother the electric blanket is the substitute for her husband, and for Dominique it is imaginary uterine regression.)

ME: *So your little sister still sleeps with your mother? Didn't your mother say that she wouldn't have her come into bed with her anymore?*

DOMINIQUE: *Well, yes, but now she's bought an electric blanket, and so the girl gets in with her for that.*

ME: *And you?* Silence.

DOMINIQUE: *Why? You think her sex could burst?*

ME: *It's you who thought of it. Tell me what you were thinking* . . . Silence.

DOMINIQUE: *Well you see, for instance, a boy six or seven years old who slept with his mother when he was little, and so the baby's sex got glued to his mother, well, can his sex burst?*

ME: *Do you think so? But you're talking about a boy six, seven years old, quite a big boy. And then you talk about the sex of the baby. I don't understand.*

---

* *Que maman lui tient chaud* for *lui tienne;* in French, a relative pronoun (like *que*) demands a verb in the subjunctive. —Translators. For Dominique this seeming grammatical mistake (he generally speaks correctly) symbolises his confusing the sex of his mother with a masculine gender. —F.D.

DOMINIQUE: *Yes, the boy can't enter his mother's body . . . But he can't get away from it . . .* Silence.

ME: *What can't enter his mother's body?*

DOMINIQUE: *Well, the sex! Because it's glued against her. A man is on the side, he's a man a little like a side. And a woman is a female side. And the sex that goes into the woman . . . They each have their own side . . . And then the sex goes in. They* (elles) *are babies first and then they grow up. With boys it's the same thing, especially when they are babies and if they stay small . . .* Silence. *You remember the cow that belonged to an Arab and he had to sell it to a nomad?*

ME: *Yes, I do.* (Dominique is referring to the fourth session: see p. 62.)

DOMINIQUE: *The nomad liked milk so much that every day he mucked her* (il la traisait).*

ME: *He mucked her?*

DOMINIQUE: *Yes, he mucked and mucked and mucked her so much that afterwards she was all thin. Or even if she wasn't thin, she had no more milk. That's the way it is when you're a baby, same for boys and girls, and afterwards you don't have any milk left . . . The mother is the cow, she's fat, fat, fat, she has milk and afterwards she's got nothing. Do boys have more milk longer than girls that have a lot? Who's better, girls or boys? . . . for milk?*

ME: *Milk* (lait) *is a food, but one also says* laid ('ugly') *for not pretty, not beautiful. What is it that's ugly?*

DOMINIQUE: *No, I wouldn't have liked being a girl, but I didn't like being ugly because I was a little boy . . .* Silence. *Well, I like to play at being a woman, but I wouldn't like to be . . . Who do they like better? Girls or boys? . . . Who do they choose?*

ME: *Tell me first who 'they' are. Maybe then you'll be able to answer that question yourself.*

DOMINIQUE: *My grandmother likes me now too, and my mother has always liked me. That's no miracle, that's just a mother.*

ME: *Yes.*

---

*   Dominique makes up the verb *traiser*, compounded of *baiser*, 'to kiss' or 'to fuck', in slang, and *traire*, 'to milk'. —Translators.

DOMINIQUE: *A mother always likes her babies, and children are always babies.*

ME: *Do you think so?*

DOMINIQUE: *Well, they grow up, but the mother's still the mother even after she's had other babies . . . A mummy cat forgets her babies after . . .* Silence. *Mummy once chose the king.** Silence.

ME: *Tell me about it.* Silence. (He seems to struggle over this memory.)

DOMINIQUE: *Mother had put a little black cat under her jumper . . .* (He sticks out his stomach and his chest under his jumper.) *Mother had put a little black cat in her jumper . . . That's it, I said to myself, I'm no longer the son of my mother. The cat's taken my place! . . . It would have been ridiculous!*

ME: *Maybe you were unhappy to have been forgotten by a mother cat, or mother cow, like by your godmother?*

DOMINIQUE: *No way, I wasn't pleased, not at all!*

ME: *That's like when your sister goes into your mother's bed for the electric blanket.*

DOMINIQUE: *Yes, Sylvie told me it's not to be with Mother, it's to have the electric blanket. Like that she is my mother too?* Dominique is confusing to be and to have (he says 'is' but means 'has').

ME: *Maybe Sylvie would like to take your father too, when he is there?*

DOMINIQUE: *That's right!* He laughs. *And she wouldn't need mother anymore, and she wouldn't need the electric blanket anymore either, because Daddy, well Mother says he's even better than us and the electric blanket.*

ME: *Then when Mother was with Daddy in bed you thought she was forgetting you and you weren't happy, not at all happy!*

---

*   Reference to the celebration of Epiphany (*Nuit des Rois*, 6 January) still prevalent in France. On Epiphany a pastry, *le galette des Rois* ('cake of the [Three] Kings'), which contains one bean, is divided up among the party. The person who finds the bean in his helping is the King (or Queen) and has the right to choose his or her partner and to wear a crown. —Translators.

DOMINIQUE: *Yes, but my brother, he doesn't give a damn. He says he doesn't like to have mother's warmth. Mother thinks he should.*

ME: *And your father?*

DOMINIQUE: *He doesn't say anything about that. It's the same to him when he isn't there. He likes boys and girls, it doesn't matter to him . . . It's women who make babies too. So it's her choice . . .*

ME: *You think they make babies by themselves? Don't you think it's fathers who give babies to women?*

DOMINIQUE: *Yes, that means something to me, I've heard it, but I wasn't quite sure whether they were making fun of me. You know, they say so many things that aren't true. But a mother is important isn't she?*

ME: *For your father, who is more important — his mother or his wife, 'your' mother?*

DOMINIQUE: *Yes, that's right. It's not my grandmother from Perpignan, but he also likes Mémé and Pépé* (the maternal grandparents).

ME: *Yes, but what woman is 'his' woman?*

DOMINIQUE: *Well it's my mother, since he's her husband. So that's natural?*

ME: *Yes that's natural. And that's why for boys when they grow up it isn't their mother who's most important, it's girls. They look for the woman they'll marry, and then they have children.*

DOMINIQUE: *That's it . . . But you have to be a student?*

ME: *You think so? . . . Think about it.*

DOMINIQUE: *No, you don't have to. Farmers and cattle merchants don't study, and generals don't study like other people, and they get married too since my grandmother is his wife.* (He is thinking about his paternal grandfather.)

No need to stress the importance of this session: it has allowed Dominique to see that individuals have one, and only one sex, and are recognised as such by their fellow men: thus entailing the repudiation of the illusion of ambisexuality, primary castration, and the questioning of phallic value so far as to cause the slip which underlines the ambiguity of being and having. Does this phallic value belong to penis-bearers? Doesn't it rather belong to women, who make and feed children? This is where the anxiety lies; in displeasing a mother who is powerful and needed, and whose neglect can cause a boy to lose his status as son; who, by withholding food and warmth, can make a boy feel ugly and useless. The sequence in which we witnessed man as a side* of woman, herself a side of man, probably refers to the story of Genesis; it also points to the ambiguity concerning the sexuality of the ideal ego, an ambiguity with which Dominique grew up.

This session had been prepared by the association-free modelling of the previous session. The present session proceeded entirely in words: neither pencil nor clay were required. An interesting association should be noted between the mother's choice of a King, and the slip between being loved (or forgotten) by the godmother,† alias grandmother: the same grandmother who had to mother her young brothers and sisters but who never mothered her daughter. It is because she was ill-loved by her mother that Madame Bel was unable to overcome primary castration, and imposed on her children the status of warming fetishes, part-objects, warm-blooded animal dolls, given her by a spouse whom she saw as her mothering elder brother.

---

*   In French coté, 'side', is close to côte, 'rib': hence F.D.'s identification
       of Dominique's words with Genesis. —Translators.
†   French marraine, 'godmother', sounds like ma reine, 'my queen'.
       —Translators.

Seventh Session: Early March

Six weeks after the previous session

They are late through some fault of the mother's. She called to say that she had missed her train and asked for permission to come later. I decide to wait for them in view of the significance of the previous session and the fact that the present one is already long overdue (two sessions missed).

When Dominique comes in, he tells me that he has not had any dreams, that he is not doing well in mathematics, and that he cannot count. I give him my interpretation: 'counting for someone' in the sense of having value for someone. (Does his treatment count for his mother, who causes him to miss sessions and almost made him miss the present one?)

DOMINIQUE: *Well, me, I count for a classmate named Georges Proteck.* (Same first name as Dominique's father; and Dominique's dog is a dachshund, *teckel* in French. Is it a coincidence or has Dominique made a mistake in the friend's name?) *But he sulks and when I invite another friend, he won't come along.* He lowers his tone. *And then he doesn't like my sister. There was a quarrel because of my sister. There was a misunderstanding, he got angry, my sister called him a little idiot. He didn't like that and for a while, he stopped coming. He said: 'I'm not coming anymore because of what your sister said: "Proteck is a little idiot."' She thinks* (Dominique is talking about Georges in the feminine), *she thinks that she thinks he's moody.*

ME: *Does she say so?*

DOMINIQUE: *No, but I know it. Somebody who isn't very normal is called a lunatic. He says that the others think that I'm a lunatic too.*

He thought the others were saying things behind my back . . . I don't like Haïta.

ME: *Who is Haïta?*

DOMINIQUE: *He's a boy I swap stamps and things with. Mother says I let myself be taken in. I don't know, maybe I do, maybe not, I don't know. But I'm not sorry about the swaps I make. Once I gave him a bulldozer, just like that, for nothing, because I said to myself, he's poor, be nice to him, give him some soldiers. Afterwards I was a little sorry. But, he's more unhappy than I am. His father is a tiler. Georges doesn't like to come here* (sic). *He says, 'Your sister says Proteck this, Proteck that.' I'm always afraid that Mother will say to me: 'Poor idiot, you let them take advantage of you.' One day Haïta took away* everything I gave him. His mother didn't want it. I said to him: 'You're going to get in trouble if you take all this home.' And he said: 'Well it doesn't matter.' You understand, I let myself be taken in because I don't have anything to play with, so I'm bored, so I let them do it and let him return everything I'd given him. Maybe I was right, maybe I wasn't, It makes me feel good to make him happy. But I'm afraid of getting in trouble with my mother, but he was the one who got into the most trouble with his mother. So that's the way it was settled.* While talking he works on a clay model. *This is a ray* (a fish, a ray with a dog's head, and another ray with an enormous, wide-open mouth: see fig. 11, p. 101). *The trouble is that the animal belongs to someone else.*

ME: *What do you mean?* He doesn't answer, and makes a third ray, which is quite realistic.

DOMINIQUE: *I think this animal is really terrifying . . .* Silence. *It has pimples on its body, it has pimples on its fins, and then a tail with a current going through it. My sister disgusted me too when she had pimples at the seaside.*

The castration anxiety can be traced here from one level to another. The 'ray' (*la raie*) of the posterior is a way French children have of describing the slit between the buttocks, or the vulva. Also note the displacement of the complementary form of the sexes onto the mouth of these animals. The fins of the fish

---

*   He doesn't mean 'take away', *emporter*, but 'bring back', *rapporter*.
     —F.D.

Fig. 11
Clay figures from the seventh session: a ray

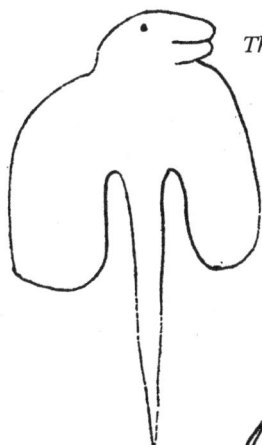

The eye is a small hole on either side of the head.

Popeyes.

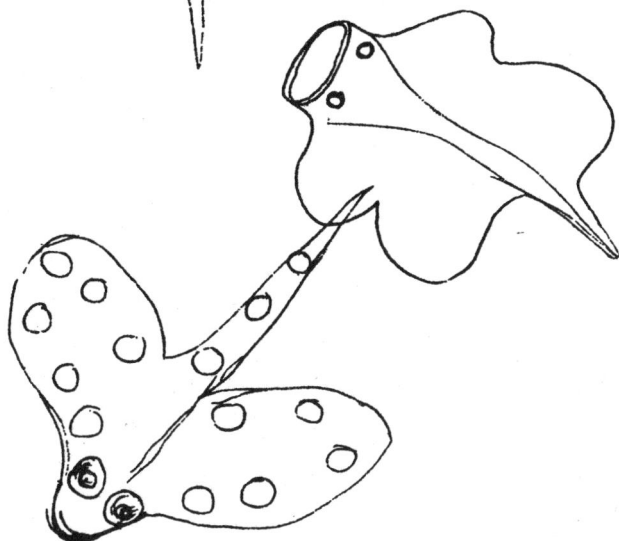

'Terrifying ray'. Wart-like markings, pimples, slit for a mouth.

with the passive mouth are in the form of a rump. The electrifying and electrified tail serves to express the danger of contact with the feminine sexual parts, the sexual mouth which electrifies the boy's penis. May not the pimples be the nipples and the clitoris? But I raise no questions concerning these resemblances to parts of the body.

ME: *You don't love your sister with all your heart, and maybe you're afraid of her.*

DOMINIQUE: *That's not right, you're supposed to love your sister. That's the least you can do to show your brotherhood.*

ME: *That's your mother talking that way. And maybe your sister is like your mother. There's something that makes you feel funny in your sex, like a tail, a current that runs through when you feel them too near you, your mother and your sister, because of their sex which isn't made like that of men and boys.*

DOMINIQUE: In a low voice: *I'm going to tell you a big secret. Well, I smoked. My friend Georges wanted me to carry him on my back, in return he gave me cigarettes. I don't know why he likes it to have me carry him on my back. He says it gives him a thrill, a current. My mother, if she knew that!*

We saw earlier that the mother destroyed Dominique's healthy narcissism by allowing incestuous games. We now find Dominique hiding sexual games and transferring his feelings onto a minor interdiction, that of smoking, a boyish game forbidden by the mother and generally forbidden to women in his family. I do not mention this, we are on the terrain of forbidden games with his sister, her pimples, problems of sex and of his tail, and no doubt of sexual games with his friend Georges Proteck, perhaps even with the dogs in the house, sexual games in which he has the initiative. His games with Georges are clearly erotic to both of them, and a betterment for Dominique. I take note of the secret, but do not interfere.

Eighth Session: Early May

Two months after the previous session; the delay was due to the holidays and to the flu which affected the whole Bel family except Dominique himself

DOMINIQUE: *You know, I sometimes still finish my work after the others. But for the last two days I've finished it at the same time. And I'm very happy when I get an exercise right. Well, I've got them all right now. Now I understand arithmetic – counting.* (Did my interpretation of 'counting for someone' have an impact, in being made at the right moment?) *Yesterday I dreamed that I was at my granny's, my father's mother's, and that I met a cat that barked like a dog. He growled like a dog. What made me laugh was when he started barking.* (He will give his associations for this dream at the end of the session.) *You know that really made me laugh.* Silence . . . *But it was also a little laugh of being afraid.* Pause . . . *A dog that meows, that would be funny too, but I don't know whether it would frighten me.* (Anxiety associated with desire without knowing whether it fits the species, here used for gender.)

ME: *And if it were a boy pretending to be a girl, or a girl pretending to be a boy?*

DOMINIQUE: *Yes.* He thinks silently. *Then I also had another dream. I was at my aunt's, my father's sister's, and I played with a boy and a girl, my two cousins. And there was a word which is 'elmoru'. I don't know who says it, but it's a word like that that says . . . it's the name of an invisible river.* Silence, then very low: *But I have a secret, I'll tell you later.* Aloud: *The best of it is that it means something, 'elmoru'; it's the name of an invisible river.*

ME: *Yes, you already told me that it was an invisible river, but how do you know that it's invisible?*

DOMINIQUE: *Well it's a river, sometimes when it rains a lot, and it's called Elmoru. It's because it's a polluted river, polluted with*

the smell of cod (morue). *Something like that.* Silence. Then softly:
*You know, it's a dirty word, 'elmoru'. There are women you see in the
evening, when they bring them in to the police station. They want to
see their identification papers.*

ME: *And what about your secret?*

He is quiet, then goes on in the usual ascending intonation
of his voice, false and somewhat mannered: *I was in the forest, I saw
three trees, three brothers. My grandmother said: 'Further up are the two
brothers,' and so on. The trees were brothers . . . What surprises me is
my grandfather takes a piece of paper and pencil to say what he means.*

ME: *Your grandfather or your grandmother?* (Doubt concerning the sex of the grandparent − but whose identity papers
could serve as a proof of his lineage.)

DOMINIQUE: *But it's my grandmother, of course.*

ME: *Just like me when I write down what you say and make a
drawing of your model?*

DOMINIQUE: *Yes . . . Three trees that might be one trunk. No,
it's not the three brothers, it's the eight brothers. Three trees on the same
trunk, that surprises me . . .* Silence . . . *Isn't that surprising, three
trees on one trunk?*

I put in some remarks concerning the trunk of the human
body, three penises or three breasts, the mammary organs, and
reminding him that he had told me that breasts were the sex
organs of men. And that he had drawn a teat like a cow's for
the penis (I tell him that 'penis' is the real word for 'prick', as
the school boys say, and he had used the wrong word: he had
called it the 'teat'.*)

HE SAYS: *Oh yes, the kiddie.*†

So we have confirmation of the meaning of *biquette*, the
word used in the previous session where the kiddie suddenly
replaced the cow; and he adds that in fact he did think that
women had one too. Then a friend told him that women didn't
have one. He's looking for me to confirm this.

---

*   I am referring to his own words, see p. 82. His answer refers to
        another session, see p. 62. —F.D.
†   *La biquette*, 'the little kid': see p. 62. —F.D.

ME: *And your sister and that other girl, your little cousin, have
you never seen them?*

DOMINIQUE: *Yes, but I still thought so. But they told us it was a
mouse, they said we were playing at cat and mouse when we ran after
each other to look.*

Probably to look and see whether she had a sexual organ
and whether he did. These are stories of what was going on in
his head or 'on top of' his head when he was with his little girl
cousin. The reader will remember that this shook up his imaginary soldiers and the imaginary tank that he hid in the chest
of drawers; the games forbidden by his paternal grandmother.

DOMINIQUE: *I've got an older schoolmate, I asked him once on the
beach whether he liked boys or girls better. He said: 'I've been around.'*
Silence, then: *I think girls' bodies are pretty good but playing with toy
cars with little girls is no fun. With girls, I like to play mummies and
daddies. My sister was the mother, her dolls were our children, and she
said to me: 'Look Daddy, she got the medal of honour.'*

ME: *And your mother, what does she say when she speaks to your
father?*

DOMINIQUE: *Yes, that's it. She also says: 'Look Daddy, how well
she's done her work.'* (His sister.) *I went to my room, I made myself
some kind of business, I ran a service station. There were a lot of cars.
Or else I was a soldier; there were a lot of medals. My mother gave us
something to eat and then we had a make-believe dinner party, because
we weren't allowed to swallow them.* (Parts of dangerous toys?) Very
softly: *Me, I like not being around.* (Identification with the absent
father?) *When you're around, you're sure to be disturbed. When you
aren't, you're invisible and then you get medals and cakes when people
come; and then the children are happy and my sister too. She likes it
when I'm the father who isn't there, she takes all the children, it's a doll*
(sic), *you understand, and she teaches them, and she allows them to
do anything they want. Then the children graw* (sic), *they grow.** (He

---

*   *Alors les enfants, ils croivent* (incorrect), *ils croissent* (correct). Here
     again, the misuse of a verb is not a plain mistake, since Dominique has
     a very good vocabulary and usually good syntax. —F.D. Dominique's
     lapsus also suggests an unconscious association with the verb *croire*,
     to believe. —Translators.

becomes a little annoyed when he realises that he hasn't used the right word.) *Anyway it means that the daddy has cars, that he has friends, that he is with the Germans. You know, in Germany they have a lot of medals. They're not bad people. They sleep in the same bed. It was Hitler who was evil. Then I used to say, I'm playing mummies and daddies and I'm called Georges.*

ME: *Like your father?*

DOMINIQUE: *She's the one who wants it.* (With a touch of justification in his tone, as if I were blaming him for taking over the role.) *She wants to be my wife, and she wants me to be her father.*

ME: *That's strange, because if you're her father, then she's your daughter, and not your wife.*

DOMINIQUE: *Anyway we took the parent's name, I took the name Georges, like my father and she took Ninette, like my mother.* (Often called Nénette: this is also the nickname of Monette, the father's sister.) *I would've liked to take the name of my Uncle Bobbi, my father's sister's husband.** *But my sister wouldn't let me. And children's names, we take the children's names, our own or our cousins'.* Silence. *Father has other things to do than to tell clothes* (sic). *I told her, a father has other things to do. And since I'd had enough of it, I told her: 'Well, take that and dress them with it.'*

ME: *And your father, does he take care of your clothes?*

DOMINIQUE: *Oh yes, he warns us, put on something extra when it's cold and take something for when it rains. Not Mother, Mother asks Father.* (Note that Dominique views his mother as if she were a child, rather than her husband's wife.)

ME: *And the children's first names. What first name did you choose?*

No answer. Instead of answering the question concerning first names: *For a while I found my name Bel a little too cute: people said 'Oh how pretty he is.' It's funny, it bothers me, but I'm surprised nobody ever called me* une belle fille ('a pretty girl'). (It was always his sister who was being admired.)

---

*   *Le mari à la soeur à mon père* instead of *le mari de la soeur de mon père*. Again the odd infantile genitive to express family relations.
—Translators.

ME: *Like your sister?*

DOMINIQUE: Silence, then: *When the friend of my brother of my father* (le copain de mon frère à mon père) *turned around and walked back, my father had no more brother.* (Note the association of his sister Sylvie's first name with the disappearance of the father's brother, no longer alive.)*

ME: *But what are you trying to tell me?*

DOMINIQUE: *You know my father's brother, who was lost in the mountains. My pépé spoke about it to my father because he was the eldest in the family. And then he also spoke about it to my sister. It was his sister and my father's sister too.* (At the time of his sister's birth, Dominique was with his paternal grandparents; the disappearance of this young man was made official and a commemorative plaque placed in the graveyard.) *My father's brother died in the mountains and his little brother swallowed the brush* (?) *of an electric train that my father was playing with*† *and he died. He was very young. And his other brother died as a young man. He was like Paul-Marie.* (A wish, or a detail concerning his age?) *My grandfather called my father to tell him all this. My grandfather went all around the Spanish jails to find his son. For a while I had an idea of my own. I thought that he had found a life, a girl, or else a job and that he had got married. And that he didn't like the idea of coming back . . . But this is impossible . . . I like to go and visit Mémé. When I go to see Mémé, I find my mémé again. My cousin Bruno, my aunt's son, is seven years old. Once we pretended to be sheriffs and I made us two nice sheriff's stars. It was fun. It must have caused Mémé a lot of suffering, when she learned that her two little boys were dead. She liked to hold me in her arms while looking at the pictures of her two little dead boys.*

ME: *Maybe it wasn't so much fun to be in Mémé's arms while she was thinking of her two little dead sons.*

DOMINIQUE: *No, it wasn't always fun and she used to scold me. I remember it was with the water hose. I'd made a hole and I'd*

---

*   It will be noted that my question about the first names in games produced unconscious associations on the first name of the sister, Sylvie (*s'il vit*, 'if he is alive'), which signify the father's brother. —F.D.

†   *Avec quoi mon père il jouait* and other infantile forms are used here. —Translators.

put the hose into it. And I wanted it to fall in. Oh how she scolded me and how she shouted. Just like a barking cat. Some voice she had! At grandmother's house when I took something, I was always scolded. 'If you want something, ask me first.' Mother isn't that way, whatever is hers is mine.

ME: *And even Mother's bed.*

He is quiet, turns serious and says: *I still like to sleep with her, in her bed, you know. But I know I shouldn't.*

He remembers his grandmother, the mother's mother, at whose home he learned to read. He felt that the grandmother with whom he had learned to read was often very strict and boundaried with regard to the young and free male he was then. But it was her interdictions of what had been abusively permitted that liberated the possibility of cultural learning, by repressing sexual, oral, anal and urethral impulses. This possibility disappeared again when he returned to his mother, who allowed all imaginarily incestuous or regressive activities.

DOMINIQUE: Silence . . . *I'd like to be a pirate, a sea robber. My brother made the* Bounty. *I wanted to be a pirate on the* Bounty. (He pronounces 'Bounty' almost like *bonté*, 'goodness'). *He's a builder so I had the heaviest granite columns.* (It was his grandfather who was a builder and drove the black people like cattle, but Dominique confuses his grandfather and his brother.) *I have the heaviest granite column. He gave me a pipe with a control system. An old electric meter. He took the pipe, wound it around some paper, made a big ball and I ran my pipe through that . . . Once with my sister, we took off from a certain point, kicking a ball. She went back and forth, back and forth. I went around the garden holding the ball.*

I prefer not to intervene, notwithstanding all the undertow of associations concerning sexual games with his cousin and his sister, caught by their paternal grandmother, and concerning fear of this grandmother, with her necrophiliac fantasies. There are no mediating elements close enough to reality. I merely stress to him that this was an important session, and that he has said and thought things useful for his treatment. There were no drawings or models.

Ninth Session: 25 May

Three weeks after the previous session

They are late again. The mother missed her train, but I waited.

DOMINIQUE: *I'm going to try and make a dog. I like coming here. I can see the shops through the window, and then the cars. We see all that in our street too, but less than here. And you've got shops here too.*

ME: *And also, here you come to see me, and your parents pay for the consultation. They pay for you to see Madame Dolto, so that you can be cured.*

DOMINIQUE: *Yes, I like that too. But not always. Today I was glad to come.*

ME: *Not always, why?*

DOMINIQUE: *Because there are days when it isn't so much fun. Yes, I had a dream, but I've forgotten it. There are times when you say things to me, and I say to myself: That was a good thing, her saying that.*

ME: *What for example?*

He doesn't reply. And then: *And then there are things . . .* (He puts on an expression of resentment, his mouth pinched.)

ME: *There are things you don't like to hear. They are hard to swallow, as they say. Or as they say again, they weigh on your heart, you'd rather not hear them.*

DOMINIQUE: *Well, you see, me, I'm stubborn; like someone who wasn't able to do something, and so his friend says to him: 'Don't do that because this or that's going to happen.'* (All this is an allusion to the fact that I told him of the prohibition of incest and told him no longer to sleep in his mother's bed.) *Well, imagine seeing a friend who's lucky in some way, and you can't have the same luck. It's not right that it should happen like that, that the other one tells you: 'It's going to mean trouble.' You don't want to believe him, and then it's too late!*

I don't interpret, I don't tell him that he is talking about his desire to take his sister's and father's place in the mother's bed. They still have the 'luck' that I talked to Dominique about: that if it troubled him when he was sharing his mother's bed, then it was the sign of a correct intuition concerning the human law of the prohibition of incest.

ME: *The story you tell me is a little like the story of Adam and Eve. It is the forbidden. It's forbidden and it's tempting. Do you know the story of the earthly paradise of Adam and Eve?*

DOMINIQUE: *Do I know it!* (He starts to act it out in mime. It is the first time he gets excited, playing all three personages, Adam, Eve and the tree. Dominique acts out the tree between Adam and Eve.) *Do I know it! Here's Adam* (to the right), *and there, there's Eve* (to the left; in between the two would be the tree, but he doesn't mention this). *Then 'he' sees* (but which he?) *to the right a glass of beer* (Adam's side, beer glass, liquid) *and to the left he sees a bread bag or a wine bag* (bread bag or wine bag; these are also the sacramental objects of Catholic worship.) *And then he wants to throw snowballs at the tree.* (He makes a snowball and says that he is throwing it at a tree, represented for him by the window.) *Maybe the devil* (he pauses for a moment), *the devil says to himself: 'They know that I'm bad, worse than the others and how happy it'll make me. Well never mind, I'll do all I can to pester him.' Maybe sometimes he hides in a tree.* (Cars, the marmots.) *And then sometimes it's in the shape of cigarette smoke or the form of the invisible.* And then, very softly: *One of them is coming out from behind the tree . . . 'Here, take this! Stumble! Take this! You're going to miss your train!'* (The train the mother missed when coming to the consultation.)

ME: *What you're telling me here is making you think of something.*

DOMINIQUE: *Yes, I saw a film, there were two demons, a wizard and a witch, who did all kinds of mean things to people. It was under Louis XIV. People, a hundred years later, see a storm and a tree cracking. Oh it was a long time ago that I saw this film.* (The reader will recall the 'crack' of the witch at the start of the treatment.)

The tree cracks and then there are two trails of smoke coming out. He tells me pretty much the story of the film which he remembers, and which is actually *I Married a Witch.* (The witch in fact is clearly myself.) *All the time in these films you see the life of a family going back to a period a long time ago, the time of Louis XIV. And afterwards you see them today. In a film about somebody's will, there was a count who lived like that in the days of Louis XIV. You saw him at first and then you saw him again dressed up like his descendants . . . It's stupid, I don't remember the dream I had, otherwise I'd be telling you. Today* (actually yesterday)*, we had a problem about a rectangle and a problem about a square. Well I understood everything, I did everything right. Luckily the teacher had explained everything a bit. Maybe if she hadn't explained it, I wouldn't have understood. What I like in school is when everybody is quiet and you can hear the flies buzz all of a sudden. People are talking, and then pop! All of a sudden everybody's quiet. It's the switch that's fun.* (Is this an illusion to the silence which occurs between parents who were talking in bed and then are quiet when they have sexual intercourse?) *It's funny too when I see a soldier.* (Sexual fantasy concerning German soldier.) *I wonder how he'd be if he were on horseback?* (These associations do bring him back to the primal scene.)

ME: *You mean if he was straddling the horse?*

DOMINIQUE: *Yes, I wonder . . . if it changes people. What I like with my friend, when he's straddling me, is making him fall.* (Remember his friend who climbed on his back in order to experience a 'current', meaning the orgasm of masturbation, in exchange for cigarettes.) *You'd think you were at war or something. Then we have to go and get an ambulance, we have to get taken care of, and then we're dead, we pretend to be dead.* Silence. *What I liked was during the war, when the Germans took him* (her) *to the police station. His* (her) *comrades were nice, they showed him pictures: their wives and children and even the Germans were nice. When she met Germans; you know, Mother* (so he is talking about her). *Well, she spoke to them. And she told me she was taken to the police station. What had she done?* (He himself is the one who asks the question.) Very softly: *I think she stayed in the street too late.* (We are reminded of the last session on 'elmoru', the dirty word, the street women being picked up and taken to the police station.) *Now, at any time of day, you don't need to be afraid that someone is going to take a shot at you. People who are hungry, the poor, my grandmother showed me the reclusion cards* (for rationing cards) *needed to buy food. But they were pretty tough anyway. They kept people* (sic, people meaning food here) *for themselves and for us there was very little.* (Amorous cannibalism.) *My grandfather used to smoke, and now he doesn't smoke anymore. That's strange. There are three smokers left, my father, Pépé's brother and Pépé* (Grandad). *Pépé's brother smokes cigarettes.* (This is what is male, associated with evil, with the forbidden: but I say nothing and just listen.) *My grandfather* (this is what he calls the maternal grandfather) *and my pépé* (the grandfather on the father's side), *when they were little, they used to walk around naked and their father whipped them with nettles . . . I like to feed the fish.*

This brings to memory the naked black people the mother talks about, and herself, naked in front of her children, who are supposed to be naked in front of her. Nakedness is idealised, compulsory on the mother's side, while it is forbidden among the Bels.

I think that Dominique is busy attributing to others something he is doing himself and for which he has a considerable guilt feeling. I think he is talking both about vomiting (feeding the fish, sea sickness) due to the fact that he smoked in secret, and also about the delights of sadomasochistic games or the fantasy of deserving a sadistic punishment – a pleasure which he cannot expect from his own family because his mother doesn't scold him – nor does his brother – his father is very gentle and distant. At the maternal grandfather's and grandmother's (Pépé and Mémé's), the grandmother was forever talking about teaching him a lesson. (The grandfather – the builder – used to whip naked black people.) Had he himself been brought to heel, says Mémé, he wouldn't have become what he is now. In contrast, it was at the paternal grandparents' house that the scene took place with the attic and the forbidden games with the hose, and the need to ask permission before taking anything. All this is running through Dominique's talk – and through my listening – without surfacing. He hopes to find in his grandfather the support of his boyish anal narcissism. But as soon as he's finished talking about liking to feed the fish he goes on: *Did you been** (usually he speaks quite well), *did you been into the Lion of Belfort?*† *You can climb around inside it.*

ME: *Inside?* (Belfort is the city where his mother went to school after her return from Africa. Also, 'Bel' is his name, 'fort', of soldiers).

DOMINIQUE: *Yes, you can go out the mouth or you can go out the rear. It's as if you were either vomit or poo-poo.* (He identifies his own body with a bodily discharge.) He laughs a little. *And then, you know, under the lion's belly there's an arrow which shows Germany and says: 'The Germans shall not pass.'* (The desire of being an oral, anal and phallic part-object, a hindrance to the rival German seducers, who, though blond and tall like the Bels, are nonetheless enemies.) *It would be nice if people put a cannon in their roof* (or in themselves?)‡ *and if they fired on their enemies. A friend told me that an Italian would push the button of a machine, that that stopped the motors of the planes and they fell down. They did that for German planes.*

ME: *Do you think so?*

DOMINIQUE: *My mother told me that the Italians were against the Germans. They were neutral (?) and then they were against us. And yet, when you see the Italians, they're nice. Mother told me that they were with the Germans, and in my mind, I didn't want to believe that. Mussolini, could be, maybe it was him who wanted to side with the Germans. My mother told me Hitler was very, very intelligent, but he was the spirit of evil. What they did in Spain wasn't right. They found somebody who'd been hiding for a long time and then they found him and they killed him.* (This session took place the week Grimau,

---

*   *Seriez-vous été?* instead of *avez-vous été?* —Translators.
†   This large monument of a lion, representing the defence of Belfort against the Prussians in 1870, is hollow, and open to the public. —Translators.
‡   *Dans leur tôit (dans leur toi?)* —Translators.

Fig. 12
Clay figure from the ninth session

the Spanish communist leader, was executed.* Dominique's
uncle disappeared at the Spanish border.) *When the Americans
saw that someone was going to lose . . . I learned the story of the begin-
nings of the United States with France . . . they decided to come and
help the French. You see I'm happy sculpting with the pencil, it's easier
than on marble. He has a head that's a little thin, just like a German
shepherd. Well, look I think it's pretty good* (see his clay model of
the dog: fig. 12, p. 114).

ME: *There is in fact a good head on your animal, but he seems
to have only half a body, half as big in volume I mean. The head seems
to belong to a dog of twice the build the proportions of the body would
indicate. He's also only half in length, he's like a paperweight in high
relief, lying down, and cut along the axis so that there are only two feet,
the right front and rear feet, a head and a tail in volume.* The reader
may be surprised at the words I use to speak to Dominique. I
always speak this way to my young patients.

DOMINIQUE: *Oh that, well I hadn't noticed.* He wants to
change it now.

ME: *It's all right, it's all right the way it is, it surely means
something. You told me earlier that you were stubborn, strong-headed,
and you see the dog has a head which is very imposing, he has a strong
head.† And you see when one is strong-headed, maybe one has a lot of
things in one's head. One wants to be grown-up, have all the privileges
of the grown-up, of men, of one's father. But one doesn't quite have
the body of a grown-up. Well, you see this isn't a person, it's a dog.
Maybe there's something in your heart that would rather not become a
grown-up, that would prefer to remain a nice half of an animal, lying
on the ground like a dog in its kennel. It's as if the earth had taken half
of its body. An animal doesn't talk, and sometimes when you speak you
don't say what you think. It would be easier not to speak. The dog sees
everything. He has eyes, nostrils, ears, a mouth that is very well made
and enormous. He hears everything, smells everything, but he doesn't*

---

*   Julián Grimau, a Catalan communist, was executed by Franco's gov-
      ernment in April 1963, more than twenty years after the end of the
      Spanish Civil War. The execution generated considerable reaction in
      the European press. —Translators.

†   *Tête* is 'head'; *têtu*, 'strong-headed' or 'stubborn'. —Translators.

say so. And also he can't act since he isn't all there. You too have ideas and you keep what you think to yourself. We'll go on working next time so we can better understand what there is in your heart that looks like your model, which is both large and small at the same time, which feels and hears, which has a head and a tail that is large, but doesn't know how to say it, and just doesn't move.

Tenth Session:
7 June

Two weeks after the previous session

In the waiting room I notice the mother who still has nothing to say to me. She waves to me in a friendly way, and Dominique comes with me into my office. The window is open and the noise from outside bothers us. I ask Dominique to shut the window. It is difficult to close; he tries, looks around, but can't do it. The building is an old one, with metal windows of a model no longer common. I go with him and make him feel with his fingers the rounded edge of the left-hand shutter of the window and the corresponding concave shape of the right-hand shutter, the two of which have to fit one into the other. A lever is to hold everything in place. He is delighted to understand the way the forms fit together, and adroitly closes the window himself.

He comes and sits down, and I put into words for him this closing of the windows using the French expressions for the female side and the male side of the window lock. I stress the way in which he has mastered the complementarity of form, and so understood by himself how to close the window and operate the lever that locked everything together. Without my verbal explanations and my manual aid to his passive hands, he would have faced an insoluble practical problem, his eyes not knowing how to build on tactile information. This way it was a practical, sensory experience, and the verbalisation of the concept of complementary genital forms, that made it all clear.*

---

*   I had to verbalise this opening of the window to make him integrate
     the sensory experience. But also, since my hands were guiding his to

Dominique is very upset and excited by the death of the Pope. He is under the impression that I have been to Rome for a professional meeting. Someone at the clinic must have discussed my absence, my inability to come to last week's meeting, which had to be postponed for another week.

He asks me whether I saw the Pope. I evade the question. He asks me whether I saw a statue of Caesar (he doesn't say a statue on horseback): *A statue of Caesar, where he looks handsome.*

ME: *What is he doing?*

DOMINIQUE: *He is astride his horse.*

ME: *Yes, he is handsome.* (We see how this session immediately links up with the preceding one: the approach to the primal scene, oedipal fantasies perhaps, sexual, phallic – and genital for certain.)

He returns to the subject of the Pope, saying that his brother and sister make fun of him *when he believes things,* and that he had been told the Pope was dead and was then seen coming back and coming to the window to give people his blessing. (We ourselves have just closed the window, as I point out to him.) (Here Dominique makes the gesture of a Papal blessing, identifying himself with that gesture.) Then his brother and sister told him the Pope was really dead, but that an American doctor had resuscitated him, *so that I didn't know whether to believe them? I thought they were making fun of me . . . I don't think you can bring the dead back to life. But what does it mean, that he was ill, and then that he was well again, and then ill again and then that he died. As if he had died twice?*

I explain the reality of historical facts. And, since his mother always told them when they were young 'to tell the truth', I think to myself that, indeed, this boy does need to know what reality is. There had been a considerable improvement in the Pope's health, though he had at first been thought to be

---

show him how to feel, I had to make sure this hand-to-hand encounter, the only one in the course of his treatment, would not be perceived as an attempt at seduction. —F.D.

dying: then indeed he reappeared at his balcony to bless the crowd, before his sudden relapse and death a few days later.

DOMINIQUE: *Oh yes, now I understand. But now I don't want to be made fun of anymore, all the time, just because I don't understand right away.*

He then delivers a speech on the popes: that such and such a pope was good to all, that towards the fifth and sixth centuries there had been French popes. And then only Italian popes, so there wouldn't be two of them. And then there was Pius XI and Pius XII and finally, John XXIII. (He seems to have really crammed, one might say, on the question of popes, and to have memorised certain sequences of their history which he may have heard or seen on television. He is now interested in TV, which used to bore him.) He tells me about something he saw when the family travelled to Italy, on their way back through the Great Saint Bernard Pass. (Bernard is the name of the father's lost brother.) It was in a small village on the border. (Bernard disappeared near the Spanish border.) What struck him were the doors of the shops, with big strings of beads of *all colours hung in front of the door.* (We know that it is in the name of Catholicism that the father, the mother and the brother justify their fear of going with girls.)

Dominique is quiet. Then: *I'd like to be a farmer, myself.*

ME: *You've just been talking about Italian shops, and all of a sudden you say you want to be a farmer.*

DOMINIQUE: *That's because I was thinking that it was very hot in Italy; there are flies and that's why you have those bead curtains which keep them from coming in. But I'd like to be a farmer; and then when it's hot, well, it reminded me that it was hot then, and that there were also flies which bothered the cows.* He is quiet and then goes on: *I'm happy because I'm going to get a snorkel and fins. Mother told me and Pépé promised too, because now I do good work in school. With what they both give me I'll be able to go swimming at Saint-Raphaël and maybe shoot fish underwater.*

ME: *Saint-Raphaël?*

DOMINIQUE: *When my sister wanted to teach me how to swim I couldn't because I always folded my feet in like a frog, but now*

I'm sure I'll be able to. Before I said to myself: 'I can't swim, I'm going to drown.' But now I know I'll be able to swim. We're going to Saint-Raphaël.

ME: *Who's we?*

DOMINIQUE: *Well, all five of us, and then Mother and Dad. I'll show you.*

He makes a sketch of Saint-Raphaël, fairly well made. I know the region and recognise everything he wants to show me. Then he makes a sketch of their caravan. The proportions are good. The parents have a large half-folding bed. For the children there are two sets of bunks. Dominique sleeps beneath his sister, and the brother under a bunk which is used for storing things. He tells me that his father has two cars, one for work and one to pull the caravan. They're very proud because the father bought a Buick which formerly belonged to the Duke of X . . . Long silence.

ME: *Well; you don't have much to say today.*

He is at first reluctant, then finally makes up his mind to speak: *I'm getting along with my sister, but I'm not getting along very well with my brother.*

ME: *Well?*

DOMINIQUE: *Well, it's Mother who's not happy. My brother is very stuck-up, he always gets himself into some foolish business or other. He's always telling my sister how to dress: you shouldn't wear this, you shouldn't wear that. He wants to give orders to my mother. He won't let her wear the dress she wants. So mother tells him to mind his own business. And don't you think she's right?*

ME: *Yes, she is. It isn't a son's place to tell his mother what clothes to choose. You know what I've told you, the mother isn't made for her sons, she's made to please her husband, to please men of her own age. But you were talking about your brother?*

DOMINIQUE: *Yes, there you are. Very often, well, my friends drop by. They see my brother's room, and so we go in without thinking. We look around, we take out a book, or touch things. One day my friend brought a record, so we went into my brother's room to play it. We couldn't find his record player — because my brother has a record player, he has a guitar and everything he needs. I don't have anything*

*myself. My father, who happened to be there, said: 'Come on in,' and
he played the record in his study.*

ME: *Your father has a study and a record player?*

DOMINIQUE: *Yes, but when Daddy's out, he locks the door.
And even when he's there and he's working, he locks the door too.
You understand, he talks to my mother a lot, he talks about his trav-
els. And when he comes back at night he has a lot of work, so we're
not allowed to disturb him . . . I'm trying to remember a dream I
had that I wanted to tell you. It was a dream about the cat that
meowed. It wasn't Mémé from Perpignan, it was my grandmother.*
('Grandmother' is the grandmother from Perpignan, from
the South of France. Dominique again makes a slip concerning the location. The grandmother from the South is called
'Grandmother', the maternal grandmother from the East of
France is called 'Mémé'.)

ME: *But you told me it was Mémé from Perpignan, the one who
had the portrait of the two dead sons, the little one and the grown-up
one, your father's mother.*

DOMINIQUE: *Yes, yes maybe I told you that, but I made a mistake. It's the grandmother, Mother's mother, we call Mémé, she lives
in the East.*

ME: *Why did you make a mistake? I don't think you made a
mistake. I think you couldn't help getting them mixed up . . .*

DOMINIQUE: *Well, she didn't want me to go into the attic, she
just didn't want it and she said: 'Don't you do it!'*

ME: *What attic was this?*

DOMINIQUE: *This is another memory, but this is a memory of
Mémé's attic, Mémé from V——, that I remember now and it wasn't
in Perpignan. They say Perpignan, but it's really in V——, not far
from Perpignan, a little village. It's much simpler to say the name of
the town next to it.*

Dominique is no longer wandering; he is relating some
memories and making it very clear which grandmother he is
talking about. He is concerned with two stories, each involving an attic, but distinct locations associated with two different
grandmothers. He is finding his bearings in time and in space
and getting over his confusion of grandmothers and families.

DOMINIQUE: *Well, then there is my grandfather, the one who lives in V——, my father's dad, the one who's a retired general. In the attic there are trunks with his uniforms, and me and my brother and my sister – you see, it was forbidden – my grandmother didn't want us to and someone had taken my grandfather's cape.*

ME: *Who's 'someone'?*

DOMINIQUE: *It was my brother who'd put it on; he made himself up like a general, and I was his soldier. We'd agreed not to say anything and well, I was very small then, and I said to Mémé without thinking about it: 'What fun we had in the attic; we found something,' and then I suddenly remembered that I shouldn't have said it, but I'd said too much. And she asked us: 'You didn't touch your grandfather's things, did you?' And so we were caught and my brother got terribly angry at me. My grandfather was a two-star general.*

ME: *You remember that you played with Bruno, and that each of you had a star?*

DOMINIQUE: *Oh yes, it was great fun, we were sheriffs. Then there were cowboys. My grandfather* – he goes right on, this parenthesis of mine wasn't what he needed – *my grandfather was a Resistance leader, that was for real. The sheriffs was just make-believe. It's like now, if we says cops and OAS.** He was the head of the party in Perpignan, and the boss of an ammunition factory in the town of X . . . This ammunition was intended for the Army. (How well he expresses himself.) *It wasn't the right thing to do to go around with too many people, because somebody might well be a spy and tell things.* (Association to himself: he gave away the story of the attic to the grandmother.) *A German spy who could have picked up five or six cartridges* (he's started working with clay now, but is producing nothing formal). *So a price was put on his head. A price of gold, because my grandfather was a head of the Resistance. Once the Pépés came* (he probably means the Germans; this is an eloquent slip) *and my pépé left from the other side of the garden by a ladder* (this particular grandfather isn't called Pépé, but Grandfather). *Then*

---

*   OAS: Organisation de l'armée secrète ('Secret Army Organisation'),
     far-right terrorist organisation active during the Algerian War;
     Dominique's sessions took place during the war's peak. —Translators.

*the Germans were really fooled because they couldn't find him, he went
right over the wall and took the ladder away. Who was to know? My
father too was in the Resistance. My grandfather had a bicycle. He had
to tell what my grandfather's bicycle was like.*

ME: *I don't understand this business with the bicycle.*

DOMINIQUE: *My paternal grandfather was in the Resistance. One
day my father went to see him. The Resistance people made him say what
colour and make grandfather's bicycle was before letting him through.*
(So as to make sure of who he was: this is the foundation of the
symbol. They feared that his father might be a spy pretending
to be the general's son.) *My father had put bombs in the Germans'
garbage cans, and then, you know, the Germans—* (Still seated, he
swings his arms to follow the rhythm of a military march, and
sings to the marching rhythm.) *This is how my mother says the
Germans used to march* (the Germans, with whom the mother had
sympathised as a young girl) *and the Germans went by and they
were blown up. I have a record of a military march, it's a military band.*

ME: *A record of German military music?*

DOMINIQUE: *No, no it's a record of French military music. You
have to play it on a tape recorder; I don't have a tape recorder myself.*
(He's making a slip.)

ME: *You're sure it's a 'tape recorder'?*

DOMINIQUE: *It's a record player, I don't know what a tape
recorder is, but I know it exists. I keep it* (the military music record)
*even though I don't have a record player, and then when Daddy allows
me to, I listen to it on his record player, because my brother never allows
me to use his. When he goes out, he fiddles with it so it won't work and
no one else can use it.*

What is interesting in this session is the very different tone of
the conversation. There is absolutely no raving; there is some
self-criticism. Furthermore, Dominique now looks me square
in the face when talking. He occasionally takes on a somewhat
troubled look when he isn't quite sure of something he's talking
about, or when I tell him I don't understand what he's saying and
want him to make his thoughts clearer for me. But then he looks
me straight in the eye again, when he's found what he wants to

say, or how to say it, in overcoming the gaps in his first account, which has been too elliptic for me to understand.

We see what has altogether changed: his right to be aggressive towards his brother, though his mother doesn't much approve of it; the possibility of being critical and combative in regard to this brother. Dominique now identifies with men – note the Pope's gesture, or the gesture of the Germans; the ideal ego is made present through the person of the father or the paternal grandfather. We must also note the recognition of the castration justified by the father. Dominique accepts the frustrations – doors banging shut – when they come from the father and no longer from the brother. He accepts that he cannot do just anything in his father's absence with his father's personal belongings, and justifies this. He accepts that his mother belongs more intimately to her husband than to her children. When the father has little time, it is for his wife that he is there, and for his work. Then there is all this valorisation of his father's lineage, his father's family. We now understand what was troubling the boy in the mother's friendly remarks about the Germans, their being very nice people; hard-working, authoritarian racists and colonialists like Dominique's maternal grandfather. And also how troubling it was to know that she had once been arrested by the Germans, those Germans who were tall and blond like the Bels themselves and with whom she enjoyed talking – those Germans who had almost brought about the paternal grandfather's death. We understand his slip when he was speaking about the Pépés who pursued his grandfather, Pépé who had displayed 'Nazi' behaviour towards black people. This represents the mother's line in him. We mustn't forget that he is the only one to take after this maternal grandfather. Everything contributed to silencing in himself the desire to identify with the masculine bearers of the Bel name. This deprived him of the educative benefit of oedipal desires.

It is also interesting to see that he made a readable map of the city of Saint-Raphaël, and a diagram of their caravan which I found very easy to understand. Only one point is worth mentioning concerning this drawing. It would have been normal to reserve a separate corner of the paper or else take a new sheet in order to draw the caravan. Instead he kept the same sheet and superimposed the drawing of the caravan on top of the city map, without seeming to take any notice. It is as if in his imagination the first image was being cancelled out by the new drawing; as if it interfered neither with the drawing, nor the reading of the new drawing. Would we be justified in seeing here an objectivisation in space of what happened for him, in fact, in time: the confusion of the phallic values of the masculine and feminine, paternal and maternal roles; the confusion between Nazi racist Germans, and the French Resistance, the confusion between record player and tape recorder.

The two interesting moments of this session are, consequently, the moments when he talks about the Pope and identifies with him by copying the gesture of benediction which he saw on television, and the moment when he expresses admiration for the mounted statue of Caesar. This time it is no longer Napoleon's Panthéon at Les Invalides, associated with his mother (see p. 82), but it is a handsome general astride a fine horse, associated with the father.

We know the sexual implications of this idea of 'astride' to a child who used to sleep in his parents' room until the birth of his little sister; a boy who was afraid of merry-go-rounds and bicycles. We also know his games, which consisted of carrying a friend on his back to give himself masturbatory sexual excitement (like current passing through the tail of the ray). Then there are the moments when, sitting, he imitates the Germans (valued by the mother) with their upright bearing and gestures of marching, and their being blown up by bombs which the father had placed in their garbage cans.

We must remember the word 'elmoru', applied to women who are taken to the police station at night. The penetration of the mother at night to deposit the semen which resulted in the little sister is really what exploded Dominique's first structure: that of the little wild man* who made himself the lord of his

---

*   The reader will recall 'the baby's sex that might blow up'. —F.D.

slave-mother, in defiance of the father, who was also defeated until proof of the effect of his fecundity, of his equestrian prerogatives within the conjugal bed, came forth.

We remember that the Germans wanted 'to keep everything to themselves'; that the maternal grandfather in Africa was a man who behaved, we might say, as a racist, and that the mother thought everything that the Germans did, including Hitler's intelligence, marvellous indeed, except that it was 'for the spirit of evil'.

Also bear in mind the moment of this session when Dominique says 'someone' had put on his grandfather's cape, and that this 'someone' was his brother. Dominique was only the soldier of his brother-general: but a soldier-spy. The sister played the role of passive fellow-conspirator. We have here a panoramic perspective of what caused Dominique's confusion from the age of five on: the lack of personal, bodily or (with respect to desire) sexual points of reference for his virility.

We see how the mother's and father's families hold opposing ideals concerning the manifestations of virile value. We have witnessed Dominique's high treason towards the grandfather; the pseudo-submission taught him by his mother has been turned into a way of spying and of getting the elder brother trapped. Some sort of trick was the only way for him to express his de-oedipalised sadistic sexual feelings towards the elder brother. We have also seen Dominique escape from the masochistic submission to which he had been driven by his phobia of pregenital magical castration by the brother and sister.

It was only from the statements and the significant family nonverbal expressions that accompanied the arrival and development of this little girl, his sister, that Dominique was able to measure the immensity of what he lacked: his lack of value, not in relation to adult manhood or paternal power, but in relation to the all-powerful magic and fetishistic phallic power of this baby girl, penis-less, her mother's part-object (still today), but symbolically endowed with phallic power by both lineages, for which she was the first girl, long awaited.

The birth of the little girl also brought significant changes
for Paul-Marie, the elder brother. I believe that he too was traumatised by this birth, and its consequences in the dynamics of the
family group, particularly in the sexual dynamics of the parental couple. For Paul-Marie, this birth confirmed his belief in his
oedipal illusion of having a child through his mother: day by day
(except during the father's rare visits) they waited for the birth
together. By identifying either with his father or with his mother,
he could now admire and adore this little phallus-sister – provided
he was willing to copy their anal and urethral phallicism, and provided also that he was willing to join the family chorus in its admiration of the aesthetics of girls' bodies and its deliberate blind
spot towards the sexual organs and, therefore, towards his own.
Paul-Marie is traumatically caught up in a passive homosexual
structure which he has borne fairly well so far notwithstanding
his difficulties in school. At the age of eighteen, with the approval
of his parents, he says he cannot understand that 'someone' can
find pleasure with girls or go to bed with them. He will, under
protest, accept the sexual act, since it is required to beget children, but regrets this injudicious whim of nature.

He cannot accept the desire for body-to-body contact,
whether it be of two bodies engaged in wrestling, or in eroticism. One desire only is valued: friendship between men in
the exchange and admiration of philosophic talk. Eroticism is
limited to voyeurism of the impersonal beauty of the 'female
figure'. Paul-Marie's repressed eroticism requires a verbal, if
joyless, build-up; children are to him but living things, four-
legged digestive tubes. At the same time, he is in love with
young children outside the family circle. The open eroticism
of this attraction is confirmed by the necessary rejection of his
brother and sister. He holds them apart. At home he is wrapped
up in himself, and does not allow his brother and sister to
speak, or to touch his things. He has no dealings with them;
only 'grown-ups' are worthy of interpersonal exchange. Girls of
any age or size are a menace. Paul-Marie was five when Sylvie
was born; it is clear that he does not make explicit to his parents, or to Dominique, the inhibiting drama of the development

of his ethos; the foreclosure of his paternal-genital ideal ego, short-circuited by the confusion with the maternal, homosexual and passive-anal ideal ego. The latter is overactivated by the magical realisation of pseudo-paternal fraternity in the absence of castration by the father, a realisation in which the fantasies of incestuous fatherhood are almost made legal by what both father and mother say to him.

I have frequently described the imaginary situation of the boy between three and seven. Independent of the oedipal conflict from which he can escape during the father's long absences, he wants to receive or bear a child – a hope of a hope of anal–urethral parturition. This idea derives from a drinking fantasy – the result of bottle-feedings and the observation of acts of human or animal intercourse, interpreted as perfusive penetrations. They invariably serve the purpose of narcissistic enjoyment. At the same time they provide an appearance of humanisation, since they involve the mimicry of the father's or mother's behaviour towards the fetish-object, the new child. All this is a way of escaping from natural castration (which is what primary castration is), a way inherent in the child's polymorphic perverse structure. It is also a cunning way of using imagination to face the natural or oedipal castration that imposes the social law of incest taboo.*

Sylvie's birth proved traumatic for Paul-Marie because it gave parental endorsement to his imaginary, magical wishes. His mother entrusted the little girl to him; he was now free to act as big brother; and since his father was never at home, he shared not only his mother's bed, but the joys and worries of fatherhood. She herself points out that his maturity – his verbal pseudo-maturity – stemmed from her having always looked to him as her companion, in whom she confided all her thoughts and worries.

---

*   Natural castration, normally called primary castration, results from the fact that the human body is monosexual and mortal. Cultural castration has a structuring force only if the subject has first valued the parent of his own sex from the social angle: if he has valorised eroticism and human fecundity. —F.D.

While his elder brother was becoming fixed on his passive pre-oedipal structures, Dominique witnessed the caving-in of everything that held his world together. Everything, even the roots of masculine narcissism bound to his sense of his own bodily schema. Paul-Marie was there in the father's absence, but he could not be the support for a pre-ideal ego. The necessary condition for the model of this aspect of personality is that it be genitally dynamic and genitally the begetter of the newborn. This implies that such a person must be dynamic in his image as genital body and not only the mother's chosen companion but eventually fertile as well; in any case he should be perceived not only as complementary to the mother, but as invested with the prerogatives of lord and master. In short, Dominique was seeking some support for his masculine structuration, and found only dangers of destructuration. Instead of a model to support him in the potential of his sex, and to value him in that sex, he found only Paul-Marie, a poor master and undynamic. To answer his need for a dynamic model, he turned to Bruno, the young son of his paternal aunt and his Uncle Bobbi. Dominique needed to keep for his libido a minimum dynamic importance in order to survive. Paul-Marie would not do; he was his rival as the affective complement to their mother, and had been arrested at the anal-phallic stage. Dominique had only his oral phallicism left, his baby-talk and body language in relating to the world, which preceded Sylvie's arrival. Paul-Marie was a bachelor by choice, by the very fact of their pairing (a new pairing in the same bedroom), a belittling pairing compared to the pairing with the mother. Dominique became the 'younger brother', an outside thing, full of incestuous amorous spite, in a body devalued and downgraded by regression. And the 'young Bel Brothers'* were both dead. It was the penis-less little sister who had the most importance in the family. The father, who did have a penis, and proved it by giving his wife a baby, was suddenly less important for the mother than her relation of dependence on the baby. The

---

*   The paternal uncles. —F.D.

father also became less important for Dominique who had regressed to positions of oral libido, shocked to see his mother feeding, with her two phallic breasts, this nursing baby who 'ravished' her.

Dominique, with his adaptive reactions to the complex trial he was living through, was now a further complication in Paul-Marie's family and public life. Only Dominique, by his behaviour, made explicit the revolution which had occurred in the family and in the dynamics of the group. It was he who dishonoured both lineages by his lack of toilet-training, by his rages and revolts which devalued the function of his brother. He set a 'bad example' for the little sister. Yet surprisingly, the mother continued to be interested in him; strangely, he was still looked upon as a son by his father, and he was beginning to gain the little sister's interest as well.

Dominique really stood in the way of Paul-Marie. For the sake of fraternity, his mother would say (I would be tempted to say it was rather a means of receiving a healthgiving castration), Paul-Marie was willing to take on the role of overgenerous elder brother.

Dominique has never been his own self. From birth he has been handicapped by his physical appearance, appreciated on the zoological level by his mother; he has also been handicapped by his elder brother's jealousy – a feeling no one mentions in connection with Paul-Marie. From the start both mother and brother have been parasites on Dominique: he was made a fetish by his mother, the replica of her father, a penis-bearer all her own, a consolation for the husband's absence; he was made a fetish by his brother as his mother's part-object, an object to be fed, protected, and a witness of his (Paul-Marie's) exemplary conduct. Until Sylvie came along, Dominique was appreciated only *qua* phallic fetish by the mother—big brother twin-couple. He nonetheless could have got the impression of substituting for the father: either because at his birth the father took on the well-paid position which made him into a 'nomad', or because Dominique's animal heat warmed the mother. Dominique was less insistent in his refusal to go into the mother's bed than his elder brother, who was too 'prudish'. He was also granted a position of honour, as Madame Bel puts it, because of his niceness and precociously perfect elocution: a little parrot able to copy his mother's words. Dominique was alienated, deprived of his freedom and his autonomy, notwithstanding his seemingly autonomous conduct and, as he stresses, not having to ask permission for anything, whereas at his grandmother's house he had to ask permission for anything he did. He became the substitute object for his mother's lack of a penis, which she has never fully accepted. Madame Bel's style of dress, which is quite proper, marked by provincial taste, dating more to the past fashions of her youth than to the present, always includes some accessories that add a masculine note: hat, shoes, gloves or handbag.

We must recall that Madame Bel was born to parents who very much wanted a boy, who were in despair when they had a girl instead. Dominique was the substitute for his mother's centrifugal penis,* while Paul-Marie was the alter ego, a sort of twin of his mother, her chosen companion on equal terms with the husband, except for coitus for purposes of reproduction, for which the husband has the prerogative. The husband, when home, is a mothering type of man, viewed by his wife as a remedy for her phobia of social contacts. ('My wife is rather gruff and unsociable, but our house is the house of God.') These phobias stem from this woman's mutilated relationships with her mother, who rejected her, and with her father, who was completely unmindful of her until her wedding day, from which time on he preferred his son-in-law to his own daughter (counter-oedipal caution of Madame Bel's father?).

---

* See my 'La libido et son destin feminin', in *La Psychanalyse 7* (1964). I have described *centrifugal penis envy* as the imaginary part-object subject to *primary castration*. *Centripetal penis envy* is the feminine pregenital desire of a part-object belonging to the father. The fantasies that lie behind playing with dolls, the fantasies of a child incestuous towards her father, are the substitutes for this centripetal penis envy. The centripetal desire in a girl, after the oedipal dissolution, is an *integral part of genital desire* for a beloved mate. —F.D.

Until Dominique's birth, Monsieur Bel used to spend all day at home. Dominique was apparently well adapted then, not conscious of his role as fetish. He became aware of this role when his mother, who had abandoned him supposedly to give birth to someone like him, brought into the world instead a truer, more beautiful (*plus belle*, BEL) child, Sylvie, blessed with all the gifts and all the powers. Dominique may have felt like a toy his mother had tired of, passed on to his elder brother, by way of his paternal grandmother. Before Sylvie's birth, the rules of the game for Dominique consisted in speaking well, so as to be listened to by his mother, and in forcing her to pay him attention, in order to interpose himself between her and his big brother. The rules of the game were now completely changed. Dominique lost his references from the day his sister was born. In comparing himself with his sister he found he had an ugly body, that he couldn't compete in the game of sphincter passivity and dumbness, that he was stupid in comparison to his brother, that he was friendless, hopeless. His grandmothers preferred Paul-Marie. His body and sex worthless, Dominique no longer knew what to do with his desires. He underwent total denarcissisation. Neither his toilet-training nor his ability to speak correctly were the effect of control or symbolic maturation, but of an imitative dependence on his mother's rhythms, through which the anal and oral pleasures he experienced were owed to his mother's welcoming of his mimicry, a welcome eroticised not only for the son, but unfortunately for the mother as well. His pseudo-control of his sphincters (in any case relative) was marked by real pleasure, which tended to become incestuous. The law Dominique had encountered was not at all that of incest prohibition, a social law. The only prohibition he knew was that of being dirty and being free, in the sense where 'being free' means free in his expulsive vegetative rhythms, free in his own movement, free in his combativeness (as he says of his sister's 'comings and goings' in school and in the garden – culture and nature). Dominique could only hold the ball (*alias* his mother's breast); or imagine himself making the baby, that is to say, like

his mother with a baby's ball in his arms, after having held it
in his belly, walking around the garden with this ball, holding
on to it, hoarding it in his arms.*

Dominique felt 'he was no longer anyone to anyone'; what
he said no longer had any meaning for him; and when this happened he could no longer transmit in words the sensory experiences he was living through. The parent's sexual intercourse,
which he had heard and seen, could be interpreted as 'straddling' games, or as a way of goading the mother 'cow' (remember
the invisible flies that irritated the cow in the first fantasies), or
the games of mounting the cow, as at the farm; or the games of
water-filled hose ends (Little Hans's plumber), but all of which
Dominique called women's games: giving milk to a woman who
is simultaneously breast-feeding a baby. The ball-pregnancy
'effect' followed by the appearance of the baby, had not been
hidden verbally from the child. The mother had suffered from
her ignorance of 'the facts of life', as she calls them, until marriage; she wanted her children to know these facts. But while
Dominique had been able to witness and to hear his parents'
intercourse, he could not without his mother's words establish
a relation between the sensations this spectacle caused in him
and the mother's joy in being the mate kept warm in bed by her
husband (warmer than by her children), and to the valorised
fruit received in intercourse, because she never 'told' them this.
She had connected pregnancy and its physiology verbally to the
mother's 'heart', and only the mother's heart. Her sibylline words
communicated some sort of parthenogenetic belief. It became
easy to associate the 'naked bodies of Blacks' and the 'women
who go out at night and are brought in to the police station'
with this system of beliefs. But while the great round ball of the
mother's body took the place of the allegorical cabbage of song
and story, the father's role as loving progenitor or beloved and

---

*   We all know that this mode of ball game – taking and keeping it and
        not letting it go – is a game characteristic of children of both sexes
        before the age of three. One gets out of the game by throwing the
        ball to someone 'beloved', in a game which is a form of conversation
        under other rules. —F.D.

desired husband, co-genitor of a child conceived by two parents, developing within the mother's womb, was never evoked. With such good results, that, with Madame Bel playing the role of both father and mother on the social and family scene, 'the children see no difference between their father and myself', between their father's presence or absence. This, at least, is what she absolutely wants them to believe; it is what they have to pretend to believe for the mother to feel safe. She has made it possible for Dominique to believe that human procreation is a woman's privilege, the outcome either of the prevailing atmosphere, or of a function akin to digestion (oral and anal), or of the magic interference of an invisible participant, or of a serpent hidden in the vegetative body.* As to his witnessing his parents' bodily encounter in bed, when he was asleep or awake and jealous of his father's presence, we know how he used to scheme to force his mother to leave her husband and come to him. The child can interpret the parents' behaviour as squatting games, or kissing games, or puncturing games, or as the petrol station attendant filling the tanks of cars – i.e., as gesture games of part-objects, such as he has with children his own age – but not as the expression of love between man and woman. The fact that the game leads to procreation is then a particular effect of the operation of filling-up, not a symbolic event.

In short, the father's role is completely foreclosed to Dominique. It was only through the discussions that accompanied Sylvie's birth and development that Dominique fathomed the immensity of his impotence in gaining recognition, from anyone, as a 'going-on-becoming man' (*comme allant devenant homme*).†

---

*   See p. 110: the tree (Dominique), between Adam and Eve; and Dominique's throwing a snowball at the window, associated with the tempting of a demon hidden in the tree. —F.D.

†   *Allant devenant*, 'going-on-becoming', is a concept of F.D.'s creation which builds upon D.W. Winnicott's 'going-on-being'. Winnicott made the point that infants need to experience continuity of being without needing to take any action to ensure their security. Dolto's point is that infants (and older children) need to experience being in a state of continuous development – their 'being' is not a static state but one in constant growth and change.

The serious obsessional neurosis which Dominique developed starting at his sister's birth turned into regression to a psychotic state when all hope of evolution (development) was refused him.

Waiting to grow up is the consoling dream of a child's narcissistic wounds and impotence: 'When I grow up . . .' is on a par with the grown-ups' consolation 'When I have time.' This had now lost its meaning for Dominique. Time had not brought the uncle home (*s'il vit* = Sylvie − if he is alive), and withdrawing from the little rival sister had failed to bring on her death. On the contrary she had acquired, during Dominique's absence, the tools of culture − the much-prized school learning which Dominique could not master, for all his efforts. Nor could he turn for help and aid to his elder brother; at the age of eight, the only course open to him was that of secondary anaclitic depression, phobic towards any kind of change.

Dominique had by now been reduced to passive oral, anal and urethral positions; the only workable way in which he could hope to preserve what remained of the narcissism of his fourth to sixth years was through passive withdrawal from desire of any kind. For this system, dosed in upon itself, any encounter in time or space, whether perceived as immediate or imminent, was fantasised as the imminence of death or of a chain-reaction of fragmentation.

After having once been a fetish (since replaced by his sister), Dominique now dwelt as an alien in his own body; he therefore escaped any of the voluntary motor realisations that would have required a subject in an autonomous body.

Dominique as subject lives in a passive paranoid world. He denies the separation from his mother's body and leads an incestuous fantasy life, induced by and included in his mother, and in a universe he has willed to immobility. In order to keep his urethral penis functioning incontinently, he fantasises that the bodily parts of mammals mirror his parents' anatomical penis-properties, but confuses who has what: 'Cows have four of them.' He lives as a sleepwalker, denying the distal, tactile and ocular references which his body feeds back to him; he no longer recognises the value of his own perceptions.

He denies that the coenesthetic sensations of the vegetative functioning of his pelvic region, or his hunger needs or instinct of self-preservation in any way concern him. This foreclosure results in the denial of his sense of observation and the loss of the sense of the relations existing between signifier and signified. Although Dominique has not lost the power of speech, he has in fact kept it only in a masturbatory style: he rants and raves without any exchange with others, asking no questions, in a language which aims at most at producing magical effects on the minds of others. He increasingly ignores direction, space and time. Unlocated in his body, he gives it an abstract fantasmatic image, strange and neither man nor animal. With what is left of his manipulative power, he objectivises this in his models and stereotyped drawings, metaphorised as labial and anal erotic objects. These symbolise the displacement of his eroticism onto his hands, which have become appendages of exchange of the eroticism of mouth to udder/breast or anus to faeces; as to his penis, this has taken the meaning of teat.* At the beginning of his treatment, we saw Dominique projecting his desire for success onto the human body of a young girl, the daughter of his paternal aunt, almost his twin, and confusedly standing for his sister, his father's sister and his mother all at once.

By escaping from the consciousness of his sexual body, Dominique has escaped the threat of primary castration and the suffering inherent in the castration complex bound up with guilty oedipal attraction. The masculine supports of his fantasies have been downgraded, if not as to their phallic form, at least in their erotic value and in an ethos that values erectile and genital functioning. Anything that may be related to the erectile masculine apparatus and to its seminal genital function has been foreclosed. There has never been a word in the family for sex. 'Popo' is the only significant word for the lower body, for

---

*   See the session in which he modelled a ball continued in a teat, and a
         Möbius strip, p. 89. —F.D.

any excremental or sexual function, in boys as in girls. Together with 'udder' (teat) it is the only word Dominique avails himself of for the lower body and for the masculine sex.*

If Dominique's regression, maintained by the naive — I might say guilty — connivance of his familiars in all passive oral, anal and urethral manifestations, leads him, as a subject, to put on the mask of a ghost, it is a matter of a ghost-member belonging to his mother, and vanished no one knows where, just like the ghost-member belonging to his paternal grand-mother, the uncle, he of whom they say *s'il vit*, who vanished when Dominique was born, which is his only symbolic point of reference; this is why he likes to dress up in a bed sheet and 'be a ghost'.

The session that marks resolution of his blinding alienation is that to which he contributed the three fantasmatic rays. The ray, it will be recalled, stands for the slit in the human bottom, the allegory of sexual glue (*poisse*)† and of the erogenous libidinal stream. We have seen the ray with the protruding active jaw; the ray with the gaping passive jaw; and, most terrifying, the so-called 'curly' ray, associated with the sister and her wavy hair — the sister who disgusts him, with her clitoris-mammary pimples, who produces a deathly current in the electric tail, an unusual presence, both death-dealing and energetic, perceived in the penis. It is in this fifth session that Dominique's talk indicates he is regaining his sexuality. Nor is this a coincidence: this was the session that led us to understand the mother's unconscious structure, as well as the brother's (based on his ideal ego as passive homosexual). We came to see the mother as pre-oedipal and cold in bed. She justifies her unconscious incestuous paederastic fixation on her own children by this phobia of the cold: they are made into substitutes for her own unquieted centrifugal penis envy, only transferred to the body of her own children and onto her husband's fertile penis.

---

*   The penis is confused with women's nipples and cow's teats: see
      p. 82. —F.D. For 'popo', again see p. 82. —Translators.
†   Cf. *poisson*, 'fish'. —Translators. See the fantasy of his sexual organs
      glued to the mother. —F.D.

The sixth and seventh sessions raised the problem of the ego ideal in relation to pre-oedipal behaviour aimed both at negating primary castration and at preventing the genital oedipal conflict connected with incest prohibition and the castration of the much-desired fruit of incest.

To know the scale of values in phallic order is a question of an ethical order.

The economic solution would be to remain passive perverse. Unless Dominique succeeds in accepting both the role of Oedipus and genital castration anxiety, his problems will lead him to a confusion in the image of his body, a confusion of age and of kind, to a false knowledge of the body and of the proper erogenous zone through which to express his sex drive. It was during the eighth session, in May (see p. 103), that we saw Dominique reconquering the image of the male body in its integrity, and the cementing of Dominique's personality – id, ego, ego ideal – into oedipal positions which he increasingly comes to accept, following a protracted period of hesitation between a homosexual and a heterosexual sense of values. Some readers may be surprised to see so few sessions lead to such a dynamic change. In my experience, I have known of cases which progressed equally fast, at the more usual rate of two or three sessions a week. I must say that though the psychoanalyst is encouraged to follow this pattern, it is not always the best nor the most far-reaching, nor even the most productive in the long run, for a psychotic subject.

It is difficult to compare two techniques, since no human being resembles another. I myself prefer several sessions a week – perhaps because it is more convenient. I must admit I would not have achieved the same style of listening had it not been for all I learned during these sessions spaced in the classic way. And we know that it is the analyst's listening which enables the subject to express the transference relationship in words, following the necessary transitory resistances. To my mind, *it is not the interpretation of resistances that leads to a truthful language*: all the more so, I would say, because *resistances always originate with the analyst when the patient's cannot be overcome.*

In the present case study, social conditions, and so-called financial, temporal or geographic conditions, limited the rate of sessions acceptable to the family. I had intended to have sessions two weeks apart, but school holidays and various material difficulties which justified the parents' resistance kept the mother from adhering to this schedule. Sessions lasted at least one hour, often a little longer. After the initial resistance, Dominique showed himself to be very co-operative, particularly and deliberately concerned with his analysis. We may also guess that the psychoanalytic therapy to which Dominique was briefly subjected at the age of six left him and his parents with a negative transference reaction to this kind of treatment. This intensely emotional transference reaction was immediately passed on to me; this allowed his urges to come into play very soon after treatment started, as we have been able to see. There was also Dominique's age, accompanied by the libidinal thrust of puberty, and his liberation from the twinship of his big brother, a liberation that modified his outer world. Both these facts worked to the advantage of a truly psychoanalytic therapy, in which the archaic wishes were revivified in the transference, along with the operational castration that made possible academic and social sublimations.

There is one undoubted advantage to spacing out the sessions — while of course retaining their intensity. Each session then acquires the distinct significance of a landmark; each is a step forwards, from the viewpoint of the libido. The speech and gestures of each session dramatically focus on a specific question and allow it to be raised in all its forms. For the subject it is a confrontation with himself, on a specific topic. We may say that the subject's progress does not depend on the spacing-out of sessions, but the emotional impact and the significance of each session is greater. Furthermore the parents are less involved with the child's treatment; this is an advantage in itself: the secondary regressive effects of the sickness and its therapy are lessened for the subject. The parents are allowed a certain distance, which they are free to use to justify their criticism and their resistances. There is no doubt that a treatment involving a fair degree of frustration for the subject aids the work of transference. This is well worth the analyst's effort: he now has to be doubly alert to all his subject is expressing; he must hear and remember all he still fails to understand, and he must be ready to perceive and interpret expressions of resistance as meaningful.

When sessions are spaced out, it seems desirable for the analyst to offer interpretations or views of his own at almost each session. When they are more frequent, such interventions are rarer: the subject then has plenty of time before him, he is less pressed by unconscious urges; he has time to develop connections between his associations and – pre-consciously but often consciously – to understand their transferential resonances unaided, and trace them to their origin. Generally speaking, he is able to tackle conflict nodes much more in his own good time.

Eleventh Session:
End of June

Three weeks after the previous session
(the last of the school year)

The mother wants to talk to me alone, without Dominique. Dominique readily agrees. She presents a summary of her son's school year.

Both the headmaster and the teacher are very pleased with Dominique. He has made enormous progress: he is the student with whom they are most pleased. The headmaster attributes this to Dominique's psychotherapy. He is now over fifteen; still the headmaster recommends that we allow him another year in the special educational needs class, rather than put him in a technical school as an apprentice. He is willing to keep him in the school, feeling that Dominique will catch up with other students during this second year. He now knows how to convert fractions, understands the units of surface, he knows cross-multiplication. The headmaster expects him to pass the *Certificat d'études* next year. The headmaster is also very pleased with his character. Dominique proved a little troublesome during the year, but calling him to order was always enough to set him straight. The headmaster says that there are children in his class who would benefit from psychotherapy, but 'You know how things are, the parents don't want it!' Worst of all are the children who don't, won't or can't listen. They constitute a permanent source of disturbance, with their continual noise.

'As far as family life is concerned,' the mother says, 'the main change is that Dominique now lives on the same plane as us.'

'What do you mean?'

'He is interested in everything, listens, asks questions, answers, takes part in conversation; he's also very interested in television, though he doesn't always understand it. But then sometimes he's the one who points out to us things we had seen, but hadn't noticed. And now when he walks down the street, he's part of the family. Before he used to walk either ten steps in front of us or ten steps behind, as if he wanted not to seem part of the family.'

'And his brother and sister?'

'Well, he takes care of himself now. The others had got into the habit of making fun of him, now he won't let people pull his leg anymore. He looks critically at what he's being told. But, you see, doctor, there's something that bothers me.'

'What is it?'

'Well, it's my husband . . . He feels we are wasting time and money. He feels we should put him in a vocational guidance centre for backward children. He feels that we are wasting our money, that there's no change, or almost no change. It is just maturity coming on and that's all. These trips to Paris and these sessions, he doesn't see how words can change anything. He says that until surgery finds a way of curing these children, it will all be no use. Dominique is abnormal as far as he's concerned. He feels we have to accept this, and that's all there is to it. I don't know whether I should follow the advice of the headmaster and of his teacher or do what my husband says. What do you think?'

'I think that whatever happens next year, he will have to go on with his treatment.'

'That's what I think too. And then, you see, at home he is no trouble at all anymore. Oh! It's a very difficult decision for me . . . What bothers me is that he's still much too good-natured, he still gets involved in swapping things and they make a fool of him and he still doesn't mind. It makes me angry. In his class too, his headmaster told me, I'd suspected it, but Dominique said no. There are some boys who waited for him when school finished, armed with thorny branches. They waylaid him. The headmaster told me that they are the bad apples of the class. Since Dominique is very careful and pays attention and gets good marks, they are jealous of him. Then those from the supplementary studies courses make fun of those in the special educational needs class, they call them the loonies. It's difficult both for the teachers and for the children. Dominique told me that nothing had happened, that he'd slipped into some underbrush, but I saw clearly enough that his legs had been scratched up. He wouldn't tell on his friends for anything in the world. When I told him that he had lied to me, and that the classmates who had done this had been punished by the headmaster (who told me), he said: "Well, that's not lying, you're not supposed to spread things like that." What surprises me is that this is the first time that I have heard about Dominique being concerned about the future. He tells me that he wants to learn a trade.'

'No doubt some of his classmates are leaving the special educational needs class to become apprentices?'

'Yes, that's what my husband would like him to do. But his teacher says that if he remains another year, he will probably get the certificate. In any case, if he didn't pass, he would get something like it, and it would be easier for him to find an apprenticeship under better conditions. Even now, she feels he is much more mature, and more interested in the class than those who are going to be apprenticed. She says it would be a pity.'

'And what does Dominique say?'

'He says he likes the class and that if his father agreed he would prefer to try and get the certificate. But, you understand, he's hardly able to believe it, it would be a miracle. He always thought of himself as being backward.'

The interview is at an end. Nothing has been decided. I have not given the mother the advice she had come to ask.

Dominique comes in. I tell him of the interview I had with his mother – the question of staying in school or going into apprenticeship – and I tell him that I hear his father finds the treatment is useless. I add that it is the last session for this year and that I hope that we will meet again to continue next school year, whatever happens, school or apprenticeship. And then I wait for him to speak.

DOMINIQUE: *You see, this summer, like I told you, we're going to Saint-Raphaël. My father's coming for two weeks and then he'll leave us there and later he'll come back to get us. I'd like to go to work on a farm myself. I don't really like staying in Saint-Raphaël when my father isn't there with my mother, my brother and my sister. I'd rather do what he's doing, leave when he leaves and go and stay with my cousin at the farm. I'd like that as a trade, farming. I'm considering two trades and I don't know which one to choose, farmer or mechanic, taking care of cars, washing them, repairing them, pumping petrol. It's a little like taking care of animals, I like it.* He's quiet and then goes on: *You know, I'm not surprised my mother said that to you about my father. He never really told me that himself, but I figured he thought it was useless, my coming here, and it costs money you know. Before that, I thought it was useless myself, but now I think it means a lot. It bothers Father that it costs so much, and it's bothersome for Mother too, who has to go out of her way to go along with me. She tells me that I wouldn't be able to come by myself, but it isn't true, I know how to. But she just says that: you know mothers. And then, she's very happy about coming into Paris.*

ME: *Does she tell you that?*

DOMINIQUE: *No, but it's easy to see. It's my sister who isn't happy. She said that they're making too much of a fuss over me, and my brother says I'll always be an idiot.*

ME: *And what do you think?*

DOMINIQUE: *I'm doing fine, I'm happy. In school I understand everything now. It doesn't bother me that the others pester me, I don't pay attention. Some kicks or scratched legs, what do they matter? I'm not a girl. And I have fun with my friends. I get along with my brother, you know, and with my father too. My brother is the great master of dressing up.*

ME: *Of dressing up?*

DOMINIQUE: *Yes, I mean of clothes. What to wear, what not to wear. That interests him, my father too. They're like fashion designers; it's something they think about, it's funny don't you think? I don't care how I'm dressed myself. This is a lovely jumper, don't you think?*

ME: *Yes, it is.* (It's a kind of Norwegian jumper with trico-
lour patterns representing reindeer.)

DOMINIQUE: *My mother knitted it for me, from a pattern my
grandmother sent her. She thought it was pretty.* He lowers his head
and looks at his jumper.

ME: *You like what is pretty, too.*

DOMINIQUE: *Yes, but for my brother, it's clothing, style, the cut of
a coat, women's dresses, everything. It isn't just jumpers that interest
him.* Silence. *I went to the Salvador Dalí exhibition; you know him?*

ME: *Tell me what you think of him.*

DOMINIQUE: *Well, he's a well-known painter. I quite liked it,
but I noticed that everywhere there were holes and there were drawers
in people, holes and drawers. They say he's a very original painter.*

ME: *What do you think?*

DOMINIQUE: *I like what he does, but not those holes and the
spots he makes on purpose. He has good ideas, but not drawers . . .*
Dominique is quiet now, at work on some modelling. *Look, here's
a man who's very, very, very ill . . . Pity you don't have a television.
. . . Whoever wins a car for the mayor of his town . . .* (one of the
gameshows currently broadcast on the television).

ME: *Tell me about it.*

DOMINIQUE: *Whoever gives the right answer, and the mayor*
(maire) *of his town wins, that's not his mother* (mère) *it's not written
the same way — I think you call it a homonym. It's the mayor and he's
a man. It could be a woman and you'd still call her a mayor; it's a
title so it doesn't change. So the mayor, you see, is lucky: all he has to
do is be a mayor of a town and if someone answers the question right,
well, he's got himself a new car. When you're watching TV it's a good
idea and fun to find out who's going to give the right answers. I like it
when they win.* Silence. *I'd like to go and live on the farm, personally.*

ME: *Now that you're fifteen years old, you could go, even on
holiday, to work there.*

DOMINIQUE: *I told Mother, but she says I'm too young.*

ME: *But you went to stay with Uncle Bobbi when you were
even younger.*

DOMINIQUE: *Yes, but it was because I couldn't go to school.*

ME: *Maybe you could go there if Uncle Bobbi thought well of you.*

DOMINIQUE: *Yes, I'd like that. My uncle sells cattle. Next to his house there's a farm and he's the farmer. There are other people to help him because he can't always stay at the farm, he has to go out to buy and sell cattle and there's work all the time. Well there's my aunt, my father's sister, she takes care of the house. It's at Elmoru.* (So it's the name of a village, this 'Elmoru' which Dominique used one day to bring up the problem of his mother: perhaps a woman in trouble who was arrested at night and taken to the police station during the Occupation because she was in the street after the curfew.) *They have three 'farms', no, two farms and a manor. It's called Trois Fountaines. That's the name of the manor. A manor is a farm too, so there are three farms, so there is lots of work. Yes, of course he wouldn't mind having me, only I don't know whether I'll be able to get away from Saint-Raphaël, whether my father and mother will let me. Mother never wants us to go away from her. Father doesn't care, he wouldn't mind. But then he'd have to pay for the trip, that's expensive. It's not expensive by car, but by train it is.* He's quiet and goes on with his modelling. *This fellow you see, he's ill.*

ME: *Oh?*

DOMINIQUE: *Yes, he's had a bad heart ever since childhood; they took him to the hospital. They gave him an injection with blue in the left elbow* (a reminiscence of a haematoma from an intravenous shot, or of the little cousin who was a blue baby, who died when Dominique was eight? He imitates an intravenous shot in the left elbow). *There you are. And then they're going to operate on him in order to cure him.* (He opens up the little man he has been modelling from top to bottom, and puts a yellow crayon right inside this split in the middle, without saying a word.) *Would you like to have a television?*

ME: *You think I should?*

DOMINIQUE: *It's very interesting. We're going to put in rivets* (?) *to keep his belly from closing up again . . .* (He does this). *Uh-oh, what's going on in his stomach?. . . Oh there's the heart.* (He models a heart and puts it in the right place.) *Tic, tic, tic* (he says this very quietly, knocking on the table with his index finger), *it's beating . . . good! The lungs* (he puts two lung-shaped organs into place). *There!* And then he hums the four notes

of the opening of Beethoven's Fifth Symphony (used during
the war to announce Free French broadcasting programmes to
the Resistance movement). *Pam-pam-pam-poom!* and he makes
the noise *MMMMMMMMMMMMMMMM . . . What's going on?
Uh-oh, at first there wasn't anything wrong and now there's all this.*
He laughs. *I don't know how we're going to get out of this mess . . .
Scalpel, my good man!* (His father would like him to be operated
on.) Again the notes from the Fifth Symphony, then noises from
the heart. *Okay, everything's fine.* Dominique is now quiet. *Then,
you know on television, we saw open-heart surgery.* During this time
he has installed something that looks like vermicelli bordered
by a long sausage. *Now there are the intestines, you see.* (A good
replica.) *You have to lift them a little in order to be able to operate.
I'm afraid he's got something weighing on his heart.*

ME: *They also say that about somebody who's sad about something.* (Dominique seems not to have heard me, but he may be
referring to the uterus, since according to his mother pregnant
women carry their pregnancy in their heart.)

DOMINIQUE: *We'll have to cut out some of it. People who have
too much heart are made fun of, they're not like others. It's a sickness.*
(His mother says he's too good-hearted and always made to
look foolish). While he imitates the noise of the heart with his
tongue like background music, he proceeds with the 'operation'.
*Yes, his heart was too big, much too big. But there are so many other
things that have gone wrong, ah if it was only the heart, but we have
to operate for appendicitis too. He eats too much and it all goes down
into the appendix, it all goes in, it might have blown up.* (Remember
the sex of the incestuous child, boy or girl, blowing up.) *Well
there, monsieur, you're an alcoholic! I'm going to get angry. What is
this supposed to mean! A big boy like you! . . .*

ME: *He's someone who likes his bottle.*

He bursts out laughing and says: *But where does he put everything he swallows? There's nothing there. He needs a stomach. I'd forgotten to put in the stomach. There. It's okay now.* (He has indeed
fashioned something like a bagpipe, very realistic, and put it in
place). *But look, part of his stomach is perforated, it's been ruined by
all that drinking. Oh là là!* Then, in a very learned tone: *This man*

has tried to poison himself; from now on, he'll have a stomach one third as large. That's the way it is. (He removes part of the stomach.) *This is a little too long.* (He removes a piece of the intestines). *All right, let's see . . .* (I note that his voice is quite normal today; it has been since the start of the session, with a proper intonation, going down towards the end of sentences for the first time.) *He's got one lung a little larger than the other, and so he breathes too fast on one side and that lung will never be any use to him again. We'll have to take it out, it's not only too big, but it's all eaten up and might give out on him; he's got one lung all eaten up by a germ. Hey . . . we'll have to do something really modern, a new kind of operation.* (What his father says should be found for children like him.) *The stomach all eaten away by alcohol, this lung all eaten away by a germ and the germ has also attacked his stomach because of the alcohol, it couldn't defend itself against germs anymore. It's 'cancirus'** . . . He bursts into laughter. (He enjoys his sadistic fantasy.) *To keep this from continuing we're going to have to remove the cancirus; take away a whole piece of the flesh where the cancirus is located.* (He works away on the entrails of the clay figure.) *There we are, we're going to close up the belly again, we've taken out a lung, we've shrunk the heart. That* (pointing to the bits and pieces taken from the doll's entrails), *those are the leftovers . . . Into the dustbin! We're going to make a plastic lung, since his was eaten away by the cancirus. There we are, he's all closed up. Now all we've got to do is wait for him to heal.* (He starts humming.) *That's it — if only it were everything, but it isn't. His leg got burned while he was trying to save a man in a fire. There, that takes care of it, that's a real person. Let's stitch him up now. We're going to have to remove the skin that's poorly, then take some skin from his healthy leg and put it on his wounded leg, and that's called making a graft. You know, all this is pretty complicated. . .*

ME: *Your father believes in surgery, not in medicine.* (Again he pretends not to have heard.)

DOMINIQUE: *The leg's going to be perfectly fixed; okay, now you can get up.* He puts the little doll on its feet. *There we are.* The

---

*   Cancer-virus; disease of lack of dynamism; prevalence of the death-
      wish. —F.D.

hour has come to its end and I want to end the session. I wish him a good holiday.

DOMINIQUE: *Do you think I'll be allowed to go to my uncle's?*

ME: *Can't you write to him?*

DOMINIQUE: *That's a good idea. But what'll my parents say?*

ME: *You'll see soon enough. Is it wrong to ask one's uncle to help on his farm?*

He takes his head in his hands. *Oh, what a tragedy! I forgot my umbrella in his belly. I'd hung it up on the coat rack, but I hung it up wrong. I hope he hasn't digested it yet.*

ME: *What a nice poo-poo* (caca) *that would make.* (Once again he pretends not to have heard, opens up the fellow with dexterity, finds all the organs he's put in, moves them about and takes out the yellow crayon that he had put in at the start, without saying anything.)

ME: *That yellow is light yellow like the poo-poo of babies, like your little sister's when Mummy was changing her diapers.*

DOMINIQUE: *Yes, and she watered it with wee-wee.* He goes on with his game and says: *I thought it was a rivet.* (His sister's clitoris? The result of an association of the woman's position during intercourse to the position of the baby girl, his sister, to whose care he has just referred, which he witnessed when he was young.) *But that's it! It was the coat hanger which was right above the patient's belly, and the umbrella fell on top of it, not into it. Well, well, it's a good thing I saw it.* He closes up everything and says: *Look, he's died of it – good riddance.* He rolls the clay into a ball, puts it into a box and says good-bye.

We make an appointment for the following school year.

When leaving he anxiously asks his mother in front of me: *I'll come back after the holidays won't I?* 'Of course,' says the mother, 'as long as you need to.' *Good, good-bye then, Madame Dolto.*

What are we to say about this last session of the school year? His style is full of wit, it puts the medical profession in its place, as well as the false claims of science; there is some admiration of surgery, but also, under cover of a clownish approach, this is a summary of what happened to Dominique. The session expresses a certain budding sadomasochism. What does the yellow crayon which Dominique put in the fellow's body at the beginning of the session represent? He said nothing about it at the start, only took it out afterwards, as if he suddenly remembered something he had forgotten. But it is clear that it was due to this crayon that the little man was able to stand up, after so many sadistic and corrective operations. Once the crayon was extracted, the poor fellow could only die. Is this a representation of the image of his own body as having 'swallowed an umbrella' (the rather stiff brother with his straight, upright bearing placed here in the father's place and his former passive homosexual ideal ego)? It should be noted that Dominique no longer holds himself in the forced upright posture of a dog sitting pretty.* Does the 'umbrella' signify the prohibition against wetting one's bed (the introjected law of the superego not to show urethral functions)? Is it the oral desire for the mother's 'udder' from which the sister is drinking? – an example of orality not marked by the taboo of cannibalism ('I thought that cows had four of them' – penises) or the taboo of cannibalism of the part-object? Or does it represent the paternal penis disappearing into the mother? Or the imaginary maternal penis which has disappeared into the little clay man (Dominique himself, or his brother)?

Perhaps the figure expresses Dominique's trauma caused by the overactivation of his oral libido while he witnessed his parents' intercourse before he was two and a half years old, reflected through his oral interpretation? Or his participation in coitus when he identified with the mother's body? I would rather think it represents a perverse form of participation in the disappearance of the father's penis into the mother's body at a time when neither Dominique nor his mother saw themselves as separable from one another. It was not the umbrella, hanging from the coat hanger (the coats themselves having the value of father and brother), but the excremental urethral penis that, in a state of erection, cannot wet the bed (umbrella), that changes

---

*   To sit pretty: *faire le beau (le Bel)*. —F.D.

shape and enters the belly, associated with the 'coat hanger', the coat peg.*

It is clear that the Dominique we saw at this eleventh session is the original personality he will remain. As he said of his robot, he has ideas of his own, but he achieved a dynamism by which his mother (*maire, mère*) and father (*père, paire*), stand to profit. I take this to refer to that in him which thinks, and that which acts. He finds the way of his other, social self again through exchange and in a sense of reality, without foregoing his imaginary life. At this last session, I was struck by how extraordinarily clever Dominique was with his hands; how exact in his observation and in his modelling. He made well-proportioned anatomical parts and placed them accurately in his clay model. Independent of his performance in school, these gifts seem to testify to an exceptional manual adaptation. I also noted the free laugh, the natural facial expressions, the normally accented and modulated voice, free of nasalisation.

The father's will to have the treatment stopped is now certainly going to come into play: he denies its value and finds it costly (only eleven sessions!).

This was the first time Dominique spoke about money; but at the same time he spoke about Uncle Bobbi's fortune and that of his father's sister, the sister who has so many advantages. The father was not able to pursue the studies he wanted because they would have cost too much, as he told his wife. He had hoped for his eldest son to support his narcissism by being successful in his secondary and university studies, but Paul-Marie has had to give up before graduating. He has given up renewing his narcissism out of Dominique's achievements. What is there left for him to hope for? Medicine would have saved the life of his younger brother who swallowed part of a toy train: surgery killed him. But he believes only in surgery for retarded children, of whom Dominique is one. There is no changing his mind.

---

*   Coat peg or *patera* (*patère, père-mère,* or *mère-père*): father-mother or mother-father. —F.D.

If the father continues to oppose psychotherapy, this may serve to wean Dominique from me — a separation without excessive trauma. Dominique is very positive towards all that comes from his father at this time. This should be taken advantage of for the sake of his structuration. I also think that the boy will return to psychotherapy if he feels inhibitions or symptoms. It is certain that he will find it difficult to evolve, free of neurosis, within the family setting that has so readily accepted his psychosis; his recovery and return to the general stream of life must raise serious libidinal problems for both brother and father, neither of whom is able to help him.

As for the mother, she mentioned while standing in the doorway, just before leaving the last session, that she might return to teaching on a part-time basis: her daughter would be making fewer demands on her. She wants to become involved with specialised teaching, identifying herself with the people at the clinic whom she sees at work, and with the teacher of the special educational needs class. 'A fine profession, taking care of problem children,' she says. Perhaps it's not so bad that the father is opposed to a treatment which threatens to modify so rapidly his wife's total dependence on her family and her house, and lead her back to the circuit of social relations, along with her son.

Twelfth Session:
End of October

Dominique missed his appointment after the end of the summer holidays. At the request of the social worker, I sent a note asking whether any more appointments should be scheduled; the mother wrote on 10 October saying that she would pay us a visit in the next week, and that it would be the last visit, in accordance with her husband's wishes. She said that the results obtained to date already went beyond what could be expected from psychotherapy and seemed amply sufficient to the husband. I shall quote extracts from this letter:

> This summer we spent two months in Saint-Raphaël. Dominique could not go to his uncle's farm. He was perfectly happy and well adjusted living with us. Other summers he had sought the company of very little children, three to five years old at most; this summer he played with children of twelve and thirteen, children of year seven and eight. Everything went very well. Parents of other children used to shoo him away in other summers, with the same contempt they always showed to retarded children – who they regarded as contagious monsters. This year, they complimented me because this big boy of fifteen was so nice and patient and showed extraordinary imagination in playing with children younger than himself. They did not even notice his retardation. This is the first time this has happened. We noted only one example of abnormal behaviour. The parents of one of his friends had offered to take Dominique to

the cinema. I had given him a five-franc bill, to pay for his seat. Suddenly, in the middle of the film, he remembered this money and told the lady: "I didn't pay for my seat." She answered, "It doesn't matter, we'll see to it when we leave." He didn't understand that his friend's parents had paid for his seat, and he felt guilty for sitting in a seat he hadn't paid for. When leaving, seeing that nobody was going up to pay for his seat, he went up to the counter himself and – there wasn't anyone there – threw his money on the counter and ran away, blushing for shame, but feeling liberated because he had succeeded in paying. Of course the money was lost, but his conscience was at ease. In one sense I am very happy to see in him a kind of honesty that one rarely sees in boys of fifteen, but it shows that he still hasn't any sense of money. He gets some thirty francs a month pocket money, but he doesn't want to keep it himself, he's afraid of losing it, so he entrusts it to me. He doesn't even think of spending it. In school he is repeating the same special educational needs class with an excellent teacher. He is very happy. His progress in French is obvious. His spelling improves day by day. It is mathematics that is still most difficult for him. He's unbelievably absent-minded if not properly watched. He draws constantly, always people in motion [compare with his earlier drawings]. This same boy, who used to seem scatter-brained, now records with extraordinary precision the smallest details he has observed. Personally I hope, as do his headmaster and teacher, that at the end of this year he will be able to take the *Certificat d'études* examination (which doesn't mean that he will pass). But this will allow him to enter a school of agriculture or animal husbandry which requires this level of education . . .

As far as his meetings with you are concerned, as I already mentioned, my husband feels that everything that has to do with the medicine of the soul is 'bunk'. He is a businessman who lives with figures and machines all year round, who is at home only two days a week, and when at home has time only to think of his work. If one of his sons had become an engineer, he might have viewed him with interest, but the eldest is only an artist [total contempt], and Dominique is merely a source of worry. As for Sylvie, she's just a girl and that doesn't much interest a man like him, and he also accuses me of having perverted her by making her literary. All that literary people like me are good for is some petty, officious civil service job. At the same time my husband is a very intelligent man in his work, and an excellent businessman; but neither literature, the news nor the arts interest him. He reads only detective stories, if at all. He has his universe and we have ours. My husband feels that there is no use in Dominique's coming to see you; the so-called jealousy which supposedly destroyed his childhood was unfounded, since our following the advice given earlier led to no progress. Thus for him the problem of Dominique is settled once and for all. Don't let's talk about it anymore. If we're going to spend money on him, it's better to have private maths lessons given him. For my own part, I'm deeply thankful to you for all that you have done for Dominique, for you have given him normal sociability. I often think that instead of bringing you the son, it's the father who should have been taken to you to turn him into a normal father!

Consultation day

I meet the mother in the consultation room where she is alone with Dominique. I thank her for her letter, which I summarise for Dominique's benefit. Dominique tells his mother that he had pretty much suspected what she had written to me.

Dominique comes into my office with me, tells me that he had hoped to take up his regular visits with me again, his mother having told him nothing about it; but that he is not surprised. His father had not wanted him to come last year either. I take note of what he is saying. (He is speaking in a normal voice.)

DOMINIQUE: *My visits to you? . . . They meant my remaining an expense for one or two more years. If it had not been for this treatment* *which allowed me to stay in school, I could have been apprenticed or employed last year and so not cost him any more money. As far as what I'll be able to do in the future, he says that no matter what, I am so far behind that it would've been better not to try and catch up. He says that you have to admit that there's an incurable problem. Well I don't want to say he's not right, he's my father, and I know he isn't wrong either, you shouldn't say that about your father, and of course I love him. But I'm awfully glad to have been taken care of by you . . . but I understand him . . . Since I'll never be an engineer,* it isn't worth spending his money. I'll earn plenty of money on my own. (I know it, I don't know how I know it, but I know it.) And then it won't be him who's paying when I come to see you. But that can't be now, so patience* . . . During this monologue Dominique's tone is quite normal, his voice normally poised, with no aggressiveness in the tone.

Silence for a spell. Then, in a wilful tone, different from the preceding tone, higher, like an episode of a story which is being continued, but still with a normally modulated voice, Dominique continues.

DOMINIQUE: *Today I'm going to make human preserves. Very naughty. It's terrible to think what will happen to anybody who ventures there!* He makes a little man in clay. *It's someone strolling calmly along who's been given a sleeping pill and falls down a trapdoor into a canning factory. (That's like a story that almost happened to Tintin.) What comes out at the end of the production line is human sauerkraut.* (He pretends to be eating sauerkraut, offers me a helping and pretends to find a hair in it.) *A blond hair! It's a factory where they only process blond men, the only ones who are good for food, whose meat rivals that of the pig! Besides the blond men, we'll send to this factory all the pests, all the tax . . . collectors*† *and all the Mer . . . cedes.*‡ (He bursts into laughter). *And the school headmasters and the priests.*

---

*   *Je ne serai jamais un ingéniéur:* the first time that Dominique uses the full negative (*ne pas, ne jamais* etc.), though he will again fail to make use of it in the remainder of our talk. —F.D.

†   French: *pères . . . cepteurs;* he has cleverly cut the word in two so that the word *père* (father) is clearly heard. —F.D.

‡   French: *mères . . . cedes;* again, he separates out the syllables so that the word *mère* (mother) is clearly distinguishable. —F.D.

ME: *Have you ever heard the expression, 'bouffer du curé'?* *

DOMINIQUE: *No, never . . . I said that to explain the black specks in the sauerkraut made out of blond men. It's lots of fun to play cannibal. Cannibals eat missionaries, they're priests, and they like it. But in this case it was an accident that a priest fell in, it was supposed to be an all-blond sauerkraut.*

ME: *But do you have anything against priests yourself?*

DOMINIQUE: *No, I don't go to Mass, neither does my father. He has too much to do to do anything but shut himself up to work or tinker all day by himself on Sundays. My mother and sister wouldn't miss Mass on Sunday, but it bores me. I had my First Communion and I was confirmed like everybody else. Even my father was a choirboy all his youth. The priest even washed his feet once a year. That was funny, and it's also the Mass I like to go to, at night, at Easter or at Christmas — those are the two Masses I like. There are choirboys there, and they get their feet washed, but I've never seen it myself, my father told me. And yes, in the sauerkraut, they take off the men's shoes before grinding them up, they'd be too hard to chop up.* He makes a model of a silhouette of a priest, and talks about TV and the recipes that some cook gives on TV. *It's a job for a woman who makes herself masculine.* He adds a big tail to the silhouette and says: *Here is the head cook.*† He cuts off the tail and then goes on: *Once there was a fellow someone else forced to go to work for the Germans. It's a film or it was like a film.* There follows a story of some women *taken along by a German, but the others he was with didn't want a woman. The people they called 'my love' were men, so the woman was furious and finally a bolt came loose in the car. Maybe it was a man who tried to cause an accident. He tried to loosen the bolt, but finally a flock of sheep forced them all to stop. Then you could see a boy kissing a girl and everybody said he's mad, he must be shot like a dog. Because they and the Germans thought that the girls, the women weren't a good thing to do.* Silence . . . *Fernandel,*‡ *in a film, found his friend's sister, a nice girl, he treated her like a doll, consoled her*

---

*   Literally 'priest-eater': to be actively anti-clerical. —Translators.
†   *Maître queux.* The homophone *queue* means 'tail'. Hence this cook has a tail. The pun is untranslatable. —Translators.
‡   French comic and actor (1903–1971). —Translators.

because the other one had left. Then there was someone who came after *him.* He pantomimes with his finger pointed towards the root of my nose. *That's what my father does, he gets a scary look in his eyes* *when you do anything dumb, and you know, I used to do a lot of dumb* *things. So he comes after him like that and by the next day he'd gone* *crazy.* Then he is quiet . . .

ME: *I think these are important stories about your way of think-* *ing, which is different from your father's and from your grandfathers'.* *Maybe the fellow who sent the other to the Germans was you, when you* *were born, everything gets mixed up with your father since your father* *began his job at that moment, and your mother was always thinking* *about him while he was away. And you think maybe your interest in* *girls isn't right because your father isn't interested in women as far as* *you can tell. Still, he gave your mother three children . . .*

Then I keep quiet, and so does Dominique. He seems to have nothing left to say: I look at the time; the span allotted to the session is over. I tell him so.

DOMINIQUE: *Wait a minute! Before I go I'm going to make you* *two cans of preserves.* This he does at great speed: he takes two cans with the lids open, fills them with the debris of the mod-elling clay, and closes them: *There you are, two blond men made* *into sauerkraut.*

I laugh: *Your father and your brother.*

He bursts out laughing and gets up. I escort him to the waiting room to take my leave of the family.

As they are leaving, the mother apologises; she would like to speak to me. I accept and we all three return to my office. 'Well, Doctor, you accept not to see him again?'

'And you?'

'I absolutely have to obey my husband.'

'And Dominique?'

I turn towards him and Dominique says: 'If I were to decide, I would come back. I'm sure it would help. But as Daddy says he doesn't want to pay anymore . . .'

The mother breaks in and says: 'Oh no, Doctor, it's not the money that makes my husband say that! For him it's all

Fig. 13
Clay figures made by Dominique during
the twelfth session

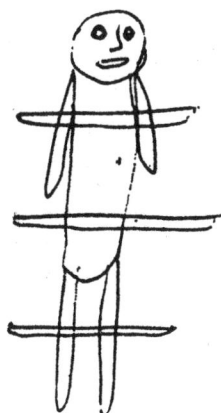

Cut up and canned

yellow
pink
blue

*The boa's head. The boa
altogether is 1 metre long.*

About 10 centimetres high

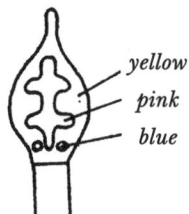

Cook, head cook (cuisinier, maître
queux). Maître queue, peres . . .
cepteurs, meres . . . cédès. *When
saying 'mer . . . cedes' he takes the
tail* (queue) *off.*

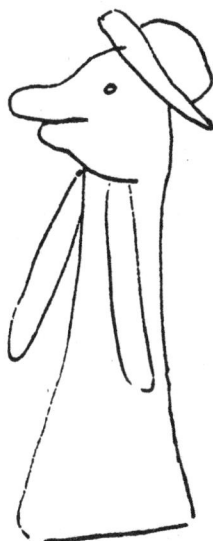

*The priests. About 10
centimetres high.*

nonsense, as I told you in my letter. He said he'd find a surgeon to operate on him if he needs it, if one can be found. For this he'd be willing to pay any price!'

'What operation?'

'Well, an operation on the centre of arithmetic in the brain! They say it exists. He believes only in that, you see, not at all in words.'

While the mother talks, Dominique makes a snake more than a metre long: blue, with a red head and a yellow cross of Lorraine. (Lorraine like his mother, or the Cross of Liberation, cf. the signature tune of the BBC?)*

'But tell us,' she says to Dominique: 'Tell us what *you* want.'

And Dominique answers: 'I told you already that I could come by myself.'

'But I told you I don't want that.'

'Well if you don't want it, then you can't come without disobeying Father.' (The mother looks at me, her eye sparkling as if she thought this were very funny.) 'But if I could come alone, well I would come every Friday and it would do me a lot of good. But too bad. Daddy wants it that way and, well, since Madame Dolto isn't angry, I'll wait until I'm older and make my own living, and then I'll come back to become completely well, if I'm still shy.'

Thereupon we part.

Epilogue

This part of the treatment of a psychotic child will be of interest to the reader who knows little about the psychoanalysis of children within the family setting. He may not be aware of the difficulties that may develop when parents are affectively immature, or neurotic, when they see analysis as a threat to the established

---

*   During the Second World War the BBC prefaced its broadcasts to
     Special Operations Executive personnel, who aided resistance move-
     ments in France and elsewhere, with the four notes of the opening
     phrase of Beethoven's Fifth Symphony. —Translators.

equilibrium that develops within the family. Children are cancelled out as individuals to become part of the carefully balanced system of unconscious libidinal dynamics in the family group, whose law requires the child to respect authority and submit to it.

We see that the after-effects of psychic traumas – even though they are absolutely personal for one subject – take their specific character only as the dialectical resulting from the constantly intervening function of the libidos of each family member. The narcissistic modifications of the subject under analysis may make demands on the narcissism of the individuals he comes into contact with. When a child is undergoing treatment, his whole family presents the psychoanalyst with transference reactions, whether concordant or discordant, which he must take into consideration.

A case such as the present one shows why the child analyst requires a much longer training than an analyst for adults, contrary to what is often said. The manner of listening to the patient is basically the same for both, but the child analyst must also consider the parents who pay for the child's treatment, and are responsible for him to society; this is a significant element in the progress of the treatment. Due to the child's dependency, the parent is naturally designated as the natural support for his ideal ego: and this is a support which the analyst must respect, since it is built into the reality of the situation and makes up part of the necessary castrating powers. The psychoanalyst's role, then, is to liberate the subject's ego ideal from its dependency on the neurotic ideal ego, but without substituting himself for the parents. He must also analyse the archaic pre-oedipal superego, but without standing in the way of the elements of the growing Oedipus complex.

Dominique has been cured only of his psychotic regression. The elements of his Oedipus complex are being belatedly structured. His sexuality has been rehabilitated as far as his narcissism is concerned, and his own body as far as its humanness. His critical sense is now finding some expression. His feelings are in communication with others. He has found a new faith in his own future. He recognises his own desire for liberation, and in its name he is willing to temporise – though still angry – for the sake of paternal authority, provided the analyst is not 'angry' and does not feel frustrated. He is aware that he is not yet satisfied with his present state – with his anxiety – and refers to it as to his 'still being shy'.

For Dominique (and all psychotic cases recovering from a similar early regression) to liquidate successfully his Oedipus complex he needs to go through certain intervening steps. and he has to live successfully through the castration anxiety imposed by the father. The subject can do this only once he has regained his oral-libidinal structure, with a real space–time dimension, distinct from that of the Imaginary. The anal and urethral libido must be oriented to the primacy of genitality. But for this to be real, the subject's anal-urethral libido must have profited from the autonomy it has derived from experience in society to become utilisable in cultural 'sublimations'. With a mother such as Dominique's, the subject can gain his autonomy only once he has become legally an adult, and has been granted the right to dispose of himself freely.

Dominique will be able to escape the cultural prohibitions imposed by his own financial dependence on his father only by learning to earn his own income – an ability which also depends on his cultural sublimations. At this time Dominique is not recognised as a valid individual by his father, who is himself the result of the trauma of childhood and youth (the only remaining son out of three), a denarcissised father, the mothering spouse of an infantile wife.

II

The Relationship of the Two Brothers and the Possible Perverting Role of the Ideal Ego

I think a study along phenomenological lines may shed light on the genesis of similar pre-psychotic childhood states: a condition which in many cases, including Dominique's, does not improve with puberty, as is too often hoped, but rather deteriorates irreversibly for lack of psychotherapy.

Our work as psychoanalysts may therefore play a role in the understanding of the prophylaxis of neuroses and psychoses, by means of therapy aiming not so much at counselling parents or at guiding children, but at recognising the meaning of the symptoms evident in children who experience at the same time both healthy sexual urges and a lack of structuring castration from their parents, who respond to the children's call, but misunderstand it.

In the analysis of children, when one child of a family shows symptoms, it is often more illuminating to study the unconscious dynamic relations among all the siblings than to limit oneself to the examination of the disturbed child alone. It is not uncommon to find the latter dynamically organised to defend his libidinal structure more ably than his seemingly well-adapted elders. The role of children who have been paired off during their development because they are close in age – as well as the role of children six or seven years apart, or twelve to fifteen years apart – is always most illuminating. The defence against structuring castration in such cases (siblings close in age) will prove particularly traumatising, if it is not demystified. The determining, humanising role in each case is determined by the oedipal situation particular to the child. Such family situations allow the displacement of the relationship with the parents onto the sibling: the emotional compensation of incest, fantasised and even sometimes real. These sibling relationships, which appear to give security, are then in fact traumatic. Sheltered by these compensations, the child avoids the healthily anxiety-laden relationship with the parents, which should lead them to face their life drives and death drives, oedipal castration and the primal scene. These are the nodal point of the humanising symbolic function, the axis of the ethos of desire whose unconscious lines of force hold together fundamental narcissism.

Until the birth of their little sister, both the elder son, Paul-Marie, and the younger, Dominique, were rivals in their talk with and conduct towards their mother. From the day of Sylvie's birth, all their interpersonal exchange came to an end, as well as their mutual mirroring relationship. There is no longer any reason for their jousting: no one is watching. No longer need one outshine the other in the mother's eyes. That desire is foreclosed, neither recognised by them, nor recognised as valid by the mother. What was involved was the heroic verbal chronicle of a tournament — a seemingly peaceful confrontation — in which speaking beings vied at expressing themselves most perfectly, in echo of their mother.* The mother never valued

---

*   Note that, in the relatively large vocabulary of this family, there are no words to refer to the sex, to the buttocks or to the lower parts of the torso. Sex and posterior have one name for both the adults (who display themselves naked) and for the children. It is simply *le popo*, having not even the common qualifications of small or large. The mother herself had never thought there was a word other than 'sex' — which she does not dare pronounce. Still, she shows herself naked to her children and sees them naked, without thinking anything erotic. For her the word 'sex' is, so to speak, neutral, one could say geographical. It means the place where the operations necessary for reproduction take place. During her pregnancies, she never referred to her belly, but to her heart containing the baby about to be born. She nursed her children, but never said the word 'breast'; she said 'to feed' or 'to give milk'. She is an unconscious voyeuse, eliminating modesty under the name of prudery. —F.D.

the love underlying this rivalry. Lacking this value, the desire in each brother to overshadow the other dried up – after it had once helped each to grow in their active oral and passive anal relationships with the mother, the object of each one's desire.

For Paul-Marie, the elder, it was a question of catching the mother's attention, and holding it, more than Dominique. By doing this, he could be on a par with her (and with the father, when he was there, who was interpreted as the big twin brother of a phallic elder sister). We must bear in mind that Paul-Marie enjoyed the advantage of his father's and mother's daily presence until he was three and a half years old, at which time Dominique was born. Dominique took Paul-Marie's place in the cot and in their mother's care, Paul-Marie was promoted to the father's place, to the role of mother's companion. When the father accepted a job that kept him on the road so much of the time, he gave Paul-Marie the eldest son's place, and even 'entrusted' his mother and brother to him. It follows that when Dominique awakened a protective attitude in his big brother, he could view him as a big brother, a pseudo-father, or a pseudo-mother. And Paul-Marie's behaviour went far to please this obsessed mother who sought conversation during the day and warmth at night from her companion, a role Paul-Marie filled perfectly at the time. The rare sexual encounters between the parents did not satisfy the mother as a woman, and were consummated by the father only with the idea of procreation.

The mother informs us that Paul-Marie and Dominique never quarrelled when they were young, and have not quarrelled since. There has never been a confrontation between them, as she has often witnessed between other brothers. She was pleased with this, not understanding that it stemmed from the absence of a father who could be the genital possessor of the mother. The father, when he was home, was not a more attractive model than the mother, nor was he a rival endowed with unquestionable genital prerogatives; nor did he stand, as a father, to prevent bodily intercourse with the mother. It follows that to Paul-Marie, the father constituted a less phallic ideal ego than the mother. The mother's phallus was Dominique, by general agreement the spitting image of the maternal grandfather.

Of the two brothers, the one who pleased her most, aping her, matching her talk, playing father-and-mother with her, was Paul-Marie. Then there was the one who gave her most pleasure as her imaginary penis, both flatterer and flattered, bodily petted but aesthetically downgraded: this was Dominique.

In her double mother-and-father role, the mother stood as adult phallic representation to the two boys. She was both mother and father at once, law-giving and overprotective; but she was also dependent on them, indistinguishable from either. It was a narcissistic trio of three maimed beings, three interdependent invalids.

The balance is upset when Sylvie is born and begins to grow up. The two boys, as pointed out, can no longer play at overshadowing one another in the mother's eyes. Dominique is no longer able to outshine anyone. The sister's sun is at its zenith and outshines all. Dominique, distressed and abandoned, lives in a state of ghostly solitude. Paul-Marie has something of a death wish towards this little brother, whose calls for help are embarrassing in public and threaten the mother's image in her own family. It follows that Paul-Marie must substitute himself for his father and mother, who appear to him as incompetent educators of their brood: he takes over the maternal grandmother's views: she is the only one of their entourage who has kept the same emotional attitude to Paul-Marie before and after Sylvie's birth.

At the time of Dominique's birth, as at the time of Sylvie's, Paul-Marie saw his father take his mother's place, alongside the mother-in-law. He saw an attentive and maternal father. He has a model. When Sylvie is born, the father grants Paul-Marie an even more attractive place than the one he gained at Dominique's birth: for a little girl is gratifying to a boy of six who can take himself for the father by adopting anal libidinal positions. As to Dominique, he is abandoned by everyone; he is in general disrepute; he loses all his cultural, anal and oral attainments; he suffers a hysterical pattern of fragmentation, for which his only reward – not surprisingly – is the outside world's phobic fear of his new ways. Paul-Marie knows quite well how his paternal grandmother would suffer if he were to hurt his little brother (his father's games once led to the death of her little son). And anyway, it is easy to see that Paul-Marie's death wishes on Dominique would, if approached too consciously, identify him with a prehistoric father, a father dating back to his own father's childhood, i.e., a father who negates Paul-Marie's own existence.* In short, a father harkening back to a time anterior to the primal scene (a mental representation of the parents' sexual relations), and who threatened Paul-Marie's destructuration, since Paul-Marie's erectile urethral libidinal positions had been neither conquered nor valorised before puberty. Dominique, then, was left with only one security: to respect his big brother while seeking to avoid contact with him. He respects him as a neutral shadow, anatomically endowed with a extra bit of flesh at the 'popo' (see footnote to p. 166), like himself, which sets him off from Sylvie, but castrated insofar as value is concerned, and almost as infirm as himself. The prize for value goes to the little sister with her penis-less popo. And, as runners-up, two idealised phantoms: the maternal grandmother and her magic rites, and the lost uncle.

At the same time, Dominique views Paul-Marie as a representative of the good old days, someone he used to know before the catastrophe, before Sylvie arrived. Paul-Marie has also been appointed – ordered – by the mother to play mother to Dominique: Dominique will try to escape this tutelage, and exploit the situation to paralyse, ridicule and devalue his elder in the eyes of his mother and of the social environment. This might have been expected to save the situation if the big brother had reacted aggressively to such physical eclipses, to the physical, psychic and verbal confusions – largely war tactics – of

---

*   This is the reason why children never want to see childhood pictures of their parents before they have reached pre-adolescence; while the family takes pleasure in comparing the children's pictures with those of their parents at the same age. —F.D.

Dominique.* Since the two brothers never quarrel, as the mother proudly points out, it is also true that they never quarrel about the fact of Dominique's psychological exploits.

The mother is too indulgent ('150 per cent a mother,' says the father), and forces her children to view regressive symptoms as worthy of respect: 'The big brother knows well enough that his little brother is irresponsible, and that he pleases me by taking care of him, as an elder brother should do for the younger.' She acts as an umbilical, pregnant, parasitic and tutelary mother; Paul-Marie must follow suit in order to please her. For Dominique he will become a perverting ideal ego, his mother's robot, and his mother's envoy to him. All his school life, Paul-Marie has had to take Dominique to school and back, making a detour of up to one hour each way, and walking ten steps behind him. The elder, Paul-Marie, persecutes and pesters his younger brother in his overprotective, sadistic style, and Dominique pays him back in kind. Dominique, his mother's own little phallus, who costs his dad so much, is only Dominique, the family's fetish-clown, who makes Paul-Marie dance to his tunes, taunts him as an ill-trained pointer taunts his master. This behaviour betrays an id connected to a paranoid ego, an ego compromised between its narcissistic desires and its oedipal desires, foreclosed ever since he was supplanted by a penis-less rival. Paul-Marie also devalues the possession of a penis, but he has remained himself, in his known identity, thanks to the shared illusion that he is serving as a husband-substitute for his mother and as a castrating mother or mothering father for the two younger children. This eldest brother can be no more than a policeman without power: he has remained uncastrated by the father, and leads his life struggling against the provocation of incest by suppressing all sexuality. He is his mother's principal companion, confidant and support, but becomes pale and insignificant whenever the father puts in an appearance.

*   Hence the danger within a family of finding fault in the elder siblings'
      aggressive reactions or lack of interest towards the younger. This
      danger is even greater for the younger one than for the elder, as he
      may be led to inhibit his sexual drives or to invert them. —F.D.

He takes his place in society by fleeing any kind of competitive confrontation. This conduct is unfortunately justified within the family in the name of 'fraternity', and beyond the family in that of 'Christian charity'.

Dominique flees from his elder brother, though he fears him and puts up with him. He no longer imitates his speech. After a phase of absolute mutism, which was made much of in the family, he started talking again, only to 'unspeak' (*déparler*). He jumbles all verbal and physical traces of himself, losing his identity. He makes himself neither seen nor heard, he hides; still, he literally pesters his brother, pisses on him one might say, radar-guided; an effective form of poisoning which persecutes the brother and inhibits him.

This is in effect the clinical picture shown by Paul-Marie ever since puberty: he wins on libidinal positions without creative results. He is closer to the Oedipus complex than his younger brother because the parents were united until Dominique's birth; PaulMarie has passed the Cape of Doubt concerning his own identity. He is a human being, housed in a body which unfortunately is of the male sex. He is bound to accept Dominique, a parasitic homunculus still dear to his parents. He has logically accepted his anal impotence to create excremental children; and he has accepted the real fact that man cannot, unaided by woman, hope to make children of flesh and blood. A man must go through with that disgusting act if he is to take part in procreation, properly the glorifying prerogative of woman. He chooses to be identified as his mother's companion. He has made himself his mother's twin, a role his maternal grandmother sanctions by looking upon him as upon the son she never had. He is the mother's twin and servant. He does not play a single game proper to his age. As he will not take the risk of appearing valiant in his father's eyes and ears, he is able to please his mother as husband-substitute, while escaping competition with boys his own age, who show their masculinity through cultural achievements or by their success at sports and with girls. His father's relationship with *his* father shows that he too never underwent castration. It was only in terms of money and emotion that the father was ever devalorised with respect to his sister. Like his father, Paul-Marie is neither socially nor genitally valorised. Due to his father's constant absences and the mysterious unknown in which he works, all Paul-Marie, this big little boy, can do is to play at being a gentleman. In this sense, we see that the 'brotherly' relationship between Dominique and Paul-Marie takes on considerable significance in Dominique's psychotic evolution, due to the lack of oedipal structuration in the elder brother – a lack which was itself conditioned by the parents' life story.

The two brothers relive the parental saga, but on the homosexual level. 'When my husband and I hold opposing views,' says Madame Bel, 'we never show it. We always seem to be in agreement.' And she adds: 'I have been both father and mother for the last twelve years, and even for the last fourteen' – twelve being the daughter's, and fourteen Dominique's age. 'Since we get along perfectly, the children see no difference, whether their father is at home or away.' Also in bed it is the same to her, she says, whether she sleeps with her husband or with a child, as long as there is someone to keep her warm. What led her to marriage was her fear of solitude, not her recognition of the need for a sexual life or for having children. But now, 'Luckily she has some children.' Beyond that, in day-to-day life, she considers herself lucky as long as there is money. When her husband's secretary phones to declare that her husband will soon be leaving unexpectedly, she submits obediently, and does not dare ask to speak to him. The husband 'has too much to do' to call his wife himself. His boss's wife meanwhile demands to speak to her husband; Monsieur Bel considers this 'odious', and her refusal to take messages from the secretary as a 'characteristic sign of snobbery'. Madame Bel has also shown us other aspects of her personality as mother, besides these traits of a totally passive spouse.

She says she has experienced all the suffering the loss of a son can entail by sharing in the trial of her mother-in-law: she was seven months pregnant with Dominique when her husband's younger brother disappeared. Her comment is worthy of Greek tragedy: 'It isn't losing a child that is terrible, it's not knowing where he died, or how he disappeared, because any public mourning rites become impossible unless the time and the place of his disappearance are known.' This long-lost brother-in-law has been made into an ever-present, disquieting ghost, invisible but clamouring for remembrance, depriving his people of their peace. Dominique has achieved nothing, and has made this exacting phantom the ideal of his dominating and perverse ego; while he is alienated – his oedipal desire in regression, and up against a wall as far as his formative, productive maleness is concerned – for the many reasons given above.

Some of these reasons are: he was born 'ugly', 'apelike', 'repulsive' (while his name, Bel, symbolises beauty), and was born just when his young brother-in-law, Bernard Bel, the cynosure of all the family's thinking and fantasising, disappeared in the mountains; he was born second in the family: the second in his father's family had died in an accident while playing with *his* elder brother, Dominique's father; he was born a boy, when everyone wanted a girl; he was born brown and hairy, while all Bels are blond.

Until the age of twenty months, Dominique's feelings of security were all based on his being part of his mother's body and on his verbal precocity. This assured him of a place in the Mother–Paul-Marie–Self triad, in which he served as a fetish able to make talking sounds, but without motor or sphincter control. His digestive tract, apparently continent both in its functions and in its desires, was subjugated by mothering injunctions and foreclosed from his own free choice, his tastes and his personal rhythm.

But everything would be all right if the little sister had not introduced the notion of the other sex, the question of the lack of a penis; what was his symbolic relation to the phallus with which this baby, a pretty curly-haired blonde girl, was symbolically endowed by all? It is she, Sylvie, who personalises phallicism for both families. Her birth took Dominique away from himself, led him to identify with his sister in his fantasies, and to his regression into outdated modes of behaviour.

He regressed beyond the prohibition of cannibalism, which he had already acquired, and so foreswore identity, his social value, and his usefulness. Having regressed past oral and anal sublimations, he was no longer able to keep up pride in his male sex, in his name, so evidently negated by his appearance. No living support from a masculine ideal ego was there to encourage a healthy and liveable ego ideal. *The death instinct reappears as dominant when the libido lacks an imaginary oedipal support, both attractive and castrating, brought together in an ideal ego, the father-image. Regression occurs at all levels of the hierarchy of body images.* A regression of the functional image and a loss of the hierarchy of erogenous zones; regression also of the basal body image, and loss of the notion of time and space. As to the dynamic image, which is without representation, it has been inverted. This inversion in turn has contaminated for Dominique the ethos of his male sex. Dominique is still defending his virile desire through the phallic phantasies with which he endows his oral and anal hallucinations, and by his ignorance of the spatio-temporal conditions of bodily contact.* Dominique no longer asks for anything, no longer calls for help; *he is entering the world of the autistic, he is passively paranoid because* everything *that tends to stimulate him or make him dynamic* sets off the wheel of danger. *Everything: olfactory perception, the lookout for incorporation, the desire of the Other;* for these are the only forms of direct bodily encounter which he can have with another being *by projecting his own residual desire onto him,* but also because his mother, in real life, refuses him the liberating break he requires, and forces the role of bed-warmer, of being stuck to her mammiferous nudity, on him. She has a phobic fear of solitude. She behaves, unconsciously, like a perverse passive masochistic homosexual, attracted to

---

*   I have described the structure of the body image as three-faceted at any one moment. It is composed of the narcissistic concordance of three elements: a basal image; a functional image polarised at the erogenous zones; and a dynamic and always present image, passive and/or active. These three images in their continuing unconscious interaction make up the subject's narcissism, the symbol of their materialisation. A bodily schema lacking a body image cannot take part in a language exchange between subjects. —F.D.

her own children while erecting virtuous verbal constructions: a sort of innocent Snow White amidst dependent dwarfs, all sworn to celibacy.

The father can clearly be described as a man traumatised in his childhood, who has found a way of protecting himself from the invading demands of family life by compulsive work, and by carefully defending his isolation when he is actually at home. His behaviour as a parent – when he acts as a parent – is that of a mother – gentle and devoted, but never castrating towards his children. An allegorical parallel could be found in the male *Ascaris*, or threadworm: a necessary male, but self-effacing, camouflaged and protected by his giant female: himself a male only through his reproductive functions.

Whatever healthy elements may be left in Dominique's ego ideal find little support in the male members of the family: only in Uncle Bobbi, the cattle farmer who is married to his maternal aunt, and Bobbi's younger son. The family name itself, Bel, 'handsome', is incarnated in the eyes of all the family in the person of the lost uncle, dating to the last months of Dominique's foetal life; he was the uncle who disappeared for having tried to recover a virile weapon – a knife – which had been lost by his friend, his sister's fiancé.

It is not difficult to see how Dominique's passive paranoid and raving structure took root. At our first meeting, my response to his first significant words to me ('I think something true happened to me' – 'Which made you untrue'), must have gone straight to his heart. He had lived through some facts inherent to his age and his developing body, but which had failed to receive value or humanising meaning because no words were there to express them, to be heard. This wordlessness left Dominique in a world of senseless sensations, in the unknown of instinctive forces which remain unrecognised as such by those around him, in their non-limitation of his desires. Maddening incest remained a possibility to him, with no checks other than those which each man carries within himself, and which were precisely what made him a psychopath, a loner, socially impotent rather than delinquent.

III

Encounter, Interhuman Communication and Transference in the Psychoanalysis of Psychotics

Interpersonal encounter, when defined in terms of the senses of one person perceiving another, is concerned with physical reality: with sight, hearing, smell, touch and taste. But any encounter between living beings, whether vegetable or animal – and even more so interpersonal encounter – can also be defined in terms of the *change* which the encounter causes in each person: a change that may be the feedback or effect of any encounter or only of this specific one. It is true of human beings that any change they experience in their perception of others, though physical in itself, is connected to psychical facts. This effect – physical or psychic – may at the same time not be perceptible to a witness: specifically when the 'encounter effect' has not led to any manifest change in the earlier way of being. It is nonetheless true that every perception results in an impression that is registered somewhere in the bodily schema. Variations in quantity or quality, in the tension or nature of the sensory signals, are perceived and become coenesthetically pleasurable or painful, giving the encounter a positive or negative symbolic character in the perception of the receiver. These perceptions may provoke a change in the way of being, and this change in turn may be perceived by another living being who reacts with a manifest, articulate and differentiated response. When this occurs, a symbolic sense develops. This is communication; it is the archaic origin of language.

For man, the organisation of language always starts within the original framework of mother and child. This is so because the child cannot survive alone for long. Like mother, like child. Having to live together and yet be separate, mother and child both experience changing tensions between them, partings and meetings; these they express through emotion-laden modulations, through signs that soon fit into a pattern. This is the first language. Moments of mutual undemanding, of misunderstanding and of recognition become identified with substantial or subtle signifiers or points of reference. A substantial or physical exchange is involved in the give and take of bodily contacts bound up with the child's needs: his feeding, toilet, moving and sleep. He gives things, or things are given to him. A subtle exchange is involved when the two communicate at a distance, through facial expressions, through the mimicry of voice and gesture, and through all the perceptions the mother and child can have of one another. Any encounter producing a sensible variation in a living organism, modifying its way of being, becomes expressive of its existence, and of the existence of another object with which it was in communication. Conversely, any change in way of being may rightly or wrongly be viewed as the effect of an encounter.

Encounter here does not refer only to encounters between humans. A living encounter can take place with all kinds of things: cosmic elements, things or objects, minerals, vegetables, animals, as well as humans. The change of impression resulting from the meeting reflects the individuality of both participants. Let us take an example from the world of plants. The tendril of a vine tends to grow in a spiral; that is the way it is; but we might also say that the tendril winds itself so as to fit around any support; this spiral growth is the manifestation of life that is specifically its own. Similarly the leaf of the sensitive plant (*Mimosa pudica*) retracts when it experiences a sudden gust of wind or the touch of a curious hand. Modes of perception are contained, as it were, in the living organism; gradual or sudden variations then come to constitute a signal for that organism.

Let us now turn to human beings. If the signal being produced has the same effect on both participants, as manifested in their pain or pleasure, their similar reactions may establish a profound link between them. The first emits a signal expressing a tension that needs release, the second a signal filling the need. This reaction, repeated over the days, builds up a link of mutual understanding and agreed-upon communication, which may be called a link of co-naturality — of a shared nature.

This exchange of signals between nursling and mother builds up a link of vital dependence implying co-naturality in both pleasure (the appeasement of tension) and pain (activation of tension). When an individual encounters no response to the variations of his internal sensations, of his perceptions, no response to his call for complementary exchange, he has failed in the encounter to find another whom he can trust, his like through shared co-naturality. This nothingness he then experiences as the solitude of a human being: he is alone in his way of being. He remains subject to the internal tensions of his needs and desires; there is no help for him. When this phenomenon of the absence of an auxiliary or complementary encounter takes place while he is surrounded by others, this nothingness that grips him is called 'nobody'. The well-known expression, 'There were many people there, but I didn't meet anybody, I met nobody' portrays this lack of a complementary emotional encounter, of true communication in a shared language, in the midst of other beings who unquestionably are fellow men.

All that has just been put forth, clumsily stated though it be, seems necessary if we are to describe our experience of so-called 'psychotic' individuals, whatever their formal age. When we meet such a person, we meet him on an archaic level, where language is either totally or partially lacking. The change in internal tensions in such individuals is subject less to perceptions originating in the environment than to perceptions derived from physiological or emotional states, without signalisation, to which no proper language corresponds. Their contacts with the environment are disturbed by strange impressions and phantasies from the past, which they mistake as signals from real presences. As a result, what they say or express, while it seems unmotivated, invariably *is* motivated, but only by their fantasies, by an imaginary life that absorbs all their energies while giving them no hold on the reality that surrounds them. Their sometimes total immobility and mutism, their smiles, their defence mechanisms inappropriate to the real situation, their shouts and gestures, their talk – raving, stereotyped, conjuring – do indeed bear witness to a language, to the fact that they are saying something. But what they are saying is the symbolic expression of their inner tensions; it is a language which no longer hopes to communicate their emotions to the 'other' that we, in their presence, represent. This mode of expression is incomprehensible to others; it has become the very opposite of what language originally was; it is a means of protective isolation in a lonely way of being which the presence of others cannot modify. Communication *seems* broken once and for all, replaced by an impenetrable curtain. I say *seems;* for these conclusions are erroneous.

All human beings, whatever may be their appearance and behaviour, perceive the presence of the 'other'; but for some that presence is the signal of a threat to their life. The presence of the 'other', which is what we are, awakens in psychotics the emotion of danger, all the more intense when we seem to want to establish with them the contact they are trying to escape, or when we seem to escape the kind of contact they want, and which seems to us disagreeable, inconvenient, or dangerous. *If we succeed in expressing for them, in a language meaningful to ourselves, and as clearly as possible, what we perceive of them, once this is clear to us, we succeed, at the same time, in structuring a field of communication between us.* The stereotype reaction, or the apparent lack of reaction of one human being in the presence of another, does not mean that the other is not being perceived by the senses, but rather that this perception is being actively cancelled. This is how the psychotic expresses the effect of meeting us; the primarily passive reaction or the active flight stem from the fact that we have shaken his way of being by unleashing the death drive in him.*

---

*   The death drive, when applied to archaic oral emotions, provokes
      a phobia of contact and a fragmentation anxiety. Applied to archaic
      anal and urethral emotions, it provokes obsessive compulsions,
      either on the level of thought and expression, leading to absolute

The person labelled psychotic behaves in a self-protective manner towards a human presence, that of the psychoanalyst — a manner that is unusual, and repeatedly focused on him. Sooner or later, after several meetings, the psychotic will display some sort of change in his way of being that is of significance to the analyst. This perceptible change is the start of a language addressed to us: we have now been included in the subject's field of perception. This is the prelude to possible communication. The psychotic recognises us insofar as he recognises himself, vis-à-vis us: we remain unchanged from one session to the next. Our presence to him is then no longer absolutely strange or unusual: it has become special. *Transference is beginning to take place; the subject's narcissism is now alert, and is the battlefield where death drive and desire dramatically confront each other.* The analyst's attention,* evident in his words or in his silence, which invites the psychotic's facial expressions, words and gestures, recognises the humanity of the other and valorises it.

A specific transference is taking place in the analyst: he believes in the humanity of the person he is talking to, and in his uniqueness as the subject of the symbolic function, the unconscious subject of the life story that is his, a human being seeking his own meaning, asking for an answer to his question. This unspoken question may not be conscious, as is the case with very young children; or the subject may have lost track of it through inhibition following a period of consciousness. In this case, a trace of the repression process will remain; a screen memory, the

---

condemnation and rejection, or on a motor level, leading to obsessions with verification, conjuring, blasphemy or scatology. Applied to genital emotions, the death drive bring on anxiety of incurable sickness, sexual mutilation, rape, kidnapping or murder. In the analytic situation, the subject may fear these acts of violence from the analyst who is the object of transference; or, conversely, he may threaten the analyst himself. —F.D.

*   It is said of the psychoanalyst that he has a 'floating attention'. The term needs to be properly understood. What is meant is not an absent-minded sort of attention, as some believe, but rather a steady availability, listening for any significant signs; an availability as free from barriers as possible. The analyst's training prepares this attitude in him. —F.D.

element of a repetitive dream, a phobic or obsessional symptom. This trace may also be a way of being, a somatisation, possibly an allergy. These are troubles of the body's language; the body is substituting itself for the imaginary or verbal language, or for the language of facial expression.

As a careful, perceptive and persevering witness, the analyst assumes that the incomprehensible, raving or mute language has a meaning; his work will consist in decoding particular instances of this language. He supposes that the gestures or the immobility which he witnesses bear the very meaning of the subject before him, though disguised under their psychotic aspect. The psychoanalyst is a mediator of the symbolic function; to the silent, to the unspeaking (*celui . . . qui déparle*), to those who passively ignore or actively deny his presence, or the presence of the 'other', he makes possible and personifies the experience of an effective human encounter. To the psychoanalyst, every other person, whatever his behaviour, is a full-fledged member of the human race; the 'psychotic' is the subject of an unconscious story which he actualises, rather than symbolising it in the form of a structured tale, as do those we classify as 'normal' or 'neurotic'. This tale is not known to the psychoanalyst. Sometimes, some factual elements are made known to him by the subject's familiars; these elements then constitute a starting point, and are enough for him to become interested in this other, this atypical interlocutor.

Even when the psychoanalyst remains quiet, his way of listening, and his careful attention constitute an act of recognition of the symbolic existence of his fellow man, who is still unable to take responsibility for, or to communicate, his desire. Yet his desire is no different from other men's: it is compounded of life and death drives, though in his case it is rather dominated by the latter. In his transference, the psychoanalyst must be prepared to receive all the psychotic would express, with a receptivity as open as possible; at the same time he must take the death wish upon himself, decode the fantasies that are the residue of anxieties, of dangerous encounters faced in the past; and which his presence now reawakens. The psychotic seeks to run away from this anxiety, or to overcome it, which he has done unsuccessfully or incompletely so far. Often the anxiety is clear to him, as it is the only eroticisation supporting his marginal narcissism.

Through his lucidity concerning his own feelings, the psychoanalyst mediates each participant's recognition both of himself vis-à-vis himself and of himself vis-à-vis the 'other'. He further mediates the freedom of each to be or not to be present. There are two selves in the human encounter, two separate bodies, each endowed with its own perception of its body and each with its own distinct perception and feedback, meeting and interfering above their separation and their contrasting perception. The encounter makes them equally, simultaneously and freely recognisable as separate; and it makes recognisable the analyst's resolve to communicate through language, but without bodily encounter, with the 'other'. This 'equally and simultaneously' here implies that they share a common time and space – the time and space set aside for their series of scheduled encounters; they have distinct perceptions of these encounters, but these perceptions find a real meaning when they communicate that distinction to one another. This meaning is modified by the listener when he hears, and then perceives and sends back what he hears. Thus, he bears witness to his openness, his availability to the 'other' he is so carefully attuned to. This participation proves to the speaker that he is being listened to, that he is welcome with his load of personal truth, and that he can make himself heard.

The language of these modifications resulting from the meeting of psychotic and analyst may remain unconscious for one or both; its expression may remain subverbal for one or for both. But as soon as both recognise the difference of perception that gives its character to the meeting, the effect of language has been achieved. The difference can be partly communicated in the here and now, according to the ability of each participant to perceive the other and to express himself at the time of the encounter. Or the same communication may be recorded on paper, or in clay, or in gestures (the autistic preverbal language);

or in phonemes or in words that can be interpreted by either or by both. *We must learn to hear, to detect meanings that have been side-tracked or deflected to language systems distinct from the spoken language, and that are alternative or parallel to the spoken language.*

The psychoanalyst applies himself to the study and deciphering of this unconscious language which underlies the language being communicated consciously there and then, during the time set aside for a session: a length of time which is shared by two human beings, one of whom is helping the other by his presence, while the other voluntarily accepts this co-operation.

But what exactly is this work that the analyst wishes to carry on? He wants to reach the living, dynamic, present truth of the man or woman before him. He achieves this through his own presence, his own listening, causing the subject's unconscious urges to surface.

In the psychoanalytic encounter with adults, whether neurotic or not, the analyst's attention is focused principally, though perhaps not exclusively, on the hidden truth, which is revealed by the flow of associations that structure the verbal delivery. When the analyst lends his ear to the subject's speech, while he is not deaf to the clearest or best-constructed stories, he listens especially for the unconscious meanings, the truthful foundation of the 'subject' that carries the conscious discourse of the patient. This is more often about the social character of each and every one, than about the irreducible authenticity of the subject of his own historical identity. The parallel fantasies, which he passes over in silence, surface in those very silences, in sudden changes of theme, in slips, in the cracks, so to speak, within his conscious delivery. The fantasies reveal the unconscious workings of desire.

When the analyst is concerned with very young children whose very survival depends upon the adult who is raising them, and is faced with functional, somatic reactions, he listens to the mother, preferably in the presence of the baby. He tries to understand the reactions that took place at home, among his brothers and sisters, at the child's birth, and the unconscious fantasies experienced by the mother in her emotional world following the

child's conception, birth and development. He tries to understand the mother's present narcissistic balance; her relationship
with the child's biological father; the child's relationship to the
mother's residual oedipal fantasies; the relationship between
the mother's narcissism and her present distress in reaction to
present conditions. In short, the analyst tries to get the mother
to talk about everything arising from the child's rooting in the
world through its mother that is likely to intensify the child's
death drives – rather than about *a priori* attitudes or answers
which are aimed at maintaining the child's life drives.

At the same time, the analyst is attentive to the child in
itself, in its existing desire. At this time, the child is all receptivity, but is destined to autonomy. The analyst uses his theoretical and clinical knowledge of the earliest stages of the libido
to speak, meaningfully, directly to the *infans* – the child who
cannot yet speak. He tries to shed light on whatever is being
expressed by the symptoms that caused the parents' anxiety and
brought them to seek his help. He speaks to the child, but in
such a way that the mother* can hear. The analyst thus recognises in the baby the subject of a desire dependent on interference waves from the familial and parental libidos. He recognises
the baby as having become, because of his somatic, emotional,
perceptive and receptive presence, the sensor of a perturbing
communication.

For some psychoanalysts – if I understand them correctly –
the newborn or young child is significant only of their parents'
desire. As for myself, while I think that the parents' desire is
passed on to the child as an effect of language, I also view any
human being as an autonomous source of desire from the start,
from the moment of conception. I think that his appearance
in the world as a living being is in itself symbolic of his autonomous desire to assume existence, as the subject Third Party
of the primal scene, the unique fulfilment of his parents' joint
genital desire, of which he is the only signifier. His first name,

---

*   The father should also be present; if not, the analyst must always
make him present at the session by referring to him. —F.D.

those sounds legally registered as his by his parents, has been a call to his individual self which he may have perceived ever since the start of his life, whenever he was being talked about, even if he has since received a childish nickname. Through the voice of the analyst, this call of his name now wakes him to a desire to separate himself from the anxiety which has been induced in him by his parents; or perhaps only by his mother. Without this call, he could not help but give in utterly to her wish: her wish that he may remain no more than what he now seems: her part-object, that is to say, the negation of the natal caesura. The child could only submit to this denial of his birth, but for the analyst's appeal to his own self-realisation. The analyst's act — of calling the child by his name, and his hearing his name from a new voice — awakens him to the fact that he is the representative of the sounds of this name: he is no longer merely the respondent to, or representative of, the mother's words, which speak only through the language of the child's symptoms; nor is he exclusively the respondent to the father's unformulable call. A father who refuses to recognise in his fatherhood the fulfilment of a desire — a father who disavows that desire — may deprive a sensitive child of his status of begotten, endowed with his own rightful desire, the desire to live. I am reminded of the case of a baby two weeks old and suffering from anorexia, or loss of appetite, in the arms of his anxious mother, sent to me, the psychoanalyst, by a paediatrician who was hardly less anxious than the mother herself. I had with the mother the kind of conversation I described earlier: I spoke while she was holding the baby nestled in her arms. Whenever the mother said anything significant, I would speak to the baby, who at first seemed to be perceiving nothing. The mother asked me: 'Do you really think that he hears you and understands you?' I called the baby by his name as I had been doing all along, and clearly repeating the mother's remarks out to him, I said: 'Your mother thinks you do not understand. If you do understand that I am talking to you, turn your head towards me, so that your mother too may be convinced that you are listening to me.' At that moment, with the mother anxiously looking on, the baby turned his head to me, giving up the nestling attitude which he had held since the start of the session.

This story will surprise no one who has come to understand through psychoanalysis that the human being is the symbolic incarnation of three desires – his father's, his mother's, and his own, all three of them language-bearers. It is not possible to be a child psycoanalyst and not have this faith in the child, the subject of a desire of his own, as borne witness to by his breathing body. And this, whatever may be the arguments of those who view the baby as a vegetative digestive tract, free of any symbolic human significance – those who do not believe that the act of living of a baby whom others view as 'preverbal' – is the expression of the word – the signifier of the verb 'to desire' – having unconsciously become flesh at the moment of conception. What they deny is that the growth and death which are this child's destiny are symbols of an energy unknowable in itself, seeking its fulfilment through the mediation of meaningful encounters, each a link in a chain of meanings, and all together testifying to a meaning which man's life and death do not, by themselves, suffice to signify. This energy is our origin as it is all about us; it is the intelligence of our flesh, of our behaviour, of our gestures, and of our words; all these are but the substantial or subtle thickening of the verb 'to be' of which we are manifestations, but which does not belong to us. We are its meaning in our appeals to our fellow men, or in our answer to their appeals; in our brief meetings with them, each aware of the powerlessness that characterises all – the one trait shared by all men, if differently incarnate in each. The emotions of love, the subtle harmonies of desire, feed us from the spring of Being; but the being we perceive is always mortal flesh, even when it is also in words, words that go beyond individual being, that pre-exist it, and that survive it in time as in space. What is said can only make sense for us through the filter of remembered perceptions, through the narrow passage of our unconscious body image. Our body image is the symbol of this carnal body which the experience of life has mutilated, worn away and lost; but the pain or pleasure experienced during our life story has been matched by words heard or exchanged with our fellow men. And if these words succeed in arousing like emotions in them, they then become pure signifiers endowed with the power to make us present to one another, even when not physically present. We then like to link those words to whatever they have come to mean to us individually: their meaning evokes the unconscious image attached to what we had felt earlier, but is now gone. Those words become supports of narcissism. As the individual grows older, he thus becomes structured through the effects of his contact with others; thanks to language he learns to humanise his drives, and can express them according to a code of affects interwoven with language. His words testify to a human psyche attuned to those of his fellow men: hence he can bear the loneliness of joy and pain, the trial of separation from others in space and time, the separation of death. It is death which by its certainty and our own waiting, gives us proof of the reality of our existence. But for language, we would apprehend Being only in its crumbling appearance of ephemeral flesh.

The psychoanalyst who deals with young children who are living badly (*mal vivants*), and sets out with them to search for their truth, is neither a teacher nor an educator (*éducateur*); he is even less a re-educator (*re-éducateur*)* or a physician. His role is in no way different from that which he fills when working with adults: the only difference lies in the subject's physiological age. These badly-living children speak through their bodies, which are forbidden, or unorganised in their motor functions. They speak also through a body whose vegetative functioning has lost its rhythm, or which suffers from an unorganised or disorganised cybernetic functioning, the symbolic expression of their anxious groping for life or of their distress. They express themselves in a language that rejects true speech; or in a language in which expression is synonymous with lack of language, with lack of communication; it is a sort of magnetic tape of

---

*   *Éducateurs* are professionals who are not teachers but who contribute to a child's education, e.g. in a boarding school, a holiday camp, a child guidance clinic; *re-éducateurs* are therapists who remediate specific difficulties: speech and language, motricity etc. —Translators.

recorded words which are void of meaning to the speaker. The psychoanalyst faced with such children must be on the look-out for the body's language and the language of facial expression. Before the child masters the use of words for purposes of expression he learns a language of the body, inscribed in the fantasies that relate to his basic narcissism, to desire, and to the needs relating to them. He retains this language well after he has undergone the imitative, passive apprenticeship of verbal and gestural languages.

It is this *language of body images* (see below) which the analyst of children and the analyst of psychotics must understand and analyse. Any human being is in possession of this language as long as he lives. The child knows no other until such a time as his autonomous movement and the seeing of his own image in the mirror initiates him to his own bodily schema. This learning from the mirror will enable him to identify himself formally with others. It is starting from this understanding of 'what he looks like' that he will further learn his language, both gestured and spoken, phonematic and grammatical, by copying the behaviour of his elders. The language of body images, which is the first of the signifiers of all his encounters, is accompanied by the kynemes* of the bodily schema and, as soon as the child can speak, by the phonemes of spoken language whenever he encounters animals and human beings. This narcissistic language of body images unconsciously resonates with every signifier, and particularly with words that reach beyond human bodies, in their irremediable separation. This language can also express itself unconsciously – wordlessly and through expressions in the bodily schema.

The attention and receptivity – not only auditive and intellectual – that children can muster when they observe adults goes beyond what adults themselves can pretend to. In general, an adult's range of attention has been reduced since childhood

*   'Kyneme' is a neologism of Dolto's, a parallel to 'phoneme'. Where the phoneme is a morsel of speech, the kyneme is a morsel of bodily experience upon which the unconscious body images may be constructed. —Translators.

to the conscious expression of self and to a sensitivity by contamination by the expressivity of others. The faculty of listening and of paying attention is, in adults, far below the readiness of children to receive impressions or to express themselves: these faculties, in children, have not yet set in the hard form of formal language — I mean in the conventional code of their surroundings. It is known that children can perceive and imitate the sounds they hear; adults no longer can.

Knowledge draws us away from immediate being. The fact that they are physically helpless and their nervous systems are still imperfect tends to give us the impression that children have no deep comprehension. This is untrue. The human being, before he has developed the power of speech, has the same degree of comprehension as the adult: but he cannot tell you, except in functional, somatic reactions. In adults, facial expressions, conscious or unconscious, are almost always specific to their social milieu or geographical region in which they were raised; this implies that adults who are called 'adapted' have in their facial expressions and gestures undergone symbolic castration at all the levels expressive of their libido. In other words, in their attempt to use many of the means of expressive signalling offered by the human body, they have found they were not being understood, and they have been inhibited accordingly. These inhibiting effects consecrate the fact that this specific human being in development has joined a specific code of expression; he has become a cohesive element of the family group on which his survival now depends, and will depend for a long time to come. The family in which he grows up informs him about himself and about the world. He must become a language-bearer, active or passive, of the desires and needs of those closest to him, whose ethos is an unconscious result of the drives of each member of the family, acted upon by those who in fact hold power in the family.

It must be admitted that adults remain forever more or less conditioned, more or less subject. Or one should say, they are alienated to a greater or lesser degree from their basic impressive and expressive truth. How often have we heard an adult say of a child that 'He only says and does stupid things' (i.e., things that have no meaning for me as an adult), while in fact the child is being true to his nature; he is being animated by his (unconscious) desire, not yet totally engaged (prior to the Oedipus complex), in his identification with a socially responsible element. He will become totally engaged only when he has integrated the law; when he has overcome his fear of oedipal castration (when the ardour of filial genital desire burns out helplessly) and assimilated the prohibition of incest into his sexual libido.

As is well known, past a certain age, adults can no longer teach themselves to pronounce all the sounds of which the human voice is capable. The unconscious image of their larynx, joined to that of their hearing, has become unable to emit and often to hear sounds which simply did not materialise in their linguistic exchange with their group, first as it started in their relationship with their mother, and then with the family. The same is true of incest. The conscious adult is unable to gratify an incestuous sexual desire.

Thus all adults – unconsciously, by their linguistic adaptation (in the widest sense of the term) – become traitors towards what they perceive: they form the habit of not really expressing it, of repressing it at an earlier or later stage of their life. What they feel but cannot express may then remain as an enclave, without means of expression. Music, like language, constitutes a means of expressing physical and emotional tensions, in sounds, in a way distinct from language; it represents a 'sublimation' of drives and affects rooted in the oral stage. It uses these drives and affects through an expressive organising of the frequencies, rhythms and modulations inhibited by the spoken language. Similarly, within any group, decency sets limits to the freedom of bodily movements; it inhibits the language of the body. Within this framework, dancing liberates the expression of what has been inhibited. It is a sublimation having its roots in the subject's former anal period. Drives and affects can all be 'sublimated'.

Whatever field of language he expresses himself in, every artist of any sort is the mediator of forbidden or inhibited expressions. It is left to his creative imagination to liberate what has been inhibited and could not find expression in its time. He is able to express what he is presently living through, not merely what he has archaically lived through. He does this in his own way, outside the usual interpersonal language. His art specifically reflects his original libidinal structure, and this often causes artists to be viewed as overgrown children. Wrongly so, because the adult's libidinal urges spring from a biological substratum connected to a genitally mature bodily schema; they differ fundamentally from those of the child he once was. He has acquired his creative and social power, and finds his own authentic unmistakable voice, by overcoming the fear of oedipal castration and by integrating the incest taboo.

An adult who has not been completely humanised through oedipal castration and has not learned to express his feelings and actions in a language that fits his parents' language, will remain marked by a structural impotence reflected in the language of his speech and gestures, and even in his somatic language; he will be temporarily or permanently maladapted. The same holds true for an individual who during childhood was mutilated in his desire through seduction traumas caused by adults, and was partly incapacitated during pregenital sexuality.

Psychosomatic, psychotic and neurotic cases can certainly all be psychoanalysed; through transference such cases can be helped to relive the principal trials of their life story; they can be helped to find their libido, whose use they had lost for communication and creative purposes. Their desires reappear during this work, freed from the fetters of anxiety: are manifest in communication with the analyst. Their desires are shaped into language in this communication, and thus acquire human value. The expression of desires in language confronts the subjects with what is imaginary in desire and with the castration provided by reality. The analysis of the transference allows the patient to recognise his desire and integrate his drives, with their symbolic function, in his relation to the world.

Psychoanalysis is often said to be dangerous in that it disunites couples and stifles the creativity of artists. Well: if the subject finds, when he reaches his truth, that his previous choices have lost their meaning, we can only say that these earlier choices were neurotic; and for a professional artist, that his creativity was not authentic. The progress of analysis has shown them that what they had built up earlier constituted a shirking of communication, a rejection of their responsibility to society; it was not what others thought it was: the proof that they had both assumed their desire and enlisted it in the realisation of responsible creativity. No real living love can be broken up by the process of psychoanalysis. Nor can the communication of an authentic creative artist be sterilised by analysis: the artist continues to perceive far more than other people, and his desire to communicate thus remains. Whatever is authentic in a human being can only be more authentic after analysis. But it is true that people who have not succeeded in communicating or in creating in social life often find lateral ways of expressing themselves, in a form of art that is a refuge or a consolation; it will lose its meaning when they find the path to their true dynamism.

Under analysis, a married man may find his marriage bond to have only an imaginary and neurotic meaning; his sense of responsibility which under analysis has been growing and refining itself may force him to face the truth and reject his marriage bond. But he will be all the more conscious of his responsibility towards the children born of this neurotic union, and he will be ready to play his part in their upbringing. It is certain that a man who has found his truth is far more responsible in his acts, in his relations with others. A completed analysis is a labour of truth – a seeking, an awakening to the respect for another man's freedom. As for myself, I have known a number of neurotic couples whose companionship and sexual life had lost all meaning, and who were able to communicate again after analysis. Before that, man and wife had long been deeply separated, often enemies or strangers, and frequently (as overcompensation) they had grown regressively dependent on one another in boredom or in victimisation – two effects that are far more harmful for the structuring and the growth of autonomy of children raised in contact with these poorly married parents than an officially accepted separation free from conflict, or at least free from deception.

But let us return to our topic – the work of analysis with psychotics. Faced with psychotic cases, psychoanalysis must apply itself to the study of fragments of fantasies, and sometimes to their traces in the unconscious slips of spoken language, in the contradictions between acts and facial expression or bodily gesture. Through careful attention, the analyst must detect archaic or displaced eroticisation, whether oral, anal or genital, in fragments of the soma: erogenous zones, organs or systems of organs that bespeak or cry out their unrecognised desire within a non-coherent personality; he must trace the lost meaning, the disturbed, distorted, enclosed meaning this eroticism has taken on vis-à-vis the whole structure. During the sessions, the analyst may seek deferred or diffracted traces of these meanings in any drawings or clay modelling made, whether or not produced alongside free-association in the form of speech. Sometimes, what is important is not expressed during the sessions, be these silent or verbose, but in messages sent between sessions.

The psychoanalyst's own analysis will have prepared him to obtrude as little of himself as possible on the encounter; this allows him to be mindful of the other person for that person's own sake, and only through his life story. For the analyst, these scattered fragments, these traces of fantasy, constitute the subject matter of the encounter, whether it be an encounter with any other person, or an encounter with this other single, chosen person, the analyst, with whom the subject is able to relive the emotions of his past – in which case we have the phenomenon of transference. But the 'encounter' can be said to be real – in the sense of a recognition of a language between analyst and psychoanalysand – only when the analyst deciphers the unconscious or creative meaning of what his subject actually feels emotionally. And this is wholly or partly hidden from the subject who communicates it to him. At the same time, it is sometimes necessary, and occasionally helpful or catalytic, for the psychoanalyst to speak, while his way of acting invariably has the value of a language which he uses better to present to the analysand the true significance of what they say.

We have been engaged in deciphering the fragments brought up by Dominique during his analysis. We have recognised them as a deferred language, the effect of an underlying desire; or else as the effect of a language diffracted into fantasies, through which the unconscious subject, going-on-becoming autonomous and masculine, expresses his desire by casting it in a set mould: a desire which before his analysis had been recognised as existing neither on the human nor on the ethical level. When we speak of deferred effects, we may mean either of two things. We may mean a desire imagined in a time other than that in which Dominique lives, a time when he could satisfy it; or in another place – elsewhere – mediated by a fantasy of a body other than his own: the body that he fantasises in alienated sensations, elsewhere or other than in the present reality of his adolescent boy's body. Such fantasies are his only means of expression during a good part of the treatment: we are concerned with emotions frozen since early childhood and which are now seeking expression; emotions that correspond to his image of his body as a child's body, a body he could not symbolise at the time he was a child and now no longer exists. Dominique's body as it now is no longer feeds back to him the same references as in the past. It is the locus of erotic feelings which he cannot classify in human terms because while he was growing up there was no symbolic interchange with parents or siblings in spoken or felt encounters, a lack which was a function of the parents' own experience – or lack of experience – of oedipal castration. It was only towards the last of our meetings that Dominique started talking to me as either a healthy or a neurotic being would; that he started talking to my person, reacting to what I said or asked him. For much of the treatment, he never or almost never referred to my presence when he asked a question or made a statement, or to his actual self. He acted mysteriously, he spoke of elsewhere, he 'unspoke' (*déparlé*) of 'people' who were to be 'non-prehistoric', to whom he attributed bodies that he made up, bodies uncharacteristic of known species outside the human race, or else sexually inverted.

A part of his libido was projected into these characters – that is, into an inarticulable erotic situation – by a need of his real body which would have, but could not, address itself to another real body. Dominique was panicked by his confusing and perverse desires, rooted in all the archaic libidinal stages. These desires, which he could not openly admit to himself in his encounters with me, were of the same kind as he had experienced again and again towards all other people he had met since he became psychotic. This appears clearly from his discourse, from his stereotyped clay figures and drawings, from his talk when he raved and ranted. He had been carrying on for years in the style which I described in our first two sessions. His ravings were full of cars (representing the autonomy of desire) that hid and sheltered in the foliage of trees (the vegetative body made to stand for the image of his own body of ineffable, visceral anxiety).

A certain change becomes apparent as early as the second session. Dominique's modelling portrays a 'person' shaped differently from earlier figures. The chest is formed of two bars of clay, on a broad surface, rather than of one, as in earlier years (see fig. 3, p. 41).

When Dominique refused contact with me at the start of the treatment, it was absolutely impossible for me to understand him, but quite possible to listen, to lend him my ear, to impress on him the fact that I was listening. Note that the ears of the new 'person' differed from those of the old, stereotyped model.

What it was that Dominique feared from all human beings became obvious towards the end of the treatment of his psychosis – when, had it been possible, the treatment of neurosis would have followed. He feared what he had experienced in his previous human contacts: the lack of recognition of the anxiety he derived from the cannibalistic and incestuous desires encouraged by his mother, by her contact with his body and sexual organs. His body no longer knew whether it was male or female, or the body of some historic, prehistoric, dreamt-up parahistoric or anti-historic species.

But I was not, when the treatment began, trying to find out what Dominique was afraid of; rather, it was how he felt in

this fear. To know this, I had to understand through transference how he reacted to my presence and came to face to face
with the fantasy which I, as everyone else, provoked in him. The
variations in the drawings and clay work served to illustrate this;
they were images both of the fantasies of the mediating body
and of the barriers erected to keep me from him.

Some statements of mine in response to Dominique's
unusual language created the effect of contact with him. Recall
his saying, as if from behind the scenes, 'Sometimes when I
wake up, I say to myself that I've lived through something true,'
and my reply: 'Which made you untrue.' And his immediate
response: 'Yes, that's it, how do you know?' A child's or a psychotic's first words are like the first dreams of an adult neurotic.
It was important for me to register these words, and see them
as holding the meaning of all that was to follow. I told him I
had not understood it unaided, it was he who had just made me
understand it. The words of my answer, which he felt to be true,
were due to my having absorbed his words; it was the proof that
he was being heard. This gave him the sense that someone was
listening; it was the result of an encounter. The silence of my
listening was meaningful, and he referred to this meaning when
he said: 'Noise, noise, and then all of a sudden a total quiet;
you could hear a fly buzz: I like that.' It is the effect of shared
silence, following the exchange of words, associated no doubt
with memories of his infancy: his parents' love-making in their
room where Dominique had his cot; the silence of the creative
meeting, the anxious flies' buzzing, interrupting the calm of the
milch cows (his mother or myself). A silence that may also refer
to the persecuting jealousy of a witness – myself – onto whom
Dominique was now projecting his childhood memories. I was
the witness who saw and heard his behaviour towards himself.
Dominique was recreating a sort of ongoing bodily encounter
which he was reliving in an autistic and sterile manner.

But this encounter still classed me as a very dangerous
person; since I was recognised as valid by those around him, I
had to be like them and in cahoots with them. No doubt I was
tainted with the same incomprehension and disapproval with

which others met his anxiety — that is, the symptomatic way of being that was the cause of his exclusion. Until the fourth meeting, he trusted and distrusted me equally; the transference was highly ambivalent.

Little by little, we met because we recognised the same meaning. I was his listener, and in the growing transference I reached his outer shell. I remained coherent, close to him, but still exterior to him. He in turn found himself becoming coherent: I did not cause him to be split; during our meetings, which were free from any bodily encounter, he mirrored himself in me; he was able to take stock of the expressive space in which he could henceforth hope to place himself, to which he could refer, or within which he could communicate (with me) without the threat of being grabbed up, or eaten up by a desire (mine) which he projected in the place of his own mutilating and cannibalistic desire.

It is in this way that, through transference, the analyst comes to symbolise the cohesion of the person who is being elaborated, the person of the psychotic. At the same time, the analyst comes to stand for the evident memory of an experience the subject has repeatedly lived through, and which now takes on the meaning of a narcissistic libidinal reconciliation. This process stems from the fact that whatever the patient expresses, the analyst invariably views as valid, even though he may not consciously understand it. This experience is in itself symbolic of an authentic meeting with another human being (*spécimen humain*),* whose appearance awakens the remaining traces of the past, but without the centrifugal effect of sensory coenesthetic destructuration. Whatever the subject perceives in his contact with the analyst leads him to recall earlier experiences that had caused similar feelings — experiences, more or less intense, that occurred under different circumstances, in encounters that took place elsewhere at other times, with other people, other things, other beings; but this encounter in the here and now guarantees the dynamic of the present body and not that

---

*   On the *Me* and its relations to the *I*, see below. —F.D.

of a body retrieved by the imaginary from its reality. All this is possible only in the phenomenon of transference, through the mediation of what the subject expresses and of what the analyst can show he is actually perceiving. At the same time, the analyst remains unaffected by these fantasies from both a sensorial and emotional viewpoint: after the session the patient sees him unchanged. Whatever anxiety or violence may be inherent in the feelings expressed by the patient during the session, the analyst remains one and the same. The patient is thus free to view the analyst as in his own place and in the imaginary role which he splits off from the symbolic field. This is the role into which he casts the analyst, rather than tackling him bodily, as indeed could happen if they were engaged in a playful or mothering encounter – if they were not involved in the colloquy of bodies at a distance between patient and analyst.

The analyst wants to study the diffracted, deferred language of his patient's behaviour, drawings, modelling and talk. In this task, he has to work with fantasies (or even with fantasies of fantasies),* with masks like the layers of an onion, with 'resistances' which he must respect totally if he wants to rescue the patient in his relationship with himself, recognised as masked, but also free to remain so.

Once the analyst sees that the patient understands that his groping expressions have been understood, expressed, how can he bring this encounter to the level of consciousness? I think he is then in a position to give words to the events which the subject effectively lived through. He can do this on the spot, during the session, interpreting these events as probably associated with a yet earlier historic event of which some outside source – the parents perhaps – has informed him. The psychoanalyst must inform his patient of his sources. I am talking here as much of a foreclosed, alienated subject as of someone who is still too young to recognise when and where the events occurred with which he was emotionally bound up and which

---

*   In the case of Dominique, see the fourth session and the cow that dreams she is an ox, p. 57.

marked him. Such a young patient will give away in his talk –
for example in the vagaries that accompany his drawing and
modelling – the libidinal style of the time when he lived these
events, without being able to integrate them. Since these traces
are again brought up in transference, we are then able to interpret them as leading back to the historic, experienced fact in
its totality. And it is this reference to the experience that constitutes the analysis of transference.

Besides this, the analyst has at his disposal his own understanding, drawn from the experience of his own analysis as well
as from his wide observation of healthy children in their pregenital period, at a time when they spontaneously react by means
of defence, through simulation reactions or creative, symbolic
or deviant reactions, or else by reactions – called symptoms – to
trials of impotence or castration. In so-called normal children,
these reactions last long enough to support their narcissism
and to help them structure their personality faced with the
real experiences and traumas that all people meet with varying
degrees of intensity.

It seems impossible to me to work with psychotics without
knowing and understanding children of three years of age or
less. Somatic disorders of adults can often be traced to the fact
that normal channels for the expression of their recurrent pregenital emotions were blocked. They were shut in, foreclosed
in their emotional relationships, which are of an erotic nature,
whether or not the subject chooses them, and whether or not
the subject himself perceives them as such. I have in mind those
psychosomatic reactions due to human encounters at work –
with the boss or with colleagues – leading to tension; or to
the resolution of the often critical tension within families in
which children of several age groups live together, each at his
own libidinal level. Some of these children caught up in such
a family situation live through experiences connected with the
conduct of their siblings that may shake or destroy their psychic structure, not so much because of what their brothers'
or sisters' behaviour is in itself, but because of what it comes
to signify in the subject's imagination, in the unconscious

judgment of the psyche. Since in this period of his life the child always exists in reference — close or distant — to a parent, he comes to feel that a brother or sister has taken a parent's role, with respect to him or to the other parent, that the brother or sister has become that parent's other self, and takes the place of his mate. The oedipal triangle which forms the basis of all human structures until the end of the Oedipus complex is thus weakened or torn apart.

Children are even more vulnerable to these shocks when they are in a state of exceptional sensitivity or overwork. At such times, the basic equilibrium of each of their libidinal stages can readily be upset by contamination; for example, between ten and twenty months of age, the taboo of cannibalism can easily give way when they see a younger sibling being breast-fed; or, at the age of two or three, the taboo of murder, when they hear an adult representative of the current ideal ego praise death in battle; or again, such a destructuration of the narcissistic bases of a child's personality can take place when he is forced to witness a parent's humiliation, or hear words belittling the parents, coming from people whom he respects, at a time when the parents still represent his ideal ego. This is the case of a child who has not passed the test of the Oedipus complex or is involved in tackling his specific anxiety. The elements which he acquired from his contact with his parents, and which constituted the point of departure, or the support of his cultural attitudes — and hence of the symbol of structuring function of his personality — can thus be weakened or even destroyed.*

---

*   The symptoms that follow these traumas can vary from 'whims' (micro-hysteria), which invariably are a sign of anxiety, to misfunctioning in language, writing, schooling, to indifference to games, and including states of organic devitalisation that lead to fear of surroundings, of medical visits, and to useless or harmful symptomatic cures such as might have been prescribed by a veterinarian. Unconscious affective symptoms sometimes weaken the organism and prepare for serious organic diseases by weakening the body's resistance to pathogenic organisms. In both early and late childhood, the psychosomatic dominates both health and disease. See my *Psychanalyse et pédiatrie* (Le Seuil, 1971). —F.D.

During human development, erotic mutations occur which are due both to the body's physiological development and to the experiences of the imagination, and more particularly to nonverbalised sensory perceptions which the child has had to assume. The symbolisation of these experiences, which the subject has to make if he is to outgrow them, partly depends on the words and emotional reactions of adults, on the confirmation or weakening, at this very time, of the ethical value of the libidinal expressions through which the child expresses what he sees or does, or what he sees others doing. The child cannot but try to identify with his parents, or with parental figures, as representing him in an adult body, as he is going-on-becoming an adult: hence their great significance. It follows that through the phenomenon of this encounter, in the transference relationship created between analysand and analyst, the subject finds and reports on himself as another subject situated elsewhere than in his own body; thus the transference inherent in the relationship presents him with the prism of a moment in history shared with people of the same human family and social group, libidinally invested with respect to the phallus, that is, with respect to the one unquestioned value.

This explains why we invariably find the patient viewing all those who have contributed to his structuration as the wilful cause of his difficulties. Feelings of discomfort, and of guilt, go searching for the responsible parties, or even the guilty ones. We still hear people who, not acquainted with psychoanalysis, or insufficiently acquainted with it, make statements such as: 'This is the reason why a certain person turned out as he did,' or 'With parents like his, no wonder he turned out that way . . .' But the real cause of psychic or neurotic troubles does not lie with what happens in reality, nor with the usual or exceptional way parents bring up their children. It is a question of dialectics. The parents or carers may have been – or may still be – failures in relation to so-called normality (which in fact does not exist in the upbringing of a child), or maladapted to society in terms of standards that are always ill-defined: or they may have died or disappeared – all this matters very little or not at all, once it can be spoken of; especially from the moment the child is in analysis.

Neither is it the real event that matters, the event in itself as it comes back to memory, or as it has remained fixed in the mind. What matters is the emotion as it has been affected by human depersonalisation, or by the distortion of values which the subject has lived through, which he has survived, and which he must now resign himself to giving up. He is up against an emotion that proved narcissising in a special way, which, it is true, he survived bodily, but which he now has great difficulty in giving up, either because its remembrance has become an integral part of his personal myth or because its witnesses are still present. To go beyond this he must experience analysis, the transference through which everything becomes real again; and then give up his analyst – his partner in the search – as lost, along with his past.

When parents, through their words or deeds, allow the child to view incest, murder or cannibalism as permissible desires, kept from him only because he is a child and subject to the limitations of childhood, they are in effect submitting him to a traumatic experience. The same is true of the protected upbringing in which a child is kept in ignorance of his parents' very real problems and in which he is treated as sexually and politically ignorant. This too constitutes a traumatising upbringing, since it fails to provide words to set off the imaginary from the real. The subject undergoes these traumatic experiences during his development, at the same time as his narcissism is being shaped; they are thus intimately connected with his being in the world. This is why an exclusively intellectual analysis, even a profound self-examination, will not by itself suffice to liberate the dynamics of the unconscious. A relation must first be established between the subject's narcissism and his analyst. After that, through the work of analysis, the unfolding of free associations, the study of dreams, the subject can be helped to relive the archaic emotional states in his relationship with his analyst; he can be helped to confront his imaginary world with reality – a painful and often greatly unsettling experience which his relationship with the analyst allows him to bear, and on which he depends to recover the lost symbolic order. Analysts who encounter patients who have undergone early traumatisation throughout a period of protected upbringing find that, sooner or later, in the process of transference, this traumatisation inevitably releases desires which seem ethical enough in themselves, but whose fulfilment, if they surfaced elsewhere than in the analytic relation, would lead to dehumanisation and negative creativity (*décréativité*), and make impossible a human conception of the self. This image of the self constitutes the usual and necessary support of an individual's narcissism in social intercourse. If this image is abolished, wholly or in part, the death drive will surface. To prevent this, the subject prefers to inscribe his narcissism into the fantasy of a Self distinct from his own body, distinct from the genital, sexual body that is his in reality; or even to fantasise a body no longer human; this may lead to delirium. Similarly, he prefers to ascribe his death wishes to another human being, specifically, to the analyst; he transfers the death drive; the analyst seems to be the re-actualisation in space and time, either of the subject himself or of a person real to him, presently or during his childhood; or a symbolic or ghostly or even magical figure.

This is the reason why the analyst faced with a patient in the grip of the death drive – which is the case with a psychotic – has to forgo any fantasies of his own in this encounter; it must involve no narcissistic value of his own; the traumatised and psychotic subjects must be allowed to pursue their dangerous choice, their daring bet on their own ability to endure as human beings, though beleaguered by so many unconscious death or life drives which they could hardly hope to keep in check if they were not symbolised in a transference.

In the psychotic, life drives allow the surfacing of anxiety about death, which seizes the body itself, paralyses defence mechanisms and may even abolish all dynamism. The death drives then emerge, freed from life drives, and anxiety disappears. But as the death drives are not susceptible to symbolisation, their prevalence weakens his ethos.

In the neurotic, on the other hand, we encounter only castration anxiety of an erogenous zone in relation to a desire which the superego forbids. This anxiety invariably confirms the life of the neurotic's own body, whose image is kept alive thanks to castration anxiety, which in adults cannot be dissociated from the sexual desire to which it gives its value. The subject's narcissism then becomes ethically over-valorised by means of anxiety; and anxiety confirms the subject in his human face, which is inseparable from his body; it establishes the subject as a being of reason, responsible for his words as for his actions. At the time of the Oedipus complex, and later of puberty, anxiety is the experience through which the subject experiences the law presented him by authority (the father or his substitute). And it is this acceptance which integrates him into society.

Such is the psychoanalytic experience to which I have been led by my work with psychotics – with particular respect to the human encounter that becomes implicit in transference, once the foreclosure of libidinal urges manifests itself in aberrant and unreasonable conduct. The symptoms are a symbolic effect, informative about a central libidinal moment during the evolution of the subject's ego ideal and its structuration by his ideal ego, which was made present by an agent of the subject's upbringing whose language was mystifying, perverting or absent.

At every moment the individual is subject to an image of the physical self. However, at times this image may be blurred; for instance, when the ego ideal, in conformity with present space–time and with a moment-by-moment subjective experience of the bodily schema, would have an ethos genitally orientated by the masculine or feminine of the bodily schema; but if unprotected and unconfirmed in this way, it dislocates the subject from speech and delivers him almost magically to the death drive. It is dislocated also from a body image which has 'lost face': the face being the place of the symbolic link between a human body and its speech

To conclude, I shall say – as is evident – that these thoughts did not come to me while I was working with Dominique. All

the thoughts I put down in my discussion of this case, and the
thoughts that follow, came to me as I reread my notes of the
meeting, which I took down as we were talking, at the same
time as I sketched the modelling Dominique was involved with.
Later, new thoughts came to me as I wrote down our sessions.
I thought about the things Dominique was communicating
through his words, through his drawings and through his work
in clay, as well as through the changing current of his transferential communications. During the sessions I was all ears and
eyes, entirely present to Dominique, the sounding-board of the
truth which was communicated to him through me, his analyst.
It would be untrue to say that the meaning of that communication was clear to me at the time. I listened; I made notes;
'it' awoke spontaneous reactions in me. When I understood, I
spoke up according to my understanding. No doubt I did understand better afterwards. In any case, it was a labour in which we
were both caught up. And following this publication, I hope it
will turn into a labour to which more – to which many more –
will contribute.

Dominique and I are the representatives of two worlds
who have succeeded in communicating. We both had the gift of
words; I was more fluent in the language of the many, he less. I
was less distrustful of him than he was of me. Rightly or wrongly
I thought that his way of being, described as psychotic, stood
in the way of his fulfilling his human creative destiny. By understanding him, I tried to help him in his struggle. The reader
has read my testimony as a witness of this symbolic relationship, which captures one passing moment in the psychoanalytic
research of our day, to which I wish to contribute.

Clarification of the Freudian Theory of the Psychic Agencies (the Structural Model), with Respect to the Oedipus Complex: Neurosis and Psychosis

A child who learns to speak speaks of themselves in the third person; they are the third person of the father–mother–child triad. When a child says 'me', they always mean 'me (my mother)' or 'me (my father)'.

For each child, the notion of their own existence is related both to themselves, located in their body, and to another person, who in turn is related to others.

Freudian analysis speaks of the ego – the ideal ego – of the superego, and of the ego ideal, as agencies of the psyche, dynamic agencies stemming from the libido, that is to say from the id – the libido focused by desire. Between these agencies is established an unconscious energetic economy.

I am going to consider the practical meaning which we are to give these psychic agencies – a meaning whose value stems from our understanding of their dynamic role as the child grows up, and which allows us to follow the elaboration of the symbolic structure of human beings, as well as to understand its pathological destructuration.

The ego

The subject of desire progressively reaches the notion of their own autonomous and conscious existence. They reach this stage consciously only when they start using the personal pronoun 'I', which appears late in their language – well after 'you' and 'he' or 'she'. This 'I' invariably refers to the subject as having its origin in the id, seen through the prism of the ego, inseparable from the body.

An 'unconscious I' seems to exist before speech. It may be considered as the organising agency of the foetus's psyche in communication with the 'unconscious I' of the parents. This 'unconscious I' exists in a dreamless sleep; it is that which wishes to live, to grow, to fulfil itself through creativity and then to die after the life drives have been spent – the drives that protect the ego itself, that protect the body ego – the mortal human specimen; the ego, moreover, that manifests both as the I identified with the given name, while also being subject to the desires of the id.

As to the family name tied to the first name, it stands for the subject's genitality; it is indistinguishable from the structure of the oedipal ego. The syllables that form a child's family name introduce them to the law which forbids their incestuous desires towards their begetters, ancestors, collaterals and descendants. The family name binds the subject through their body to a lineage; it legitimises the child's parents' tutelary responsibility towards the child in their youth and the child's own responsibility to the parents in their old age. At birth, the subject rightfully becomes a narcissistic extension of the parents' joint ego(s) – whether joined legally or not – by the law, the same law implicit in the family name. The family name thus connects the subject's existence to the parental Oedipus on the levels of language and of the unconscious (before becoming conscious) and confronts them with this Oedipus. By passing on the family name to the child, they tell the child of the law of chaste love within the family, inscribed in language, and they do this even before the child's desire awakens to test this law.

While the first name is symbolic of the subject beyond their death, the family name stands for the castration of incestuous desire towards those of the child's lineage. The prohibition of incestuous desire represents the filiation which makes, out of an individual limited to their body, a representative of the lineage which binds the individual to all other men as they bind others to the individual.

The ideal ego

The ideal ego is another unconscious psychic agency. It is *always represented by a living being whom the subject strives to resemble*, as if this model human being represents the fulfilment of a stage of their own development, and which in their desire they hope to become. A subject always selects their ideal ego from tangible reality. The ideal ego attracts the subject and supports the structuring of their drives. The person who incorporates this ideal ego acquires symbolic phallic value, that is to say an absolute value for the subject's libido. Before the discovery of sexual differences, this ideal ego by definition resembles the subject in their own eyes; it is by definition of the same sex. Thus, in very early youth, the ideal for a child of either sex can be either the father or mother, or any other individual who is respected or valued by those around the child, a feeling which the child comes to share by contamination. Thus, the subject finds an ideal ego in a body like their own, a co-natural body; they endow it with a state of perfection, ease or naturalness, and power greater than it possesses in reality.

In short, the ideal ego is an image, a *narcissising image* built up in a subject who, until recently, existed in a totally powerless and dependent body; they are now developing according to a pattern which is that of the subect's species, and of which they already appear to have the intuition. They are, as it were, called forth, drawn by an image of themselves, an image that is mature on the biological as on the emotional level, and which they see first as manifest in the form of a parent, and later in whatever shape is praised and built up by general approval. The ideal ego is therefore exemplary. It confronts the imaginary of the child with reality. The child's imaginary dependence on this reality narcissises them, and stimulates their drives to flow in the direction of the achievements they see in their ideal ego. What does 'me' — the subject localised in this specific body of theirs, and which calls itself 'me' — want? It wants to 'be like', 'have the same as', 'act like' and 'become like' this living model. We have here a 'pre-ego' (*prémoi*); the id in the process of being organised, by way of the body image fashioned by desire. The body images of this pre-ego evolve as the individual evolves from infancy to the walking stage. We will not analyse here the structure of the body images. Let us say only that these images are not visual or scopic, and that the face and neck are not included – they will be only after the subject has viewed themselves in the mirror. The body images of this pre-ego are triple at all times: a basal image; a functional image; and an erogenous image. The erogenous image is focused by the subject's desire for the ideal ego, as mediated by the losses and recoveries of erotic satisfaction that mark neurological evolution. The desire in its successive stages can be called oral, then anal-urethral for both sexes; then penile-urethral for boys and oral-vaginal for girls. In the subtle communication with the ideal ego, this desire stands as a metaphor of the bodily communications that spring from the subject's needs. For each stage of development, a narcissistic body image develops from which an unconscious ethos, in turn, emanates. This ethos changes from one stage to the next when, as is usual, the person who is the support of the ideal ego of this archaic pre-ego ceases to find satisfaction by the mere fact of relationship with the child. When the opposite occurs, the ethos of the child is blocked narcissistically at an archaic stage. In the case of a development that has not been blocked, the neurophysiological and psychic evolution of the child is supported by the passing through of a castration at each stage:

— the cutting of the umbilical cord (and the start of breathing, of smelling, of hearing, of feeding);
— weaning from the breast;
— weaning from bottle-feeding and from an all-liquid diet;
— freedom from functional physical dependence;
— unaided walking;
— toilet-training;
— total bodily autonomy.

As the child grows beyond each castration, their narcissistic ethos undergoes a mutation that structures the taboo of vampirism (foetal stage); then of cannibalism (oral stage); then of sticking to the mother (anal, urethral and archaic vaginal stages). What is born out of these taboos is the acquisition of metaphor – first, the perceptive emissions of healthy respiratory functioning is phonematic and oralisation develops; then, as the hands become prehensile, analisation develops, including the ability to give and reject: this receiving, keeping and producing of phonemes, and taking, keeping and throwing with the hands, become organised as a language with the mother; progressively the child grows independent in their movements, starting with walking – a revolution – and this independent mobility leads to the exploratory stage and the intelligent play-oriented use of hands and body.

The baby and young child invariably looks upon the mother as the person to imitate. But until the age of two and a half or three, the child cannot say 'me'; thus we talk of the 'pre-ego' stage. At the same time, the child notices that the mother too has a preferential object – the other of the mother – and the child takes this object as incarnating the mother's desire, valorises it, and endows it with the symbolic phallus. Any person more mature than the child can temporarily be assigned this role of accessory support of the ideal ego; but they all remain subordinate to the mother's appreciation: she remains the preferred co-existential object. Any object to which she shows preference takes on a meaningful phallic value for the child, and hence it becomes an unquestioned and unquestionable power. Siblings also play a role. The father is also closely associated with the mother in the child's mind; he is perceived as different from all other familiars, as preferred by the mother. More than anyone else, he is given the role of the ideal ego, jointly with the mother.*

---

*   This two-headed ideal ego, before the child formally perceives sexual difference, plays a role in initiating them into the desire to communicate; the nursling is subjected to empathy when, merged with and co-animated by the adult who carries them, the child co-communicates with the other adult. This triangulation is a matrix for language; it is necessary for the efficiency of the symbolic function whether or not the parents are the child's biological parents. —F.D.

Primary castration

When the child reaches the age of two and a half or three, and becomes aware of sexual differences, their drives have to face the problematic opposition of the imaginary and the *reality*. The boy first attracted by girls sees them as strangely mutilated in their sex; he sees them as a threat of *penis mutilation*. To girls, on the other hand, the discovery of the male organ, represents a mutilation, with the formal significance of desire, which in this place has no expression; the penis which these fascinating 'boys' possess is either an attractive horror (if seen as 'wee-wee': *pipi*) or as a wonder (if seen as an expression of genital desire). When a child asks a representative of the ideal ego the question concerning the absence or presence of the penis as representing sex,* its answer brings them the revelation of 'destiny', inseparably bound up with the complementary nature of man and woman in procreation; that is, the revelation, for the subject, whether boy or girl, of the dynamics of desire bound up with its irreducible reality. The ideal ego reveals to the child that they have the destiny of an adult to conquer: it is through or beyond this revelation that the child of three reaches autonomy. This statement establishes a conditional relationship between the real and the imaginary; it sets aside what is possible from what is not for the first time. It separates the never and the forever of time's reality; it does this through the body which the child knows to be theirs in space, and whose structure comes to represent the *Me* for them. From there on, the child is then able to associate the syllable *Me* to the grammatical *I* in the acts and thoughts which their language takes on.

Further change follows primary castration. The ideal ego, valued above all else, becomes a human being in a body which, while it is more developed than the child's, is nonetheless subject to the laws of the same reality, as it is of the same sex. The child now seeks to identify the ego with the ideal ego; this leads them

---

*   As contrasted to the penis's role as part of the urinary system.
—F.D.

to cultural acquisitions that spring from the oral and anal libido which at this time is fully engaged in its apprenticeship to identify with the child's model. Not only does the child take the ideal ego as a model, not only does the child try to imitate it in all ways — the child even seeks to contest their specific role with respect to the other parent, in such aspects of their behaviour as are perceptible to them. With this example before them, the child initiates themselves within their ethnic group into the language-value of the libido, either male or female. Thus the child is led to express their desire someday to beget a child with the parent of the other sex. This desire to identify with the valued adult of the original father—mother—child triangle naturally leads the child to the fantasy of incestuous procreation as they promised to their desire as the child is going-on-becoming an adult.

A child will experience normal auto-eroticism, which from the time of primary castration until oedipal resolution is centred on the genital region. If they are not blamed for it, the child's masturbation, unless they are bored and do it in public, will normally be restricted to the times when they wake up or go to sleep.

For children who have not yet experienced the sexual learning I have described, a transitory period of exhibitionism may exist. It is a mimicry through which they silently ask the meaning of the pleasure they have discovered. We must remember that the three-year-old child asks questions about everything: 'What is it?', 'What's it for?', 'What's it called?'

The boy twenty-one or twenty-five months old finds that his penis can give pleasure in erections and that erection cannot take place while he urinates. He wonders about these things. He is no less puzzled by his scrotum, his testicles and their exceptional sensitivity; left to himself, he speculates that they might be little reservoirs for his excretions. The irritation of the tip of his penis perplexes him, particularly if the foreskin is tight. He needs to be informed about these things. He needs to know that everything in him is all right, and that he will grow into a man like his father.

Negative remarks about his sex, using such adjectives as 'dirty', or 'not beautiful', words which seem to confine it to excremental functions, now that he has learned its function in relation to girls, are traumatising; this is so even more for boys, whose sexual parts are more apparent, than for girls. The boy's sex, for this very reason, is more vulnerable – literally and figuratively – than that of girls. Erections are frequent and unexpected, and focus the boy's narcissism. The little girl too must be told the truth about the sensitive and erectile portions of her genital anatomy; though these parts are less visible, she has a tactile knowledge and a subjective erogenous recognition of them. She is entitled to know the true names of the vulva, the lips or labia; and the name clitoris for what she calls a button – as she calls her erectile nipples, with which she naturally associates the clitoris. She must know that the word vagina applies to her hollow female sex, which she otherwise calls a hole, and which she experiences as circularly erectile at particular moments when boys cause certain emotions in her. The girl must be told the real names of her sexual anatomy; she should be told this by her mother, who initiated her into language in the first place and who named the other parts of the body, in adult terms; these names bestow a humanising meaning and value to the region on which a girl's womanhood is founded, and to the precise and subjective feelings which she has been experiencing but whose functioning still escapes her. From the age of three, intelligent children are curious about their parts, which are so thrilling and, to them, so near to the dereliction of excremental functions in their ethical value at that time. Self-confident children invariably ask questions concerning this mysterious region which, intuitively, they feel to be endowed with a considerable future role, and which is all the more interesting to them once they have learned to compare it with that of the other sex: not only as a urinary function, as they once believed (boys standing, girls sitting or squatting), but a sexual matter. Why? What's it for? They want to know what their body and their sex will be like later, and whether boys are like their father when he was their age, and whether all boys when they grow up will be like their fathers? Is this beautiful? So, their sex is all right, too? And girls, will they be like women when they grow up, will they have breasts like the ones they see on their mother and other women?

All this information which comes to the child in reply to their questions increases their interest in the sexual region, up till then considered a part of the anatomy specialising only in the necessary elimination of waste.

Their first name, the way they dress, are now seen as confirming their sexuality. It is not whether Father or Mother would have preferred a little boy or a little girl, but that each of them carries the truth in their body; the child expressed it when they were born, whatever adults may think, who may be misled by their face or the things they wear.

The meaning of the pleasure localised in that region becomes clear from this information concerning their own anatomy. Once they have been made conscious of their destiny, these children are now free to verbalise, draw, play or act out their fantasies. These illustrate their desire to be like adults of their own sex, whom they see as crowned by a great power of seduction that supports both the grown-up's identity and their own identification.

Once the primary castration anxiety has been overcome, the child has been initiated into the realities of their masculine or feminine body; the child has been introduced to the problematic inherent in their sexuality and to the desire to reach their full adult stature in the hope of replacing the parent of their own sex in the other parent's affections. This is a hope which the child forms as early as their third year, when masturbatory fantasies liberate the components of their heterosexual desire and set them on their way to the Oedipus complex.

The direction pointed to by this new step leads the child to take as model the parent of their own sex: in this way the child will please and attract the other parent. At the same time the child must handle the parent of the same sex gingerly because, firstly, this parent, associated with the other, still incarnates the ideal ego; secondly, because this parent also still stands as the guarantor of existential continuity, and of the regressive satisfaction the child requires. As a basis for its narcissism, the child needs to be able to turn back to the comforting basal body image; this will help them through the vicissitudes of the future, and will lead them to seek the protection of both parents who jointly represent the child's archaic structure.

Oedipal castration

After a few years of working through these issues, the child develops their narcissism as a small person taking their place in and outside the family by mastering language, acquiring manual and bodily dexterity, and by discovering even more precise auto-erotic genital sensations accompanied by oedipal fantasies. At this time, a new anxiety threatens the child: *the fear that they may not be able to attract or seduce a parent adult* – this parent always seems more attracted to his or her mate. The child never really succeeds in becoming a real competing rival: they play at being a little lover or little mistress, but it is not 'for real'. In fact, the child is sexually impotent, manifestly so. Reality hits them in the face whenever their desire rises up, and makes them try to conquer the object of their incestuous love. Oedipal castration anxiety follows: the feeling of being threatened with destruc-tion in one's own person or of mutilation of the child's sex – a fantasy linked with the projection onto the adult of the child's own rivalrous feelings. At the height of the Oedipus complex (at around the time of the loss of the baby teeth), the child faces the narcissistic dilemma of being punished with death or assaulted in the place of their desire; and threatened by their own death drives and the loss of ethical reference points, may be affected to the point of neglecting or damaging themselves.

Castration anxiety is perceived as a threat of mutilation: of evisceration to the little girl, of detesticulation to the little boy. It will be all the stronger if the child's sexual desires are strong, and if the parents are prone to giving in to the child's excessive demands, or are ready to grant them bodily encoun-ters – whether in the form of excessive cajoling or petting, or of repressive physical punishment. The child perceives both as seductive love, or as the mark of jealous rivalry towards them or towards the other parent; both have a perverting effect. The attitude that will least trouble an oedipal child is one of discreet affection coupled with an upbringing that makes demands but still respects the child's human dignity.

If from the age of three to seven, the time a child's sexual desires develop, one of the parents is absent (or is emotionally or sexually frustrated), that child will be slow to progress towards the primacy of a genital desire not guarded by the rival adult. In the same way, at the age of seven, when the child is facing the castration anxiety springing from their oedipal desire, it is the parent's attitude that can overload the child with anxiety and so check their evolution.

This is what occurs when a child perceives that their parents disagree about the way to bring them up. The child may then unconsciously be drawn into a position where they exploit and manoeuvre the tender weakness of the one, and the repressive, overaggressive strength of the other. This is a real danger to the child, as it perversely maintains them as the abusive one in the oedipal triangle, the chief actor in the home, the general centre of interest. The child is then confirmed in an oedipal castration anxiety which is both guilty and enjoyable and will lead them to stagnation in an infantile psychosomatic or affective stance. It is impossible for the child to overcome the drama of their oedipal desire, and the fear of castration which it sets off in the unconscious balance of their libido, if their anxiety perturbs the equilibrium of the parental couple, and if the parents are more concerned with the question of how they are to treat their children, than with their own social or creative roles, or with their togetherness as a couple.

The child's integrity as a person, as well as the integrity of their sexuality, are completely involved in the incestuous desire that dominates them around their seventh year. It is fortunate that at this time the child experiences a physiological slowing down of the sexual urge that will last until puberty. They are — at seven — entering a period called the period of physiological latency. If at this time the *law of the prohibition of incest* is not clearly impressed on the child, *as a law imposed on their parents and brothers and sisters as well as on the child themselves,* they are likely to remain in a state of latent oedipal conflict from which they may not be able to free themselves until puberty. At that time physiological drives inherent in puberty will unleash the major latent conflict between incestuous desire and the anxiety associated with it until a resolution through the renunciation of genital desire as such (not only incestuous desire), which can from then on be completely repressed for the duration of adolescence: something that entails certain neurosis. On the contrary, when around the age of seven the child is given a clear notion of the prohibition of incest, they are initiated into the common law to which their parents and siblings are equally subject, like every human being, and an overhauling of their libido occurs before their entry into the latency period. The dissociation between genital desire and chaste love for the parents and siblings allows the person's narcissism and ego to give up imaginary infantile aims. There is an abandonment of total dependency upon the aggressive and sexual drives towards the two primary representations of the ideal ego, and at the same time the emergence of an autonomous ego submitted to the genital superego, keeper of the prohibition of incest and called forth by an ego ideal which is no longer mixed up with the objects of the oedipal triangle. The ego ideal will be free to develop as the pole of attraction for an ethos of the prevailing genitally sexual desire – an ethos that is an autonomous moral conscience, the child's awareness that they are responsible for their acts and for their words.

Before the oedipal period the child, though moved by masculine or feminine sexual urges, still has a fluctuating set of moral beliefs that change from day to day to fit in with the tension between – on the one hand – their drive to conquer and enrol the parental object of their fixation and – on the other hand – their fear of the other parent, the rival whom the child looks upon as an unwelcome *Third*, perhaps a threatening Third whom they must either win over or else neutralise. The child, boy or girl, who has resolved the Oedipus complex, stands on the ruins of their hopes for parental or fraternal seduction. It is only then that they can start to seek outside the family for the kind of friendship — more or less amorous friendships, towards a member of the same or of the opposite sex — to which they will be able to transfer the last traces of their incestuous desires. Towards a third comrade who then seeks to join the couple, the child will show themselves to be aggressive, possessive and jealous. The child will seek out 'auxiliary selves', comrades-in-arms — friends of their own sex who have also experienced the incest taboo, and with them the child will strive for cultural achievements in society.

The child will find these 'auxiliary selves' in comrades of their own age, whom they look for outside the family circle.

From the age of eight or nine, and discounting cousins or children of neighbours, a boy or a girl will prefer to befriend children whose parents are unacquainted with their own. Friendship holds no interest for them when their parents meddle (the child's horror of the question: 'What does his father do?' — as if it mattered!). Children's sociology does not correspond at all to the criteria of their parent's sociology. In this regard, a remark may be made concerning one of the phenomenological aspects of the dissolution of the Oedipus complex. Too many parents postpone the sublimation of the Oedipus complex during the latency stage by trying to control their child's games and emotive life outside the family circle. Secretly it is often with respect to adults that children seek to love, to quarrel, to build up relations of respect, or of bickering and reconciliation. This is for reasons that parents cannot understand. Children quarrel with their peers, with their friends, about their teachers, about their elders whom they may have seen at school, about the sporting heroes, the heroes of music and television who are in fashion among their group, a child will seek out positive or negative 'models' to fit in with a narcissistic choice — as far removed as possible from models that may appear as oedipal models, and which change with the seasons. For a child, each of these crushes or fixations is the support of transitory identification fantasies which help them in the search for self-knowledge in social life, by learning from those they admire.

The superego

We have seen the autonomous ego arise, castrated of the incestuous desire that so far had organised the psyche. At the same time,
the superego develops, heir to the revelation of an ethos that pro-
hibits incest. The oedipal superego stands warrant of the fact that
survival is possible, at the cost of giving up the incestuous sexual
urges: it is a repressive, prudential agency of the psyche whose
purpose is to warn off the subject from a return to castration anxiety. It is an agency of the psyche made unconscious through the
assimilation of the law connected with the primal scene, which is
the child's origin, and the key to their filiation.

The superego is thus the posthumous heir of the pre-oedipal
ideal ego. Its role is to uphold the incest prohibition by means
of the castration anxiety that is awakened by masturbatory fantasies with an incestuous object. The superego inhibits the sexual desires that, in the most frequent instance, create an unconscious taboo out of the fantasies of incestuous intercourse and
the desire for incestuous offspring. The superego thus has the
effect of awakening the castration anxiety in case the Self is
tempted to outwit this anxiety, or to escape the law, if only in
daydreams. The sexual superego does not forbid sexual desires
directed towards heterosexual objects outside the family. On the
contrary, it helps the subject's narcissism develop along the direction proper to their sex: towards amorous conquests outside the
family and competitive successes in their career and culture.

The ego ideal

Faced with the castrating effect of the prohibition of incenstu-
ous desire, the child's sexual desires detach themselves from
their parental objects. Inhibited, they are now cast back on the
narcissism attached to the child's own body, which becomes precious to the child; the child looks forward to a future which they
know will bring them the secondary characteristics of sexual
maturity. Certain cultural requirements exist, associated with

this state; these the child now masters. The future which the child is promised is the pole attracting their fantasies during the period of latency. The fantasies turn into long-term projects, focused by a new form of the psyche sprung up alongside the oedipal resolve: the ego ideal.

Arising from the ruins of incestuous desire, the ego ideal stimulates the ego to acquire the kind of culture prized by the society outside the child's family; the child now knows a pleasure different from that of charming father or mother, of 'pleasing' them. The ego ideal is all the stronger, the more forceful in helping the subject to inner integration, if they can find in their peers and elders of the same sex an echo of the same values which pull them towards the realisation of the ego ideal, even though they cannot ever, by definition, fully achieve this ideal. They cannot achieve it because the ego ideal is not incarnate in any human being. It is an ethos whose effect is to focus desires through daily actions, through a series of specific creative initiatives whose worth is recognised and appreciated by the group: sublimations. The superego's effect, by contrast, is to inhibit the desires that would tend to distract the subject from the main line of their desires that lead them to court, by means of these sublimations, a sort of success acceptable to their ego ideal.

Effectively, if the law is unspoken by a valued representative of the child's sex, responsible for and guarantor of its truth, it leaves the child in a state of confusion with regard to their value in society as a sexed being, and their desire, masculine or feminine.

This is why children who have not been sexually structured during the physiological oedipal stage will remain subject to oedipal castration anxiety during the latency period, and be very readily influenced by the example and the sayings of those they admire or fear, of their peers or elders. These 'auxiliary selves', when they themselves are outside the law, are then apt to confuse the child's ego ideal by continuing to present them with the model of a seductive ideal ego of oedipal style, and which by rights should by now be outdated.

In fact, one continuous line runs from the genetic possibilities included in the libidinal capital of the id to the ego ideal. The genetic potentials of the id may have been thwarted, until the time of the Oedipus complex, by individuals who served the child as ideal egos. But once the child has clearly given up their hope of identifying the child's desire with these individuals', the child's ego in fact comes to lack a sexual parental ideal for their desire; particularly if the parents no longer project themselves in their child. The child has lost their hope of finding some fulfilment of their sexual desire involving their close family. Hence, their ego can finally give up its concern with incestuous conquest, and grow according to its gifts, without seeking to please the parents.

A boy or girl suffering from an unresolved Oedipus complex can evolve towards a perverse or delinquent structure if the father, still fixed on his own mother, is unable to undertake his child's oedipal castration, or if the mother, still fixed on her own father, 'plays doll' with her children. During the phase of latency, a child can regress to earlier homosexual or narcissistic positions if the father or mother, who to them represent adults who have apparently reached the level of sexual or creative communication, are in fact immature, phobic, obsessional or hysteric. To such parents, the fact of having an oedipal child at home may awaken a repressed homosexual and narcissistic libido, a libido daily driven from sexual to pre-sexual positions. The children of such parents enter the period of physiological latency, around the age of nine, not proud of their sexuality, but rather as neuters, individuals of weak sexuality. At puberty they will meet with serious problems resulting in neurosis.

This neurosis will be all the more pronounced if it is matched by continued success in school.* This success, while giving satisfaction to the parents, will pre-empt the libido of the child, which is unclaimed by any relations with the child's peers. The child will shy away from and fear those who should be

---

* The child's success in this case represents a kind of success through obsessive fixation on competitive results. There is no real cultural gain. The pupil's homosexual or heterosexual fixation on their teachers tells them not to fail in the tasks they set for the pupil in school; the pupil's success in this case becomes their one and only concern,

their playmates, absorbing themselves with masturbation and the fear of oedipal castration associated with it, fear resulting from the fantasies which accompany the child's onanism and centre on the conquest of imaginary or unreachable objects, the hidden substitutes of parents.

What we are describing is a case where the ego ideal is thwarted by the surviving oedipal ideal ego, either still represented by the parent, or exemplified in the lifestyle which the parents present as a model, or represented by the parents' moralising, which completely replaces any attempt at setting up a personal code of ethics. The guilt feeling strangles narcissism.

This thwarted ego ideal is not able to become the focus of the desires of the archaic erogenous stages, or the desires of the present sexual stage. All the aggressive drives, active or passive, that should pursue in concert with the sexual drives some object of desire and some creative work (creativity and reproduction) – all these drives, without exception, are inhibited, forced back by the false superego, which is stuck at the pre-oedipal stage. *This retrograde superego forces desire to fit in with an ideal ego – that is, with the model of an individual – rather than with an ego ideal –* on pain of castration anxiety, which is often somatised in the form of exhaustion, insomnia or visceral troubles.

It is true that this ideal ego is no longer completely the father, but it is a thinking-master, a 'trustworthy' individual outside the subject and who tells the subject how to act; a parent or religious figure, or a worker figure, or a doctor, when it is not simply an open homosexual fixation on an older person.

This results in a dependence of the ego; and, inevitably, in a lack of the total dynamic of the sexual drives. Part of the ego has remained infantile (and often heroic in its unquestioning attachment); in this, the subject cannot find what they need to structure their wishes. When there is an ego ideal, the subject's projects

---

excluding all other concerns of their age; they are over-preoccupied with marks; their wounded narcissism would make them view low marks as the frustration of the teacher's desires, with which they identify their own; they are filled with anxiety. This extreme tension can lead to chronic depression. —F.D.

serve the sexual urge guided by the honest call of pleasure; lack-ing this, they become a fog of fantasies that keep them from see-ing reality as it is. Their projects fail − either because they are simply not fulfilled, or because they derive no enjoyment from them. Their sexual competition is feeble and guilt-ridden; they cannot harness it in a responsible way, to serve what they really want. They fear failure so much, spends so much energy fore-stalling it, that failure follows, confirming their guilt feelings and leaving them broken. They are dominated either by apprehension, or by procrastination; or else they are concerned with not being in absolute agreement with the ideal ego − i.e. with someone's opinion, which their superego forces them to pay attention to. Compare this to the individual who *has completely freed themselves from their oedipal fixation.* Such a person is able to pursue their sex-ual drives and feels responsible for them. *Their libido moves freely, along an axis which proceeds from the id to the ego ideal, passing through the ego as it is guarded over by the superego of the law, which they have successfully assimilated.* Desire is focused and no strength wasted; the person moves with a feeling of freedom towards success; they find pleasure in fulfilling their aim. And when they fail, they are not driven to a feeling of guilt, not affected with a narcissistic wound. They turn their failure into a lesson about the world, and keep the aim of their ego ideal. From here on, their sexual urges will be even better fitted to their purpose: the object of their desire in obtaining pleasure. This is the form libidinal 'health' takes in maturity. This until the physiological age of menopause for women, and of andropause for men. A new (natural) castra-tion follows, which brings on a new symbolisation of desire, free from anxiety as from symptoms of regression.

Neurosis and psychosis

A clear understanding of *neurosis* follows from the above. Neurosis occurs in a human being whose libidinal disorder took root only after they have successfully overcome primary castra-tion. That is to say, in a person who is proud of their sexual characteristics, who has lived through the Oedipus complex without being able to resolve it altogether; hence their latent anxiety of sexual castration, unconscious most of the time, and expressed in symptoms of which they are conscious both because they feel troubled by them and because they feel guilty at being unable to dominate them. But in any case, what is characteristic of the neurotic is that they cannot imagine, even in their dreams, and they cannot regress to, an ego who is not of their sex, or not human.

Psychosis, on the other hand, attacks a subject who in the pre-ego stage, before they were three, did not benefit from having as support of their ideal ego a mother who is proud of her femininity and a father proud of his virility – proud also of having begotten the child and proud to have the child be of the sex they are. This situation occurs when the father and mother have not resolved their Oedipus complex and form a neurotic couple, closed in upon itself and on the material support of its children. These adults inhibit their sexual urges. They 'work', they are 'educators'. Their children are the fruit of desires which they are ashamed of having shown; they bring them up childish and afraid and ashamed of sexuality. Such parents are invariably timorous with regard to other adults, and mix little with them. When the grandparents, who are at the origin of this neurosis, play a role in their children's family, or in the upbringing of their grandchildren, this third generation is then exposed to serious traumas that threaten their libidinal structure.

It takes three generations for a psychosis to appear: two generations of neurotic grandparents and parents are required to form a psychotic. One of the parents must lack a pre-oedipal or oedipal libido structure, and they must have encountered a similar lack in their mate, also derived from at least one parent. A psychotic has been unable, from their earliest years, to see their ideal ego in a parental adult who is part of a sexual couple either in reality or symbolically. Such a child is an eroticised part-object within the father–mother–child triangle; the weakness of the parental objects that served to structure their ideal ego, and the inconstancy of the oedipal rival in the real world have bred anxiety and insecurity about their own sexuality in them. At the time the child's Oedipus complex was resolved, their parents' sexual libido was not polarised in a satisfactory adult sexual life: they had a fixation on their offspring, due to the castration anxiety inherent in their infantile pseudo-superego. As they had not been erotically liberated from the emotions of their own guilty childhood, they made their child feel guilty for any expression of independence which the child might attempt. It is normal for such parents to behave either as policemen or as excessively doting and anxious guardians. They deny their children any chance for libidinal freedom in play outside the family, and any autonomous creative initiative.*

What is not well known outside the world of psychoanalysis is that it is possible, and not uncommon, for adults to have psychotic and perverse structures that go quite unnoticed, phenomenologically. They are hidden behind patterns of behaviour that are more or less acceptable in society, and can therefore be readily ignored. The unconsciously perverse or latently psychotic character of these parents is revealed only through their effect on the children they bring up. It is in the children's inability to reach the proper structure at some stage of their growth that we begin to detect the parental death drives to which they are unconsciously subjected. The outward or apparent words and behaviour of these parents do not correspond with the perverse desires — conscious or repressed — which privately motivate their personal relations with their children. Furthermore, the very fact of having one or more children who are *visibly* maladapted to society allows these parents to overlook other neuroses, whether it be the neurosis of their other children who appear 'adapted' because they are 'adapted' to school, or their

---

* The nurses and nannies of very young children also play the role of pre-ideal ego, and are able to either correct or to amplify the deficiencies in the parents' libidinal structure. The same is true of educators during the phase of latency and at puberty, if the child is sent to boarding school before having acquired pride in their sex, or resolved their Oedipus complex due to insufficient information concerning the incest prohibition. —F.D.

own neurosis or latent psychosis, 'adapted' as they are to their jobs. This is why the treatment of psychotic children requires psychoanalytic work with all brothers and sisters, as well as with parents: in short, with all those who have served as representatives of the psychotic's ideal ego, and who have therefore not been able to sustain their narcissism in the symbolic communication of the psychotic's emotions towards them. For this communication, as we have seen, is impossible when the parent eroticises their relationship with the child – which is precisely what occurs when the parent has not undergone the successive stages of the humanising castration.

In such a family, it is the child most richly endowed with libido that will show the gravest trouble. This is the child whose desire was greatest, and whom these fragile adults will have found hardest to bear. The child's natural precocity and fine sensitivity threaten to upset their precarious unconscious libidinal balance; this is the child whose desire they will naturally repress.*

When it comes to treating a psychosis, and therapy is limited to one 'patient', including their familiars, it is surprising to see that as their condition improves, one of these familiars – parent

---

*   This is readily apparent. During development, desire takes shape around those erogenous zones which are most valued in the course of evolution towards neurophysiological maturity. At each stage, some of these libidinal drives fail to find full satisfaction, either because of the natural course of things, or because their manifestation meets with only a certain tolerance from adults. But the significant fact, that which marks a mutation in energy and the passing on to the next stage of organisation, is the clear and total prohibition of certain aims of the drives characteristic of that stage. This absolute prohibition of certain aims of the drive results in a separation of the functional body image from a part that shared its nature, and was necessary to the fantasies of its desire, even though, up to then, it was situated in another body. This, in psychoanalytic terms, is called a castration. The castration has an impact because it can either play a structuring role for the subject's symbolic representation, or alternatively, it can hurt or mutilate. Its effect will depend on the particulars of the event when it occurs; and on the subject's affective relation to the person who is, or seems to be, its mainspring. The humanising value of this castration also depends on the fact that it is shared by the person who enforces it; the all-important question then is whether this person does or does not respect the child as subject of desire. For the castration to have positive effects, after it has deprived

or sibling – will start compensating by a neurosis, or by acting out, either by having an accident or by developing psychosomatic disorders. Parents will then frequently terminate the child's therapy, or else compensate by losing all interest in the child, now better adapted and on the way to recovery, while formerly the child's recovery seemed to be the parents' prime concern. It is important to foresee and understand these reactions; if by curing the psychotic we destructure the closest members of their family, we run the risk of giving them a second guilt feeling by feedback, and so arresting their evolution or even leading them to wilful or accidental death. This can be prevented if we take care of the family and allow the parents also to progress in their neurosis, while the psychotic is undergoing their cure.

We have seen that a neurosis is cured by analysing and overcoming the Oedipus complex; the cure of a young psychotic, however, is not completed when they have relived and reorganised the archaic stages with the help of the analyst, and have

---

the subject of the fulfilment of some of their wishes, it is necessary for both taker and giver of the castration to respect one another, and to recognise one another's dignity as individuals and indeed as individuals of a specific sex. Given these conditions, the castration can then have the humanising value I mentioned: it can sublimate the forbidden desires into humanising patterns of behaviour, patterns such as are encouraged and rewarded by the group.

It is natural for an individual who finds their desires thwarted by such a prohibition to suffer, but at the same time they will come to view the promulgator of the prohibition as a valued image of what they themselves will be some day. Such is the case of the child vis-à-vis the adult. They find a way of fitting the expression of their desires into allowable drives and new aims which, thanks to their particular stage of neurophysiological development, their drives will soon discover and learn to exploit. When parents or educators are maladapted to the children in their charge – who later, in turn, will be maladapted within the social group – it is that for some reason unknown to themselves they have retained from their own poorly castrated early youth an anxiety which is now projected onto their relationship with their own child, whenever the child expresses their desires at the oral, anal or genital stage. The unconscious emotional relationship between parent and child in this case is reminiscent of communicating vessels in physics; they effectively place their own child in a relation of insecurity vis-à-vis the child's own desire. The child's desire knows of no prohibitions; no structuring can result from it. —F.D.

rebuilt their structure accordingly. This is because, compared with their own age group, they have fallen behind considerably in sublimating their oral and anal drives, drives which grew disorganised during their maladapted and delirious state. They will be even further behind if the period of maladaptation occupied a significant part of childhood – the time when most basic learning is absorbed, between the ages of five and eight, and the time of the cultural learning following the Oedipus complex.

Even if the psychosis appears during adolescence or maturity, the sexual drives will prove destructuring of what had been thought structured, because of the pre-oedipal regressive elements which had gone unnoticed. The individual, once their oedipal structure has been belatedly re-established, must now live through a late and artificial phase of pseudo-latency, usually interrupted by a period of acting out which can rarely be dispensed with, and must assert their own creativity, acceptable to their society, as a function of their desire, their family and social milieu, and their age group. This is not strictly speaking the business of psychoanalysis proper, but of a combined psychotherapeutic and educational or professional effort. At this point, these individuals recovered from psychosis are still weak in their ability to compete with others of their age; and yet, they depend on progress for the genital fulfilment of their urges in the scholarly and professional fields. This then becomes primarily a social question, depending on social means. This is equally the case with social and cultural contacts which must be established before the subject can choose a mate who is more than a momentarily compensating narcissistic choice; to be successful in this the subject must be able to assume the responsibility of becoming a mother or a father.

This is why the analyst should try to enlist the support of the family of the psychotic child or adolescent, and why it is always important to be concerned with this family so that the child, adolescent or adult, once cured of their psychosis, will be able to find auxiliary support in their family or in the social group with which the subject is involved. Unfortunately, even today, our so-called developed countries are not yet equipped to allow access to education or work that doesn't require a diploma to adolescents who, because of psychosis, have been unable to benefit from regular schooling or professional training. This is also true for adults who because of psychotic decompensation have lost their jobs. Our society still does not provide for these needs. What solutions do exist are in fact individual, very costly, and available only to the privileged classes.

Conclusion: Can we hope for a prophylaxis of infantile neuroses or psychoses?

The arguments presented above all plead the case for the spread of psychoanalysis. They stress the need to apply therapy early where it is needed. We must spot those children well below three years of age who, unknown to their parents, are already maladapted to the social life of their age group, and whose normal schooling will only compound their problems unless parent–child psychoanalytic therapy is begun.

We must also be on the lookout for children under eight who are apparently free of trouble, who are able to cope scholastically, but who are retarded on the sexual and affective levels. It cannot be sufficiently stressed that a child's or adolescent's scholastic or intellectual level is in no way a measure of their affective, moral or mental health. Neither is a poor scholastic and intellectual performance a mark of neurosis, though the feelings of inferiority and social failure to which they lead may favour passive adaptation or adolescent delinquency.

A child who is behind at school but affectively healthy, good with their hands, and who knows how to get along with people is in far less danger, in the years to come, than a child who is successful in school, but is anxious, phobic, scrupulous and unable to function autonomously outside the protected world of the family or school.

It is not true, as is commonly said, that a maladapted child is born every twenty minutes. What is true is that the extension of city life, the drop in infant mortality, the absence of a policy for children or of assistance to fathers and mothers (of generations, in France, traumatised by two world wars) — all this results in depriving some 45 per cent of babies and young children of a playful, vocal, active and imaginative life. They lack the contact and communication with others of their age which they require to develop healthily before they are three. Man depends on his relations and communication with his fellow men;* he must be able to freely express himself and to be involved in exchange with them.

Medicine, surgery and the prophylaxis of physical illnesses have made enormous progress; this must now be followed by an equally great emphasis on educating doctors and other medical personnel on the need *not* to take the child out of their family background, while enlisting specialists in the strengthening of that background by providing suitable early education to children between the age when they learn to walk and kindergarten age. Similarly, attention should be given to the prophylaxis of affective and sexual disorders during the early school years, up to the ages of eight or nine. What is needed is an enormous effort in the education of boys and girls, to open their eyes to the cultural possibilities of music and similar activities, as well as to sports and creative manual skills and games, from the ages of eight to fourteen, during their school career and before their professional apprenticeship. Finally, children need sexual education; they need to be given the legal and civic knowledge they require to prepare them for adolescence — when they will want to take on responsibilities, and participate in communal or civic life. They must be prepared for this by progressively being included in the labour force, while they pursue their intellectual, cultural and professional training.

---

*   To appreciate this, we must understand education. The child is able to humanise themselves during their growth only by undergoing operational castration. They must not only experience this, but experience it at the right time, when they are able to organise some of the desires inhibited by society into solid unconscious taboos, whereas free desires can accede to pleasure in their conquests during the next libidinal stage. —F.D.

Parents and educators are too exclusively concerned with the newborn or young child's organic health. They do not sufficiently focus on the psychic causes for anxiety, originating in disturbances of the symbolic father–mother–child relations; or on the mental pathogenic consequences that result from the child's anxiety over separations – either before they are nine months old, being separated from the mother in the maternity ward; or later, during early infancy, because the child or the mother are hospitalised; or because the family are separated for reasons of health or other reasons. These separations bring on language and motor disorders, phobic and compulsive states and false learning disabilities which will later appear as the signs of early traumatic neurosis.

The problem is that paediatricians are so little informed about the psychosomatic development of very young children of the first or second age groups. Paediatricians have no need to know psychotherapy, but one can only regret that they are so little informed about mental prophylaxis for psychic and affective disturbances in children from zero to seven years, particularly in the child–parent relationship. When troubles first begin, a few wise words by a physician to the child themselves and to the parents, some simple advice to the father and mother, can help the child pull out of the regressive reaction pattern into which they have sunk. They could still emerge from this if they could speak out (*parler vrai*), and be understood. A few months or years later the same results will require a long therapy because by then new symptoms will have been added to the early inhibitions, symptoms which will organise themselves into a pattern of adaptation to the world whose overall effect will be the child's maladaptation to the kind of creativity and communication characteristic of their age: behaviour which signifies a growing dehumanisation.

Too frequently we meet with parents who come to us after having repeatedly sought professional help and understanding, but have been able to find only medicine and the advice to be patient: 'He will be all right with time,' 'Keep her at home as long as you possibly can.' Or else they will have been given a firm diagnosis of incurability; or they will have been told to place their child in one of those classes for maladapted children in which children are segregated from others of their age group and their family, and are tutored by teachers who are no less segregated from their own colleagues. These teachers often show remarkable talents, talents that would be most welcome in the education of so-called adapted children. But with this class of the 'maladapted', though they may succeed in teaching their pupils something, they cannot hope to give them the healthy symbolic structure they lack. What these children suffer from can only be taken care of by psychotherapeutic work. And the efficiency of this work will depend as much on the parents' involvement as on the child's. Unless the child specifically requests it, they should never find themselves separated from their family; the family must be made to take responsibility for them until they have come to the resolution of their oedipal conflicts.

No doubt we psychoanalysts are responsible for not having sufficiently worked at keeping paediatricians informed. We have not been sufficiently articulate in warning against the *instrumental* re-education programmes designed for object-children. We have been unable to show convincingly that the children's symptoms bear witness to structural troubles having their origin in the *foreclosure of desire*, and that we must be concerned, not with 'correcting' the symptoms of this foreclosure, but rather with analysing it, and not just removing the visible instrumental impotence. Today, these children are deprived of their reality as individuals, they are 'trained' to academic and professional behaviour which diverts them from their autonomous libidinal desire. Their future looks dark indeed. When they grow to adulthood, they will beget children for whom they will not take responsibility, even if they manage to make their own living. These children in turn, born to parents who have been deprived of the chance freely and humanly to assume the responsibility of their own desires and role in society, will be headed for failure. 'Social' education and 'national' education, in their euphoria of 'aid to maladapted children' utterly ignore this.* We are forever being told that every day seventy-five maladapted children are born in France. But the fact is that (except for children who are physiologically handicapped, and even then) there is no such thing as a child born maladapted. These are children who become precociously traumatised in the symbolic function of desire; their maladaptation is their way of adapting symbolically to parents who themselves are unconsciously traumatised or anxiety-riddled. The present ways of coping with these children – the paediatric, maternal, academic or alimentary disciplines imposed on these children – are in opposition to the emotional structure of the growing human being: a little boy or girl who is primarily a being of language, who cannot, without symbolic danger to their life, be cut off from their first name – most of all – nor from their family name; nor from their mother, father, brothers and sisters. The child must not be cut off from the basic milieu into which they were born and in which they first developed – until the age of eight, or at least five. And if, at the age of five, a separation is inevitable, they must remain in the same tutelary educative environment until puberty.

We need day-care centres located at the mother's place of work, so that mothers may be able to go and feed and visit their children during the day until they are old enough to walk. We need small nurseries which fathers, mothers, brothers and sisters will be allowed to visit frequently: we need special rest

---

*   A word should be said here about the French system of social security (*sécurité sociale*). Among other things, this covers parents for the better part of their medical, re-educational and psychotherapeutic expenses. A free consultation service is available to 'problem children', or such children may be 'taken over' free of charge for a period of three years. These children are then separated from their families on the pretext – sometimes justified and sometimes nor – that they may harm their families or that their families may harm them. They are placed under the guardianship of 'specialised educators'. These men and women are sometimes well prepared for this task, but are frequently just as vulnerable on the emotional level as the parents were, seeking their personal satisfaction in surface results – 'adapting the child to society' – rather than loving the child for what they are – the necessary first step. —F.D.

homes where tired mothers can go to stay, hotel-style, with the young children still dependent on them, and where the father can join them at evening time or during the holidays. We need numerous nurseries for children from toddlerhood to kindergarten age, nurseries open to parents who can come to see their child play with their peers, and can discover the importance of their behaviour in school. Parents need to witness the example of specialised educators for the very young, and need a chance to talk to them. Each of these specially trained women should have charge of four or five youngsters; they should be conscious of their role in education, as the parents' auxiliaries, specifically in charge of children's games and of their mutual adaptation. All this should take place in an informal setting, quite unscholarly by present standards. These nurseries would be tolerant towards the temporary recuperative regressions which, in children under three who have been shaken in their affective lives, are natural and needed. They would help the child to autonomy in a number of respects: the child's care of their own body, their spoken language, cleverness with their hands and body, and rhythm in music. Through such nurseries, children reaching kindergarten age would already be integrated into their age group, without having lost the benefit of close family life. The age of entry into kindergarten can vary from three to five; it is often earlier under present conditions because children need to be around others of their own age, or because mothers have to go to work. At the present time, this cannot be remedied. But it is impossible for a schoolmistress in charge of a kindergarten class – however perfect she may be – to do her work usefully if she has more than fifteen youngsters to take care of. And even so this number assumes that they have acquired the necessary language skills and are ready to communicate among themselves.

I am arguing for a policy that will allow the young child to remain within their family at the same time as it makes it possible for the child, from their earliest years, to mix daily with children of their own age group. The child's temporary or even permanent maladaptation must not be made grounds to separate them from their peers and family, at least until a certain age, which varies from seven to nine, and notwithstanding the accidents of their physical health. A new policy is needed which will consider the pre-oedipal needs of the child. They must not be isolated; they must not be separated either from their parents or from their peers.

It is not difficult to foresee the objections that will be raised against this. Some will say that the family setting is in many cases intolerable, quite impossible for the upbringing of children; others, on the contrary, will invoke the parents' right to bring up their children as they themselves wish. To these objections, I answer that the authority of the state requires medical prevention and control; that a civilised country boasts of its public health, of the drop in infant mortality rates. Why should not the same concern be shown for cases of morbidity or symbolic death represented by neuroses, psychoses and most of the problems of mental and affective development? The state at present feels no responsibility towards such troubles, even when they are detected early, and when their early structural origin is evident. This lack of social responsibility reflects failure of real human communication, of 'education', in the sense of answering the child's call for humanisation. Must we continue to cure and correct, when we could so easily prevent?

Would it be Utopian in this age to express the desire for a coherent policy towards infancy and early childhood? A policy that would respect the basic integrity of each father–mother–child triangle, that would refrain from withdrawing the child from their parents before the child themselves wishes to be separated? The child is able to achieve this wish or desire only when their pre-oedipal structuring is very strong – when they have had a chance to grow up within their family, and have learned to find joy in the company of their peers from other families. There is no opposition between social life and home life, but complementarity.

A civilised society such as ours should assign itself the following purposes in respect to its youngest members:

— Society should assume responsibility for the protection of every child; it should help prepare the child to master their language, and to participate in creative exchange with other members of the community.

— Society should help the child to become aware of themselves and their own worth; it should help introduce the child into the group, even before adolescence, by offering them readily accepted remunerative work. At the same time it should foster their creativity in culture and leisure, and should provide the equipment this requires. It should prepare for their success outside the family by organising periods of residence in similar families, or in groups offering opportunities for both structured and unstructured leisure. The experience of such parallel groups will give the child a chance to observe and contrast different family situations, and they will grow by having to adapt to these new settings. The child will be obliged to broaden their judgments, which inevitably tend to be limited when they know only their own family and the style of language and behaviour of their own family.

— Starting in primary school, society should sustain in each child the conscience of their interpersonal, sexual, political responsibility; society should support the adolescent who finds they are of age to assume responsibility for themselves, and to be emancipated from the framework within which they grew up. Homes ought to be created in large numbers for older children and adolescents, to which they can go to get away from family settings that have grown stifling; at the same time they should be given protection from the dangers of the street, or from exploitation by employers or from perverse so-called protectors. These homes should make them feel welcome, and encourage them to follow supplementary schooling or training within a framework that is flexible and yet gives them security.

— Society should help each adult become aware of the responsibilities incumbent on parenthood; each adult should be made aware of their responsibility to set an example for their children through their behaviour as a citizen or parent. Groups of parents should be organised to help understand each other's difficulties.

— A similar need exists concerning the oldest members of society. Through a wise communal housing policy, particularly in cities, older people ought to be helped to find a place in society; their experience of life and age has prepared them for many responsibilities that go untended-to today. Life expectancy has been considerably lengthened, and 'retirement' comes much too late, after the individual has grown adapted to a pattern of activity from which they find it hard to change. Thus retirement comes to many people as the trauma of symbolic death, as a rejection. As if old age itself were no longer human. Aged adults would be much healthier if they felt useful. I am not referring here to the very old who are no longer active: many local authorities are concerned with them, as are many private philanthropies and organisations. I am thinking of healthy men and women between sixty and seventy years of age who have been reduced to solitude, who have nothing to do, who develop psychosomatic disorders or who, when they live in the larger towns, exist as parasites on their children's homes, conscious of their dependence, embittered, and complicating family relations in cramped quarters.

Isn't this chain of communication among all the members of society the symbolic source of life of a culture which is structured only by language, by the interhuman, interfamilial language which it weaves between all its living members? The major concern of legislators and of men in power today should be the very opposite of bureaucratic affective anonymity; it should be the respect of each man's free development as an individual.

Only this gives value to the laws which a society develops to secure its living cohesion.

Françoise Dolto (born 6 November 1908, Paris) was a psychoanalyst and paediatrician. Alongside private practice at her home, where she saw adults and child, Dolto practised in four institutions where she saw only children patients: the Polyclinique Ney, the Centre Claude Bernard, the Hôpital Trousseau and the Centre Étienne Marcel. From 1967 to 1969, Dolto answered adult and child listeners of the French radio station Europe No. 1, live and anonymously under the name 'Docteur X'. The programme enjoyed excellent ratings, but Dolto found dialogue to be hindered by the demands of live broadcasting and advertising. In 1976, she agreed to return to radio with *Lorsque l'enfant paraît* on France Inter, on the condition that she replied to listeners' letters, which enabled her to go into depth. The programme was a huge success, and would make her a household name. In 1978 Dolto retired as an adult psychoanalyst: her fame had become such that it distorted the therapeutic relationship with patients. She now devoted herself to prevention, training of young analysts, group and individual supervision, publications, conferences and radio and television broadcasts. She also continued her work with children in the care of the Aide Sociale à l'Enfance, some of whom she received at her home until the end of her life. In 1979, along with a small team, she founded the Maison Verte, a place for early-years socialisation welcoming children from ages zero to four along with their caregivers, for sessions of play and talk. This model spread throughout France and Europe, to Russia, Armenia and Latin America. Dolto is the author of more than a dozen books, and several essays, interviews and seminars. In English, her books have been translated as *Psychoanalysis and Paediatrics* (Routledge, 2013) and *The Unconscious Body Image* (Routledge, 2022). Françoise Dolto died on 25 August 1988 in Paris.

Ivan Kats (1926–2008), naturalised American, worked as a translator, editor, teacher, publisher and journalist in France and the United States. He graduated with an MA from Yale University, New Haven, in 1969. In 1970 he founded the Obor Foundation, dedicated to the publication and dissemination of books to book-poor countries, which he directed until his retirement in 1996.

Lionel Bailly is a practising psychoanalyst of the Association Lacanienne Internationale, an academic associate of the British Psychoanalytical Society and a child and adolescent psychiatrist. Trained in medicine and psychiatry at Salpêtrière Hospital in Paris, he is honorary professor at University College London Psychoanalysis Unit where he is particularly involved in the doctoral school. He led the Sainte-Anne Hospital Centre's bio-psychopathology unit before moving to London in 2000. Bailly is the author of two books, one on psychotrauma in children (in French) and *Lacan: A Beginner's Guide* (Oneworld, 2009).

Sharmini Bailly is a psychoanalyst (member, British Psychoanalytical Society) and a senior member of the British Psychotherapy Foundation. She translated Françoise Dolto's *The Unconscious Body Image* (Routledge, 2022) and has edited two books on Lacanian theory. She works in the NHS and in private practice, and teaches and supervises psychodynamic/psychoanalytic practitioners.

Michael Ryzner-Basiewicz is a doctoral candidate in clinical psychology at Duquesne University, Pittsburgh, Pennsylvania. He works psychoanalytically with children, adolescents and adults.

Other books out with Divided

Disorganisation & Sex by Jamieson Webster
Who knew the hole was what Freud had in mind when he
invented psychoanalysis and wouldn't stop saying 'sex'. Take a
tumble into Wonderland with Dr Webster and decide for yourself
what counts as real. —Courtney Love

In Thrall by Jane DeLynn
A beguiling account of the perversion, angst and ego of
adolescence. —*The Irish Times*

In Pursuit of Revolutionary Love:
Precarity, Power, Communities by Joy James
Revolutionary Love is umph-degree love; or love beyond measure
. . . It is love that dares all things, beyond which others may find
the spirit-force to survive. —Mumia Abu-Jamal

Bosses by Ghislaine Leung
Few artists dig deep into themselves like this: an extraordinary
insight into the process of producing art. —Cosey Fanni Tutti

Stage of Recovery by Georgia Sagri
Insightful, passionate, flowing and jarring . . . a creative journey
that invites the reader to reflect on and reimagine society.
—Marina Sitrin

How to Leave the World by Marouane Bakhti
Translated by Lara Vergnaud
A rare book that depicts the isolation and poetry of rural life.
—Annie Ernaux

Let Them Rot by Alenka Zupančič
This brilliant account of Sophocles's *Antigone* breaks new ground
for philosophy, psychoanalysis, and political and feminist theory.
—Joan Copjec

Wave of Blood by Ariana Reines
Her voice – which is always more than hers alone – is a dialectic
between the very ancient and the bleeding edge. —Ben Lerner